THE THIN MAN

MURDER OVER COCKTAILS

CHARLES TRANBERG

THE THIN MAN
MURDER OVER COCKTAILS
©2009 CHARLES TRANBERG

PUBLISHED IN THE USA BY:

BEARMANOR MEDIA
P.O. BOX 71426
ALBANY, GEORGIA 31708
WWW.BEARMANORMEDIA.COM

ISBN-10: 1-59393-400-9 (alk. paper)

BOOK DESIGN AND LAYOUT BY VALERIE THOMPSON.

TABLE OF CONTENTS

FOREWORD

W hy are the *Thin Man* films as fresh and alive today as they were more than sixty-years ago when the final sequel was released? Yes, they had the MGM gloss and unlike most movies series (such as *Blondie, Crime Doctor, Boston Blackie*, etc.) they did not have "B" picture budgets and were not designed to be fillers, playing second fiddle to another film on the bill. Of course the scripts were hugely entertaining and written by superb writers like Frances Goodrich, Albert Hackett and Robert Riskin (not to mention being based on a Dashiell Hammett story and characters). They had fast-paced direction — especially the first four which were helmed by "one-take Woody" Van Dyke. I should say fast-paced, but not careless. All of this naturally adds to why these films are still fresh, but I believe, and I think most people would agree with me, that the primary reason as to why *The Thin Man* series continues to be highly popular with people today is because of the chemistry between the two leads — the brilliant William Powell and Myrna Loy.

By the time Bill Powell and Myrna Loy were selected to play Dashiell Hammett's witty and slightly tipsy protagonists, Nick and Nora Charles, they had already appeared in one picture together, Woody Van Dyke's *Manhattan Melodrama. Manhattan Melodrama* was more or less a Gable picture. Clark Gable was Metro's hottest male star and was top-billed. William Powell was on loan-out to Metro from Warner Brothers where he was demanding and getting a huge weekly salary but the studio executives were unsure of his commercial viability in recent years and wondered if he was still worth the investment. Myrna Loy had been in pictures (like Powell) since the silent days, but had often been cast as villainous exotic types. However, thanks to Woody Van Dyke, and a picture he directed called *Penthouse*, Loy was on the rise at the studio. *Manhattan Melodrama* may have been a Gable picture, but from the time

Myrna Loy falls into Bill Powell's arms as she is getting into a taxi cab, they completely seduce the audience in a five minute scene of effortless charm, wisecracks and repartee. Van Dyke knew it then — a new screen team was born. Lucky, he had the perfect story too — the screen adaptation of Hammett's popular new novel, *The Thin Man*. MGM had Loy under contract, and Warner Brothers showed no reluctance to allow Powell a second loan-out at the Culver City lot — they were making money on his loan-outs, so why not?

The film of *The Thin Man* was shot in fourteen days! Van Dyke loved to print the first take because he felt that the actors were at their freshest then, and he did offbeat things, too, like telling his actors that they would rehearse a scene and then motioning to his camera operator to give the sign to "roll-it" and rather than rehearsing a scene as the actors believed, Van Dyke was shooting the scene. The result is that the film does have an extemporaneous look, feel and pace to it — and still very professionally done. Van Dyke hasn't received his due as a director (despite some very impressive films on his resume), but movie-goers worldwide owe him a great debt of gratitude in his foresight in bringing together William Powell and Myrna Loy. For Van Dyke saw the sense of fun they invested into their characters and thru them a truly new cinematic experience was created — a married couple who truly demonstrated their love for one another — sometimes in unorthodox ways — but always with affection and a large dose of humor. There can be no doubt, too, that despite their twin beds, that these two connected in more than one way. Nora, the heiress, with the adventurous streak, and Nick, the ex-detective, who was now content to sit back and enjoy her money, could go back and forth with barbs which kept them both on their toes:

NORA: You know, that sounds like an interesting case. Why don't you take it?

NICK: I haven't the time. I'm much too busy seeing that you don't lose any of the money I married you for.

One of the reasons for this untouchable chemistry between these two polished actors is that they liked and respected each other as people. Here is Loy on Powell, "Two of the most important things about Bill Powell are his ability as an actor and his sense of humor, which are unfailing, often biting, always objective. With all the outward manifestations of a lazy, luxurious person, he is essentially a vital, supremely intelligent man." Bill reciprocated, "Her poise is fantastic. It's unbelievable that anyone could work as hard as she does, be on her toes always, accomplish things with dispatch and efficiency, buck the exhausting nervous strain of stardom and still — through it all maintain such quiet, assured calm."

While Powell and Loy were the films most obvious assets the other actors involved add substance to each and every one of the films. This is why this book takes a close look at nearly fifty of the supporting players who populated these films. *The Thin Man* films featured some of the best character actors in Hollywood history: Nat Pendleton, Porter Hall, Minna Gombell, Edward Brophy, Edward Ellis, Jessie Ralph, Sam Levene, Paul Fix, Joseph Calleia, George Zucco, C. Aubrey Smith, Otto Kruger, Louise Beavers, Anne Revere, Lucile Watson, Harry Davenport, Donald Meek, Leon Ames, Keenan Wynn (among many others). Some of those names don't ring a bell? Well, just watch the films and see their faces and in many cases, hear their distinctive voices and you'll say, "Oh, Yeah! I've seen him (or her) in lots of movies." *The Thin Man* films helped launch some top Hollywood actors early on in their careers. James Stewart, Donna Reed, Gloria Grahame and Dean Stockwell are the most obvious examples.

The films have also been hugely influential. It's difficult to come up with a sophisticated film prior to *The Thin Man* which involved a happily married, usually wealthy couple, merrily solving crimes. In fiction we have Tommy and Tuppance, Agatha Christie's crime-solving duo, but they had not yet made it to films. Afterward we would have a glut of such couples both in films and on television. MGM even produced another series, which was more in the "B" vein as a filler between the two and even three years between *Thin Man* films about a rare book collector and his wife who solve films (*Fast and Loose*). William Powell even had a couple of excursion into this type of story minus Myrna Loy in *Star of Midnight* (opposite Ginger Rogers) and *The Ex-Mrs Bradford* (opposite Jean Arthur). On stage we had *Mr. and Mrs. North*, which later had an adaptation in films (which starred Gracie Allen! As Mrs. North, but not George Burns as Mr. North, rather it was William Post, Jr.). There were also radio and television adaptations of the North's adventures. Ida Lupino and her real-life husband, Howard Duff, were Mr. Adams and Eve. For more contemporary television viewers certainly *McMillan and Wife* (with Rock Hudson and Susan St. James) and *Hart to Hart* (with Robert Wagner and Stefanie Powers) were greatly influenced by the *Thin Man* films and characterizations. And why not? If you're going to borrow (as opposed to steal) why not borrow from the best? Of course, *The Thin Man* itself made its way to television (as one of MGM's first excursions into television) for a couple of seasons in the late fifties with the Nick and Nora characters played by Peter Lawford and Phyllis Kirk, unfortunately that show didn't quite capture the flavor of the original, but did produce 72 episodes, some of which are available today on DVD.

No book is a solitary effort and I need to Thank, as usual, my publisher Ben Ohmart, who keeps alive the stars and character actors of yesteryear thanks to his BearManor Media. I also want to give a big Thank you out to Scott O'Brien, the writer of a marvelous biography of Kay Francis (*I Can't Wait to Be Forgotten*) for providing me with several articles and pictures from his collection as well as his memories as a young college student — meeting the wonderful Myrna Loy. Another big Thank you to Laura Wagner, the author (with Ray Hagen) of the wonderful book, *Killer Tomatoes: Fifteen Tough Film Dames*, for photographs from her collection, including the cover photograph.

We are lucky to live in an age when we can own or just go to a video store and rent a *Thin Man* film and enjoy at our leisure. These films have been delighting audiences for more than seventy years and will continue to go on doing so. I hope this book will give the reader more insight into the history of the films and the actors and creative teams behind them, but most of all I hope this book will reintroduce the reader to one of the finest series of films ever produced by Hollywood.

CHARLES TRANBERG
MADISON, WISCONSIN
DECEMBER 29, 2007

William Powell and Myrna Loy — the screen's greatest team.

CHAPTER ONE

WILLIAM POWELL: A TOUCH OF CLASS

"Possibly the most attractive man I ever met."
JACK LEMMON, 1984

William Powell is one of the bright lights of the American cinema. His best films are as alive and sparkling as when they were first released. Film critic Roger Ebert made a very astute statement when he wrote, "William Powell is to dialogue what Fred Astaire is to dance." They both represented the quintessential '30s man about town — both often decked out in top hat and tails. Astaire could be tongue tied with dialogue, but got his message across in dance — and how. Powell was the master of witty conversation and double entendres. He is droll and debonair. Neither was classically handsome, but Astaire captured the hearts of his leading ladies through his feet while Powell did it through his wit.

". . . I was born in Pittsburgh, Pa. July 29, 1892," Powell wrote in 1964 to somebody inquiring about his family roots in West Middlesex, Pennsylvania. "My father was Horatio Warren Powell, who was born Aug. 10, 1865 in West Middlesex. He was the second of seven children born to William S. and Harriet Powell . . . Until I was fourteen I used to spend my summers with my paternal grandparents at their home on Main where, as I remember, all their seven children (my uncles and aunts) were born. Next to their home (toward the railroad station) lived my great uncle Frank and great-aunt Lucy. They had a farm a short distance out of West Middlesex, where I used to ride (bareback!) a genial old mare called Bess. I have no remembrance of the James Powell's who moved to Nebraska, but I do remember great uncle Elija and great-aunt

MGM publicity shot of Bill, circa 1935.

Elizabeth . . . I am greatly indebted to her for having loaned me $700.00 in 1912, which enabled me to attend the American Academy of Dramatic Arts in New York City and launched me in the acting profession. I have never been back to West Middlesex since 1906 (or '07), but I have very idyllic memories of my boyhood summers there, now fading, I fear, into a more and more distant past . . . ."

We can add a little more to the story. When Powell was nine, his father, an attorney, moved the family away from Pittsburgh, settling in Kansas City, Missouri. Powell enrolled into Central High School in 1907. One of his teachers, Preston K. Dillenbeck, who taught elocution and public speaking, was impressed by Powell's strong voice and urged him to consider a career as an actor. This, as is usually the case, was counter what his father wished for him. His father wanted Powell to be a lawyer. But in high school, Powell seemed more inclined to take his instructor's advice and appeared in school plays, pageants and the glee club, which often made regional tours. He was so focused on the theater and other extracurricular activities that his grades reflected this, resulting in what Powell would later say were, "verbal skirmishes, in which my father insisted on the bar and I on the stage." (*Picturgoer*, 4/10/37) Among the plays Bill, as he was most usually called, performed in were *Twelfth Night* (as Malvolio) and a four-act comedy, *An American Citizen*, which was his school's Christmas presentation in 1910. He played his part with "genuineness," said a review of his performance. He also served as the president of Central's Shakespeare Club in his senior year.

Upon graduating, Bill decided to placate his father by enrolling into the University of Kansas to study law, but he quit within a few weeks. He then took on a job as a clerk for a telephone company, which paid $50 per month, and ushered at a local opera house which gave him the advantage of seeing the shows for free. Bill wanted to pursue the theater, but his father would give him no support in that aspiration. Bill spilled out his heart to a wealthy aunt (Aunt Elizabeth, who he spoke about in that 1964 letter) with a twenty-three-page letter in which he attempted to convince her to loan him $1400 so he could go to New York and study at the American Academy of Dramatic Arts. Aunt Elizabeth was touched, but was no pushover. She sent him half, $700, and told him he would have to earn the rest of the money and that she expected the money to be repaid — with interest — six percent. Bill happily agreed to this, and, while it would take him thirteen years, he did pay her back, and he never forgot her generosity.

He was accepted at the American Academy, one of the premier acting schools in the United States, and at that time, probably *the* top school. One of his classmates was Edward G. Robinson. (Future stars to come out of this school include Spencer Tracy, Ruth Gordon, Agnes Moorehead, Lauren Bacall, Kirk Douglas, Lee Remick and Robert Redford.) It was tough going and he described the winter of 1912-1913 as the "harshest of my life" as he tried to concentrate on his studies as well as earn a meager living, sharing an attic room with another young man. His first professional job as an actor was playing three bit parts in a play called *The Ne'er-Do-Well* at a salary of $40 per week. It ran only two weeks.

After leaving the American Academy Bill joined the road company of the play *Within the Law* and met the woman who would be his first wife, an actress in the production named Eileen Wilson. They married in 1915. While they loved each other, it was a stormy relationship with several separations. On one such separation they both (unknown to the other) sailed to Italy to forget. They ran into each other in Venice and reconciled. In 1925, a son, William David Powell, was born.

In 1917 Bill made his Broadway debut in the play *The King*, which ran for five months into March 1918. He then began working for two years in a stock company headed by a famous actor of the time, Leo Ditrichstein, who wrote, adapted and starred in several plays with Bill as one of his company of stock actors. Bill would later credit Ditrichstein for teaching him more about acting than anybody up to that time. They toured the country, and it is estimated that Bill appeared in more than 100 plays in stock — even appearing in a Civil War play with the future screenwriter of *The Thin Man*, Frances Goodrich. The budgets for these stock productions were often shoestring.

His big break came in 1920 when he appeared in the Broadway production of *Spanish Love* which ran for more than 300 performances. *Variety* reviewed the play and called Powell's performance "a personal triumph." Bill himself later said that *Spanish Love* represented his big break "because it brought me to the attention of movie people."

Bill was cast opposite John Barrymore in *Sherlock Holmes*, for Samuel Goldwyn. There have been stories over the years that he played Dr. Watson, but he actually was cast as a villain in the film, an assistant to the chief villain, Dr. Moriarty. This seemed to type him for he spent most of the '20s as cads or suave villains. He was then signed by William Randolph Hearst to play opposite Marion Davies in *When Knighthood Was in Flower*, appearing as the King of France, and *Under the Red Robe*, playing the Duke of Orleans.

Richard Barthelmess (who would become a lifelong friend) hired him to play in two films for his Inspiration Pictures: *The Bright Shawl* (which was filmed in Cuba) and *Ramola*, which featured him trying to seduce both Lillian and Dorothy Gish while wearing a pageboy wig. He was so effective in this role that Paramount offered him a seven-year contract in 1924. They actually gave him a chance to be the hero in *Faint Perfume*, but it was clear that they, too, saw him at his most effective when playing it nasty. He dumps his good wife in *Sea Horses* for another woman; abducts the heroine in the Western *Desert Gold*; and then was featured in one of his most important films to date, *Beau Geste*, as the thief who, in the midst of being tortured, commits suicide. He then appeared in the first film version of Fitzgerald's *The Great Gatsby*, as the gas station operator who shoots the hero. Other significant roles: the gangster in *New York*; yet another ethnic heavy (Spaniard) in *Senorita*; good guy Gary Cooper's rival in *Nevada* and appearing as an Arabian sheik in *She's a Sheik*. He was a far way from the Bill Powell that filmgoers of the '30s would come to know and love.

He then came to the attention of Josef von Sternberg who cast him as the sadistic movie director in *The Last Command*. It was not a happy film experience (Powell came to despise the tyrannical von Sternberg), but it was an effective role for Powell, and, despite his bad-guy role, his rakish good looks made feminine hearts aflutter. Von Sternberg would later write, "As an actor who was to portray the cruel and supercilious film director, I choose William Powell, who with that performance, which, to use his own words, was forced on him, was lifted from the ranks of minor players to become a star in his own right. He acknowledged his debt to me by specifying in the new contract that he was offered that he was never to be assigned to one of my films again." Not quite because Powell did work with von Sternberg once more, in *The Dragnet*.

Despite his busy resume in silent films, talkies would make William Powell. His was the perfect voice for this new sound medium. He made his first appearance in a talkie film, in 1929, playing a philanderer in *Interference*, and his cultured, stage-trained, but not stagy voice made a big impression. "His cultivated and expressive voice, his smooth, polished manner," wrote Elinor Hughes in the *Boston Herald*, "and easy assumption of emotion masked under flippant cynicism, made him the outstanding person in the cast."

Then somebody at Paramount finally got the bright idea that with that smooth voice and his general good looks he might actually make an appealing hero. Paramount brought the rights to the first two Philo Vance detective novels by S.S. Van Dine. The self-important and pompous sleuth of the Van Dine novels was marginally humanized by Bill, and *The Canary Murder Case* became a big hit for the studio. Powell later stated that Vance, "made a mint of money for the studio and did very well by yours truly," but felt that the character itself was too much of a snob. Van Dine enjoyed the money that Hollywood was paying him, but was contemptuous of the studio executive, telling a friend that all they knew how to do was to sign checks and make promises. As for

Bill as Philo Vance in *The Canary Murder Case*, with Louise Brooks, 1929.

Powell, Van Dine wasn't impressed, feeling that Powell's playing of Vance, "had the grace and subtlety of a Sicilian fisherman." But Van Dine's own biographer contradicts him, writing that he thought that Powell "was confident, efficient and debonair. He looked and sounded right." Louella Parsons said that Bill was delightful "playing that flippant bore with the pretentious British accent." Bill would play Vance in three more Paramount films over the next two years, *The Greene Murder Case, The Benson Murder Case* and, in a guest shot, in the all-star *Paramount on Parade*.

It was at around this time that his marriage to Eileen faltered for the final time and they were divorced after fifteen years of marriage. In 1931 Powell worked opposite a young blonde actress, Carole Lombard, in *Man of the World*, and they were soon seen around town, but the headstrong Lombard announced that she wasn't going to marry any man, "not even William Powell." Bill countered, "She's marvelous! She's the one girl for me. I want to marry her. I'm going to marry her." By early June of 1931 they announced their engagement and on June 26, 1931 they were wed in Lombard's Beverly Hills home with Bill's father acting as best man. At the time Bill commented of those who scoffed at the age difference between them (16 years), and how their marriage wouldn't work, "It's a lot of nonsense . . . we are in love with each other . . . and what then does a few years difference mean as long as Carole enjoys doing the same things I do . . . and I enjoy the same things she does."

In 1930 Powell had one of his last villainous turns in the film *Behind the Makeup*. His leading lady, Fay Wray (who would also work with Bill in *Thunderbolt*), recalls him as having "grace, style, wit and technique. He was not absolutely handsome, so that he was believable as a leading man or as a villain or whatever role. He was Olympian in the sense that he seemed to have achieved an elegant arrogance. When I see photos of him in splendid profile, I think of how he told me how he achieved that taut chin line, 'I start a swallow but don't finish it.'"

It was with *Behind the Makeup* that Bill worked for the first time with the up-and-coming actress Kay Francis. They would form a teaming which, although not quite as memorable as his later run with Myrna Loy, is no less effective. Powell later told Adela Rogers St. Johns that as an actress he found Kay, "as responsive as a violin

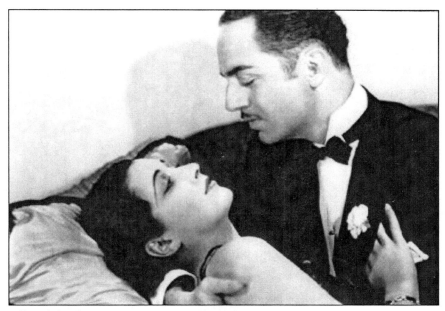

Bill with his first great screen partner, Kay Francis.

. . . I . . . love to talk out scenes and business with her. She's wonderful really." The feeling was mutual. "He's generous to work with," Francis said. "Has an unfailing sense of humor, is witty, has a fine code of honor, and is so essentially a gentleman under all conditions. We always laugh and joke when we are together — our humor seems pitched in the same key." They did get along beautifully off camera as well as on. For a time, before Bill married Carole Lombard, he was often seen squiring Kay around town and rumors of a romance were rife. But they were only friends. After *Behind the Makeup* they would appear opposite each other in five more films over the next two years.

A major difference between the Powell-Francis teaming and the Powell-Loy teaming is that at this time in his career Bill was not known on screen for his comedic work. His work is darker and the films themselves are more serious with fatalistic consequences between the leading man and leading lady. The later MGM films and the relationship between Bill and Myrna are lighter and more amusing and the endings inevitably more uplifting and leaving the audience with a smile on their face rather than a tear in their eyes.

Bill with Kay Francis in *One Way Passage*.

At this point Bill and Kay Francis were among the Paramount stars that were "raided" by Warner Brothers and put under contract. Warner Brothers knew they had a good thing and cast Bill and Kay in two more pictures, *Jewel Robbery* and *One Way Passage.* The latter film provided both stars with a hugely popular swan song. They would work together one last time in the late '30s in a radio adaptation of *One Way Passage.*

At Warner Brothers Bill also played Philo Vance one last time in *The Kennel Murder Case* and then was cast opposite a young Bette Davis in *Fashions of 1934.* But a significant film during this time was *High Pressure* which has the distinction of being Bill's first out-and-out screen comedy and, as such, it's very much a landmark. It was directed by Melvyn LeRoy and features Bill as a fast-talking promoter who makes money making rubber out of sewage.

At around this time Bill's two-year marriage to Carole Lombard was fast approaching an end. They would always be devoted friends but they were too dissimilar for their marriage to survive. Bill was basically shy and enjoyed staying home while Lombard was a free spirit who enjoyed dancing and partying. When the divorce became final Lombard was asked if she had any plans to marry again. "I am not planning to marry anybody. I prefer my career in pictures to marriage, and besides, I respect my former husband too much to want to wed again — not for a long time yet — and maybe not at all." (*Oakland Tribune*, 9/21/33) In time she would find the love of her life, Clark Gable. Bill, too, was telling reporters that he was doubtful that he would ever want to wed again and, in fact, was even contemplating retiring from the screen.

Warner Brothers then loaned Bill to MGM to appear opposite Clark Gable and Myrna Loy in *Manhattan Melodrama.* The film is very entertaining but it's the scenes between Bill and Myrna which really crackle. Director W.S. Van Dyke was convinced he found the team for his upcoming film an adaptation of Dashiell Hammett's best-selling novel *The Thin Man.* Some executives at MGM thought of Bill as an aging leading man, and Myrna, was best used as exotic vamps — not ideals for Nick and Nora. Van Dyke imposed his will and Powell and Loy became forever linked as one of the great teams in motion picture history as former detective Nick Charles and his socialite wife Nora who solve murder amid wisecracks and martinis.

Roger Ebert would later say that Bill plays Nick Charles "with a lyrical alcoholic slur that waxes and wanes but never topples either way into inebriation or sobriety. The drinks are the lubricant for dialogue of elegant wit and wicked timing, used by a character that is decadent on the surface but fundamentally brave and brilliant." The film became a huge hit and Bill was nominated, for the first of three times, for an Academy Award as Best Actor (losing to Clark Gable for *It Happened One Night*). When Warner Brothers, in an economy move, reduced Bill's salary to (a paltry!) $4,000 per week, Bill moved to MGM where he became more famous than ever as the studio's definitive light leading man.

Bill's services were in huge demand and he was put in one film after another. Powell and Loy were reunited in the heavy drama

Bill with Luise Rainer in *The Great Ziegfeld* 1936.

Evelyn Prentice; he was loaned out to RKO and Ginger Rogers for *Star of Midnight*; he and Jean Harlow were paired in *Reckless* which led to an off-screen love affair; and he was also very good with Jean Arthur in the *Thin Man*-like *The Ex-Mrs. Bradford*.

1936 was William Powell's year. He appeared in five memorable films: *The Ex-Mrs. Bradford*, *My Man Godfrey*, *The Great Ziegfeld*, *Libeled Lady* and *After the Thin Man*. Three were nominated for Best Picture of the year: *The Great Ziegfeld* (which ultimately won), *Libeled Lady* and *After the Thin Man*. Powell himself was nominated for his second Academy Award, for his superb performance in *My Man Godfrey*. With the exception of *The Thin Man* and *Life with Father*, *Godfrey* is probably Bill's best-remembered film. *My Man Godfrey* is the story of a bum, or the so-called Depression-era "forgotten man," who becomes a butler for a wacky heiress, and her equally crazy family. The film was shot at Universal, and Bill, who had script approval for all of his films made on loan out, insisted that only one actress could capture the wackiness and humanity of Irene and that was his ex-wife, Carole Lombard. It was a big publicity value at the time for ex-spouses to team up and this was no exception. The director of *My Man Godfrey* was the underrated Gregory La Cava. One story has Bill and La Cava having a script disagreement with the two spending the evening pouring over the script, with a bottle of scotch between them, attempting to find a consensus. The next morning La Cava arrived on the set, with a mighty hangover, to find no Powell. He soon received a telegram stating: WE MAY HAVE FOUND GODFREY LAST NIGHT BUT WE LOST POWELL. SEE YOU TOMORROW. The film proved a huge success with heavy profits for Universal which badly needed them at the time.

Libeled Lady is a real treat and Bill had the pleasure of not only working with Myrna Loy and Spencer Tracy, but his real-life love, Jean Harlow — making for a happy and fun set. *The Literary Digest* called the film "the cinema season's most piquant and daring comedy also is the funniest."

Coming off of the peak that was 1936, 1937 would be one of Bill's worst years. In fact, the next three years would be quite trying for the actor, now in his mid-40s. Two of his releases had less than stellar runs at the box office, *The Last of Mrs. Cheney* (with Joan

Bill with his great love, Jean Harlow.

Bill and Harlow in a candid moment.

Crawford) and *The Emperor's Candlesticks.* He then reunited with Loy in the enjoyable *Double Wedding*, in which he plays a bohemian artist. It was while filming *Double Wedding* that Jean Harlow suddenly became violently ill. She was on another set filming *Saratoga* with Clark Gable. She became so weak that she literally had to be lifted up and taken home. Harlow continued to decline while studio officials and Bill urged her Christian Scientist mother to admit her to the hospital, which was finally done. But it was too late. On June 7, 1937, Harlow died, leaving Bill devastated and, perhaps, a little guilty because Harlow very much wanted to marry him, but Bill hesitated due to his past track record in the marriage department. United Press International, in an article, would write, "Jean's mother and her latest suitor, dapper William Powell, appeared today to have suffered the severest shock over her death. Both were at her bedside in Good Samaritan Hospital urging her to fight harder for life when she sank into her last coma yesterday morning." At the funeral another report said, "Powell was pale as he escorted the bereaved mother to the chapel." Bill had "wept unrestrainedly" at the funeral and had to be supported as he left. After a few weeks Bill returned to the *Double Wedding* set. "Bill and I tried to carry on with this slapstick comedy," Myrna Loy recalled, "but he collapsed and the picture kept being delayed. He blamed himself for Jean's death: he had loved her but hadn't married her and taken her away from her mother. He'd call me for comfort when he got low. One day he phoned, moaning, 'This is a good throat-cutting day.' I put on my hat and ran, but he was over it by the time I arrived. 'It was an Irish funk,' he explained. 'It's just the Irish in me.'"

In December 1937 Bill was loaned out to Twentieth Century-Fox for another forgettable comedy, *The Baroness and the Butler.* Little did he know but, when that film wrapped in January of 1938, he wouldn't be on another soundstage shooting a new movie for nearly 21 months. What happened to Bill was long kept secret from the public. It was only known that he was not well, but he, nor the studio, went into any kind of elaborate explanation. It was only in the early '60s that Bill came forward, then in comfortable retirement, with his story of his beating cancer. In March of 1938 the papers announced that Bill had gone into the hospital for an operation for an intestinal obstruction. What he was really suffering from was rectal cancer. The doctors wanted to operate immediately and remove his entire rectum. He underwent extensive testing over the next few years, but the cancer never returned. Despite beating cancer, he was quite weak, but he felt the need for some work and while he couldn't for the time being endure the difficulties of making movies, he did appear on some radio programs. (One of the films that he had to turn down due to his health was *Ninotchka* opposite Greta Garbo; the part ultimately went to Melvyn Douglas.) Bill would later say of his fight against cancer, "I was one of the lucky ones."

In the middle of July 1939, he finally was well enough to begin acting in front of the cameras again. MGM was happy to have him and they put Bill in comfortable surroundings with people he genuinely enjoyed working with — director W.S. Van Dyke and Myrna Loy — for the third *Thin Man* adventure, *Another Thin Man*. Bill would never work as hard again. By this time he had been making films for 17 years and had appeared in 70 motion pictures. In the fifteen years remaining of his active movie career he would only work in 21 more films, two of which could be described as guest appearances (*The Youngest Profession, It's a Big Country*).

Bill acted, too, like a man given a second chance in his private life. He had given MGM permission to do some publicity stills around his pool with a young actress. On the day that the studio arrived to do the photographs he had forgotten and was at home when he caught sight of a young, attractive blonde, the subject of the photographs, twenty-one-year-old Diana Lewis, who had only appeared in a few films. He was taken by the 5'1" blonde, and between shots he teased her about her relative short stature (Powell himself was only 5'6"), telling her, "You look like a little mouse." He asked her out and she accepted. His nickname for her would be from that point forward "Mousey." Within weeks of their introduction they eloped to Nevada and were married before a Justice of the Peace at a ranch near Las Vegas. The marriage would be a long (44 years) and happy one.

During the early forties Powell continued to be one of MGM's highest paid actors and he appeared in four straight films opposite Loy (*Another Thin Man, I Love You, Again, Love Crazy* and *Shadow of the Thin Man*). In 1942 he was cast opposite Hedy Lamarr for the first of two times in *Crossroads*, then, in 1944, MGM put Bill and Lamarr together again, this time in a comedy, *The Heavenly Body*. The teaming of Powell and Lamarr just didn't have the sparkle of his teamings with Loy and Kay Francis. Both films were disappointments at the box office. What wartime audiences wanted was more *Thin Man* and in 1944 Myrna Loy gave in and returned to the MGM fold for her one and only wartime film, *The Thin Man Goes Home*, which is one of the funniest of their outings, and most domestic, with Powell's Nick Charles not drinking a drop of alcohol in the entire film. In one scene, poor Nick is reduced to drinking apple cider!

In his next film, *The Hoodlum Saint*, Bill was cast against type as a huckster who finds religion. The film faltered. At this point, Bill very much needed a big hit, since, with the exception of *The Thin Man* films, he hadn't really had any huge successes at the box office since the early '40s. When Warner Brothers bought the film rights to the hugely successful stage play *Life with Father*, Bill appealed directly to Louis B. Mayer to loan him out to Warner

Bill and Myrna in one of their non-*Thin Man* collaborations, *I Love You, Again*, 1941.

Brothers to play "father" — a change-of-pace role, which he felt would reinvigorate his career. Since MGM hadn't really anything on their plate for Bill, they loaned him out (along with young Elizabeth Taylor) to Warner Brothers and the result was one of Bill's biggest successes, and most remembered films. Needless to say, this film became one of the year's biggest successes and Powell won some of the best notices of his career. Bosley Crowther, of the *New York Times*, put *Life with Father* on his list of the ten best films of 1947, and in his review of the film wrote, "Even his voice, always so distinctive, has taken on a new quality, so completely has Mr. Powell managed to submerge his own personality. His Father is not merely a performance; it is character delineation of a high order, and he so dominates the picture that even when he is not on hand his presence is still felt." Bill was nominated for the third and final time for an Oscar. While he didn't win (losing to pal Ronnie Colman), he was awarded the New York Film Critics Award for his performance in this film and the one he gave in *The Senator Was Indiscreet*, which was released the same year.

Add *Song of the Thin Man*, Powell's final co-starring film with Myrna Loy, to the mix and 1947 was Bill's strongest year since 1936. Powell later called his role in *Life with Father* the favorite of his career.

He was now in his mid-fifties and graying. His days as Nick Charles were over. The final *Song of the Thin Man* did well at the box office, making a profit for MGM of more than $500,000, but the studio was now discontinuing their series films. Increasingly, Bill began appearing in character parts. It seemed that despite his personal successes with *Life with Father* and *The Senator Was Indiscreet* MGM didn't know what to do with an aging William Powell. Of his eight final films only two were made for MGM. For Universal he played a fisherman who hooks a mermaid in the enjoyable *Mr. Peabody and the Mermaid* (Ann Blyth) and entered the realm of film noir with *Take One False Move*. He then went to Twentieth Century-Fox to play a faded ex-movie star in *Dancing in the Dark*. He had one of his most unusual roles as an eccentric medicine man in the Universal Western *The Treasure of Lost Canyon*. In 1953 came his final film as an MGM contract player, third billed as Elizabeth Taylor's father in *The Girl Who Has Everything*.

Bill holds onto Myrna Loy, while Spencer Tracy has a lap full of Jean Harlow, on the set of *Libeled Lady*.

He ended his film career in style as the distinguished older man (Texas millionaire, though Bill uses no trace of a Texas accent) who Lauren Bacall should have married in *How to Marry a Millionaire*. He then went out strong playing Doc in the screen adaptation of another long-running stage hit, *Mister Roberts*. It was not a happy shoot. Henry Fonda, who had played Roberts on stage, didn't like the direction that director John Ford was taking the film. He felt it was getting too slapsticky and losing the subtleness and nuance of the play. Perhaps capitalizing on Bill's Nick Charles persona, Ford wanted to make Doc a drunk. Ford left the film, claiming illness, and Melvyn LeRoy came in and reshot scenes making Doc sober, and one of the rocks that Roberts and the rest of the crew could depend on. Bill enjoyed working with the great cast (Fonda, James Cagney and young Jack Lemmon); Lemmon would recall that Bill

Bill and "Mousie" Powell in his Palm Springs retirement.

acted as the "den mother" for the cast and that he shared quarters with Bill when they were on location shooting the picture. The film went on to be a huge success at the box office and critically.

Bill made no announcements; he just suddenly decided to call it a day. Myrna Loy knew something was wrong when she received two dozen roses from Bill and called him up. "So what's going on?" Powell explained to her that he wouldn't be doing a proposed TV program with her. He was done with acting. Bill and Mousie quietly lived out their years in Palm Springs. It seemed like every decade or so he would allow an interview.

In 1968, his son, a struggling writer, committed suicide.

He remained remarkably healthy except that he did become rather deaf. A day before he died, he was admitted to Desert Hospital in Palm Springs after experiencing trouble breathing. He quietly passed away on March 5, 1984, at age 91, from "infirmities of age" per his physician. "I'm very grateful to have had him 44 years," said Mousie. "I think it was very fortunate for all of us that he was with us for so long." Jack Lemmon memorialized Bill, "He was not only filled with qualities of decency, but he had a sense of compassion, humor and gentleness, and above all, he had grace and elegance. That man spread an awful lot of sunshine." His frequent screen wife Myrna Loy said, "I never enjoyed my work more than when I worked with William Powell. He was a brilliant actor, a delightful companion, a great friend and above all, a true gentleman. I shall miss him more than I can say."

CHAPTER TWO

MYRNA LOY:
A WOMAN OF CONVICTIONS

"A great star and a woman of accomplishment who is angry about all the right things."

LENA HORNE

"Even my best friends never fail to tell me that the smartest thing I ever did was to marry Myrna Loy on the screen." It was the smartest thing William Powell did, or, rather, MGM ever did. The teaming of William Powell and Myrna Loy rejuvenated his career and enhanced hers. The sloe-eyed, freckle-faced, copper-headed girl from Montana with the slightly tilted-up nose came to epitomize the modern woman. The critics called her the "perfect wife." Loy scoffed at that. "I prefer Gore Vidal's description of my image, 'The eternal good-sex woman wife' which removes the puritanical connotation of perfect. What man would want a perfect wife, anyway?"

She was born Myrna Williams on August 2, 1905, in Helena, Montana. Her father was a rancher and former Republican state legislator. But there was nothing "stand pat" about him, for he was a Teddy Roosevelt progressive. Her mother was a Democrat who was active in the community. Myrna grew up in an atmosphere in which current events were discussed and community activism was encouraged. Loy later said that she developed her own innate social consciousness as a child, ". . . it was part of the air I breathed . . . I was taught early in life that there was a relationship between the world and me." Myrna later recalled that when the first black family moved into their neighborhood, most people shunned them, but not the Williamses, "Mother made no distinction. She welcomed them and encouraged us [Myrna and her little brother, David] to play with them."

The Screen's Perfect Wife was pretty sexy.

Her father and mother didn't live their lives as stereotypes of what a man's role was and what a woman's role was supposed to encompass. According to Myrna, her mother "loathed" cooking while her father rather enjoyed dabbling in the kitchen, "and was darn good at it too, having learned over a campfire at round up time." They lived up on a hill and were considered well-to-do but not exactly rich. Their neighbors in the big house down the hill, Judge and Mrs. Cooper, were considered among the more prosperous families in Helena. They even sent their son, Gary, to school in England. Little did anybody know at the time that Myrna and Gary would eventually become two of the biggest stars in Hollywood.

Myrna's mother wanted to live in California, but her father preferred Montana. This caused some strain in part because Myrna's mother needed an operation for a hysterectomy, and felt it would be safer if it were done in Los Angeles. Myrna's mother did go to Los Angeles for her operation and took along Myrna and her brother and they stayed for some weeks as she recuperated. It was while on this trip that Myrna got her first look at a movie studio — taking a tour of Universal and watching them make a Western. She said at the time, like many kids her age, she wanted to be an actress.

While in California Myrna was hit by the dancing bug. She watched marvelous dancers at theaters and began to emulate them. She later described herself a "natural" dancer for all she had to do was watch a routine and she could pick up on the steps. But her father wanted his family to come home as soon as possible. When they did, Myrna began taking lessons in Helena.

In the fall of 1918 Helena was struck by the Spanish influenza which was afflicting much of the country and, in fact, much of the world at the time. "People walked the streets with makeshift surgical masks over their mouths," Myrna recalled. When Myrna's mother and brother came down with the flu both Myrna and her father nursed them. As they were recovering, it hit Myrna and her father was alone — caring for all of them. Myrna would recall the look of pain in his face as her father nursed her.

Just as she, her mother, and brother were practically recovered, it hit her father — and it hit him the worst. He began hemorrhaging. Myrna was taken in by some neighbors across the street. In her autobiography, she wrote of an old Swedish saying that when a bird hits a window, somebody is going to die. While at the neighbor's house, a bird hit the window. Within minutes the phone rang; her father had died. Myrna would recall that her father had once told her that if anything ever happened to him he wanted her to take care of her mother and little brother. Myrna never forgot that and pledged to fulfill his wishes. She was only thirteen.

With her father gone, Myrna's mother decided to move to California where she felt the year-round sunshine would be good for all of them, especially David who had a mild case of TB. The family settled in Culver City. Myrna continued to dance and put on shows in her front yard. She also began to study ballet. Her mother enrolled her into the Westlake School for Girls. Her mother, to supplement her income, began giving music lessons and working at a friend's dress shop. Her mother was able to get discounts on clothing and dress Myrna well when she was attending the exclusive Westlake school. Myrna recalled that the girls at Westlake were "uppity" and eventually she switched to Venice High School where she became interested in art.

To help the family's finances, Myrna began teaching dance at the Ritter School of Expression in Culver City. "My salary, of forty dollars a month," Myrna recalled, "went directly to my mother." She also earned some extra money working as a splicer at the Hal Roach Studios.

In 1923, shortly after she graduated from high school, Myrna got a job as a dancer at Grauman's Chinese Theater in Hollywood. One day a photographer took pictures of the dancing girls. Rudolph Valentino saw one of the pictures and, taken by Myrna's beauty, thought that she would be perfect for a small part in a film of his, *Cobra*, which eventually didn't pan out. Instead, he suggested Myrna to his wife, Natacha Rambova, for a movie they were producing, **What Price Beauty?** It became her first film role. She then tested for the part as the virgin in **Ben-Hur** but instead was cast as the mistress of one of the senators. Her next film, **Pretty Ladies**, featured her as a show girl with another who had yet to hit it big — Joan Crawford. The two would form a lifelong friendship.

It is ironic that Loy, considered one of filmdom's "good girls" in her real life, spent so many of her early years in films cast as vamps, probably because of her distinctive cat eyes. It was felt that the name "Myrna Williams" was not exotic enough for that image so a new last name was given to her by a writer friend — "Loy." Myrna Loy. It had a ring to it. She signed a contract with Warner Brothers and played an Indian girl in **The Black Watch**; a Mexican in **The Great Divide**; an island native in **Isle of Escape**; and, most unusual of all, was one of several white actors appearing in blackface in an Army comedy, **Ham and Eggs at the Front**. She had a walk-on as a dancer in **The Jazz Singer** and then worked with John Barrymore playing a maid, one of the few women not seduced by **Don Juan**.

Myrna in one of her early Oriental vamp roles.

"I worked with the two greatest lovers in the world at an age when I was too young to appreciate it," Myrna recalled of Valentino and Barrymore. "Valentino was a great gentleman — and so was Jack Barrymore, but Jack was also a rascal." She was then cast in major roles in *Bitter Apples*, playing a girl who marries a man out of revenge but slowly comes to love him, and then came the first in a series of Oriental vamps in *Crimson City*. In 1929 she had a role in the classic *Noah's Ark*, in which she played a dancer in the modern part, and a slave girl in the Biblical portion of the picture.

She was let go by Warner Brothers, but, having no problem adapting to sound, made the rounds of the studios and in 1930 appeared in no less than nine motion pictures, including *Cameo Kirby, Under a Texan Moon, Cock 'O the Walk, Bride of the Regiment, The Jazz Cinderella* and *The Truth about Youth*. At the end of 1930 she had a big success playing the woman (donning a blonde wig) Ronald Colman sacrifices for Loretta Young in *The Devil to Pay*. She was in an even bigger hit the next year opposite Will Rogers in *A Connecticut Yankee*. Producer Sam Goldwyn liked Myrna's performance in *The Devil to Pay* so much that he asked for her to play the part of Joyce Lanyon, in one of her last vamp roles, opposite Ronald Colman and Helen Hayes, in the John Ford film *Arrowsmith*.

By 1932 Myrna had made over sixty films without really becoming a star. One producer in Hollywood believed in her, though, and he was an important one — Irving Thalberg, the boy genius at MGM. When Thalberg signed her to a contract in 1932, he told her, "There is something holding you back. There seems to be a veil between you and the audience. You've got to cut thru it. You must reach out there and grab them." Her first picture of the MGM contract was opposite Metro's most popular leading lady, Marie Dressler, playing the spiteful stepdaughter in *Emma*. She was then cast as Neil Hamilton's girlfriend in *The Wet Parade*. But she also had her last stands with evil in the films *13 Women* (where she murders the sorority sisters who had snubbed her years before) and, her final Oriental, as Boris Karloff's evil daughter, in *The Mask of Fu Manchu*. But it was on loan out from MGM that she had her most significant roles to date, delicious as the horny countess in *Love Me Tonight* for Paramount and Leslie Howard's self-centered wife in *The Animal Kingdom* at RKO. It was these two roles that she finally, and effectively, cut thru that veil that Thalberg spoke about, and he was ready to give her some important roles at her home studio.

She was third billed as the lady novelist in love with Frank Morgan in the enjoyable *When Ladies Meet*. She was cast opposite John Barrymore in *Topaze* playing a Baron's mistress who takes an interest in a simple school teacher. She then worked for the first time with the man who was probably most responsible for her finally becoming a star, director W.S. Van Dyke, in the pre-Code *Penthouse*. Loy's first day on the set with Van Dyke on *Penthouse* cemented their relationship. Loy walked on the set, apprehensive about the film and the director. The first scene would be shot without a rehearsal, "Okay, gang. Let's go," Van Dyke called out. Soon after the cameras began rolling, Van Dyke called, "Cut!" He felt that Myrna was overacting and trying to be too melodramatic. "Ah, that's a lot of nonsense, Myrna. You don't have to act." Myrna was shocked by his frankness and buoyed by the way he built up her ego. He was smiling at her and putting her at ease. "This part," he told her, "calls for a typical American girl and you're certainly the type yourself, Myrna, and that's what I want." For a girl accustomed to playing exotic and ethnic roles, this was a revelation. From then on the shooting went smoothly and when the film wrapped Van Dyke told her that she was going to become an important star. He went to Thalberg and Louis B. Mayer and told them that it was time to stop misusing Myrna Loy and making her appear as exotics and vamps and begin to cast her as she is — an all-American girl. He told them that if they did this she would be the most popular feminine star on the screen.

Bill and Myrna with Clark Gable in *Manhattan Melodrama*, 1934.

They took Van Dyke's advice and soon Myrna was cast as Clark Gable's leading lady in *Men in White* and then Van Dyke asked for her to be the leading lady opposite Gable again in *Manhattan Melodrama* which, of course, also starred William Powell, on loan out from Warner Brothers. In her autobiography Loy says, "I don't recall much about my scenes with Clark" and that the "picture doesn't get going until Bill comes in." From their first scene together both Loy and Powell could feel the chemistry between them; "from the very first scene, a curious thing passed between us, a feeling of rhythm, complete understanding, an instinct for how one could bring out the best in each other. In all our work together you can see this strange — I don't know what . . . kind of rapport. It wasn't conscious . . . Whatever caused it, though, it was magical."

But this film was only the beginning. Van Dyke liked what he saw on screen between Powell and Loy and insisted, over some studio objections, that they be teamed again in *The Thin Man*. That elusive something that they had in *Manhattan Melodrama* was now in full bloom and as Nick and Nora Charles was something new — a married couple on screen that actually enjoyed being married and enjoyed all aspects of married life — not the least of all, sex. The affectionately bitchy bantering with one trying to top the other with witticisms, not to mention their post-Prohibition love of alcohol, captured the hearts and funny bones of Depression-era audiences. Loy's Nora was the instigator of the action. Born of wealth, she was captivated by the whole idea of investigating murders amid chic conversation and cocktails. Nick wanted nothing more than to retire and enjoy his wife's money. She loved the thrill of the chase as well as the eclectic friends that Nick collected over the years as a detective — people who he had invariably put away but held no hard feelings toward. "There was a spontaneous gaiety which had much to do with the understated incisiveness of the stars' playing," David Thomson later wrote. "Their styles matched perfectly and it is obvious . . . that they loved acting together. The team became one of the keystones of MGM in the '30s." They enjoyed each other as much as people as they did as a team. Powell was impressed by Loy as a professional. "I never saw Myrna go into a temperamental tantrum, rave and rant, or walk off the set in a huff. She never lets her emotions come too near the surface, and remains calm and poised in the most difficult situations. There were days on the set when she liked to sit alone, and other days when she felt rowdydow and wanted to play pranks."

While Powell and Loy would be increasingly cast together, they both continued to enjoy rich solo careers with each of their careers enhanced by their teaming. Loy, with the success of *The Thin Man*, finally became one of MGM's top female stars. Powell, who left Warner Brothers, was signed by MGM where he became the classiest of light leading men. Myrna was loaned out to Columbia and Frank Capra for *Broadway Bill* and Paramount to play opposite (for the first of three times) a young Cary Grant in the aviation drama *Wings in the Dark*. She was cast opposite Spencer Tracy (in a role meant for Powell) in the comedy *Whipsaw*. "I couldn't figure her out," Tracy later said. "I'd just come from the *Riffraff* set, where Jean Harlow had spent her leisure time making life merry for me and the rest of the crew. But here was a girl who finished her scene and retired into a corner to study her script. There must be something wrong with one of us. I prowled around for a day or two, then I marched myself up to her: 'What's the matter with me? Have I got leprosy or something?' Myrna smiled. 'I've been wondering when you were going to come and pay me a little attention.' That was all I needed. Twenty-four hours later we were on ribbing terms."

When she wasn't playing opposite William Powell, she was often cast opposite the King of the MGM lot — Clark Gable. By 1936 Loy and Gable had already appeared in three films together: *Night Flight, Men in White* and *Manhattan Melodrama*. She was now cast opposite Gable and Jean Harlow in *Wife vs. Secretary* (naturally, Myrna was the wife). She later said that she played off her leading men in very different ways, where she was "detached and a little incredulous" with Powell it was a different story with Gable. "Clark . . . suffered so much from the macho thing," she later wrote, "that love scenes were difficult. He kept very reserved, afraid to be sensitive for fear it would counteract his masculine image." With Gable she had to compensate and rather than being detached had to be "a little tough with him, giving him what-for to bring him out, because he liked girls like that." While Jean Harlow played "the other woman" in *Wife vs. Secretary*, it is Myrna as Gable's wife who oozes sex appeal. Loy later called her "perfect wife" in *Wife vs. Secretary* "the sexiest wife I ever played."

In 1935-1936, as Myrna's films were becoming bigger box office hits, she was still stuck in a contract which was paying her much less than her marquee value was worth. She went on strike and took off to New York and Europe while MGM stewed. They threatened her with everything they had but Myrna had all the bargaining chips in her corner with her newfound popularity. MGM renegotiated her contract, with her new agent Myron Selznick, brother of David, and one of the top agents in the business, and she was now paid $3,500 per week.

On the personal front her life took a further change. Up to this time Myrna had continued to live with her mother and younger brother. She had had her romances but by the age of thirty she had never married. She was too caught up with her career to consider it. All that changed when she met the producer Arthur Hornblow, Jr. They had actually met at the time of *Arrowsmith* and while he was giving her the eye, she was warily trying to avoid him because he was still married, and to a good girl like Myrna to date a married man was a definite no-no. He and his wife finally separated and Myrna, also attracted, was smitten and against her mother's wishes (her mother still wanted to control Myrna's life) they married on June 27, 1936.

In 1936 Myrna and William Powell were teamed together in no less than three very popular and classic motion pictures. It was the peak of their popularity as a team. First up was her impersonation of Billie Burke, complete with blonde wig, in *The Great Ziegfeld*.

Much better, however, was their second collaboration, and one of the best of all screwball comedies, *Libeled Lady*, which also starred Spencer Tracy and Jean Harlow. *Libeled Lady* became a hit, earning $2.7 million at the box office, and was well received by the critics. "Count on an hour and a half of almost continuous laughs . . . in a bubbling French-type farce, tailored in the smartest American mode, that sparkles and twists, and enough witty dialog to stock five ordinary comedies," wrote *The Hollywood Reporter*.

The Powell-Loy team ended the year with *After the Thin Man*, reprising their roles as Nick and Nora Charles, and in the opinion of some critics this film even superior to the first. Also in 1936 Myrna

Myrna was by 1936 one of MGM's most popular actresses.

had appeared in a less well-known film which may, nevertheless, contain one of her most effective performances, *To Mary with Love* opposite Warner Baxter. It is a story which looks back on ten years of a marriage which is now on the brink of divorce. So popular at this time was Myrna that she began to appear in the list of the top ten box office stars. In 1937 Ed Sullivan would conduct a

Myrna proved she was capable of playing even slapstick comedy.

well-publicized poll (in some 400 newspapers) to name the "King and Queen" of Hollywood. When the results were tallied, the King was Clark Gable and the Queen was Myrna. They were crowned on a national radio broadcast.

In 1937 Myrna slowed down a bit and appeared in only two pictures. She replaced Joan Crawford opposite Clark Gable in *Parnell,* based on the true story of the Irish politician whose career was jeopardized by his affair with a married woman (Myrna). Audiences didn't seem to know what to make of the film with its two stars playing so far from their acknowledged screen personas. Myrna would later write, "Disgruntled fans wrote to the studio by the thousands — they did that in those days. Some of the critics complained that we played against type. We were actors, for God's sake. We couldn't be Blackie Norton and Nora Charles all the time." Myrna's other assignment was with Powell in *Double Wedding,* a piece of fluff but definitely a letdown after *The Thin Man, Libeled Lady* and *After the Thin Man.*

By this time Myrna had appeared with Bill Powell in seven films over a span of three years. But they wouldn't appear together again for over two more years due to Powell's bout with cancer and depression following the death of Jean Harlow. Powell would be off the screen for most of this time only to reappear in late 1939, opposite Myrna, in *Another Thin Man*. In the meanwhile, Myrna appeared in a string of films, including *Man-Proof* which had her top-billed over Franchot Tone, Rosalind Russell and Walter Pidgeon. She then did two very popular back-to-back films with Clark Gable, *Test Pilot* (cited by Myrna as her favorite role) and *Too Hot to Handle*. This was to be Myrna's final screen teaming with Clark Gable, one which is almost as much fun, but not quite as memorable, as her teaming with William Powell.

Myrna then went into one of her lesser films, *Lucky Lady* opposite Robert Taylor, and then into one of her all-time best, on loan out to Twentieth Century-Fox, *The Rains Came*. Myrna plays the shallow Lady Edwina who is later redeemed in part due to the selflessness of a young Indian doctor after a series of natural disasters. The film certainly gave Myrna more to do than some of her "perfect wife" roles did and she made the most of it. She works well with Tyrone Power, cast as the young Indian doctor, Major Rama Safti. The film ended up being a huge box office success.

Myrna would appear in only four more films before the United States' entry into the Second World War. Three of them were with William Powell: *I Love You, Again, Love Crazy* and *Shadow of the Thin Man*. The one non-Powell film was a comedy with Melvyn Douglas (MGM's William Powell-lite), *Third Finger, Left Hand*.

Shortly after *Shadow of the Thin Man* opened, the United States was attacked at Pearl Harbor and the country entered World War II. Myrna went to the MGM front office and told them that for the duration of the war she would not appear in any films as she wished to devote her time to the war effort, in particular, volunteer work on behalf of the Red Cross. MGM was reluctant to agree to this because, after all, Myrna was one of their top female stars, but they finally agreed. By this time, too, her marriage to Arthur Hornblow was flagging; in her autobiography, she would write that she was worn down by Hornblow's constant put-downs. She had been pursued for some time by John Heinz, Jr., the son of the car rental king. They were married soon after Myrna's divorce from Hornblow became final. Heinz encouraged Myrna's retirement from the movies, not so much due to her work on behalf of the war effort but

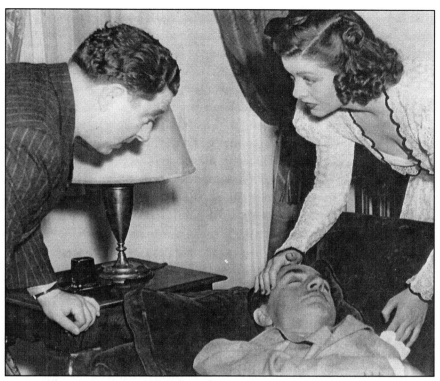

Myrna and Bill in *I Love You, Again*.

Myrna and Bill in another non-*Thin Man* film, *Love Crazy*, 1941.

because his fragile ego couldn't encourage a wife who was more prominent than he. It was a marriage doomed almost from the beginning, and would end in divorce within two years.

But in the meanwhile Myrna did devote herself to the war effort by participating in promotional films on behalf of war bonds and Bundles for Britain. She went on countless war bond tours throughout the United States. She visited army hospitals and cheered up the troops and gave of her time at the Red Cross. Many male stars gave up their careers and enlisted in the military, but it can be said that the only female star who almost exclusively gave up her career and devoted her time to the war effort was Myrna Loy. All the major female stars gave of their time, but none of them stopped making movies. This goes back to her sense of being part of a world that was bigger than thinking only of herself, which was a part of Myrna's upbringing. But, needless to say, the public did clamor for Myrna and so did the studio to make just one more *Thin Man* film. And in 1944, Myrna reunited with Bill Powell for *The Thin Man Comes Home* by popular demand. It would be her only wartime film and one she only reluctantly agreed to.

When the war was over and actors resumed their careers, a lot of thought went into their first post-war films. For some of these actors it had been three, four or even five years since they last appeared on the big screen and they feared that they would be forgotten. Myrna decided to go back to work but it seemed as if MGM didn't really know what to do with her. They seemed to now only want her for the occasional *Thin Man*. She had been slated to star opposite Spencer Tracy in *Sea of Grass*, which would have been perfect for her with her western background, but was surprised when she was abruptly replaced by Katharine Hepburn. She felt if they weren't going to use her she may as well go elsewhere and asked for her release — which was reluctantly granted.

When Olivia de Havilland decided that the part of Milly Stephenson in Sam Goldwyn's *The Best Years of Our Lives* was too small for her talents, the producer wisely went to Myrna. It made perfect sense. Myrna was the epitome of "the perfect wife" and in *Best Years* she would represent the wives who had spent the war years keeping the home fires burning waiting for their husbands to return. Goldwyn's biographer would write, "Even though Goldwyn

A glamorous Miss Loy.

doubted she would ever accept so small a role, it took only one dinner at Laurel Lane (his home) to discover that her arm needed no twisting. 'I read the book,' Miss Loy remembered, 'and when Sam Goldwyn asked if I would play the part, I said, 'Yes' — fast.'" The only apprehension that Myrna had about accepting the part was the reputation of the film's director, William Wyler. "My only reservation about doing *The Best Years of Our Lives* concerned working with William Wyler — because of all the stories from Bette Davis and other actors about his endless retakes and bullying. 'I hear Wyler's a sadist,' I told Goldwyn. 'That's not true,' he replied '. . . he's just a very mean fellow.'" Needless to say, they got along fine and Myrna delivered, perhaps, her finest screen performance. When returning husband Fredric March comes home and the camera captures the look of joy on her face, it was something that all G.I. wives could relate to. The film was an immense international hit and was well received by critics. It won a truck load of Oscars, but, once again, Myrna was ignored.

She and Powell teamed for the final adventures of Nick and Nora Charles in *Song of the Thin Man*. It would be their final co-starring film together, though Loy would appear in a cameo playing — what else? — Bill Powell's wife in *The Senator Was Indiscreet* later in 1947. Of their teaming Myrna would say, "Perhaps it's because it isn't like working. Bill and I seem to be kidding along. And the next thing you know, the picture is finished." She did two delightful back-to-back comedies with Cary Grant, *The Bachelor and the Bobbysoxer* and especially *Mr. Blandings Builds His Dream House*, where Myrna has one of her funniest scenes ever being ever-so specific in picking out the colors used to paint each room in the house.

But it seemed that by this time Myrna's chief concern was still on behalf of the government and fostering peace and understanding among the peoples of different countries and cultures. She accepted a post as a delegate to the United Nations Educational, Scientific and Cultural Organization (UNESCO). "UNESCO's work is unspectacular," she said at the time, "and doesn't attract nearly the attention that it should. Naturally the debates before the main body of the United Nations are much more dramatic. But UNESCO is doing a constructive work which has as its goal a world where peace and plentifulness are not subjects to discuss but such accepted facts that no one thinks about them." She also married again in 1946, to screenwriter Gene Markey, a marriage which would only last four years.

Myrna never made any bones about her liberal politics, supporting FDR and criticizing the work of the House UnAmerican Activities Committee (HUAC). She was firmly in support of civil rights. Naturally, in these times of the Communist witch hunts, her name came under scrutiny. When a frustrated playwright, Myron C. Fagan, published a pamphlet alleging that various Hollywood liberals were Communists, most of those named decided to ignore it; Katharine Hepburn, for example, thought it would bring more attention than it was worth. But not Myrna; she sent her lawyers in and ultimately won a retraction.

By 1950, 45-year-old Myrna had no problem accepting parts other actresses, like Joan Crawford, might hesitate in taking — such as a mother in *Cheaper by the Dozen*, based on a best-selling novel about the adventures of an eminent psychologist and his wife and their rambunctious life raising 12 kids. The film was a huge hit and spawned a sequel two years later also starring Loy, *Belles on Their Toes*. This would be the final starring role of Myrna Loy in a major motion picture and, in fact, the final film that she would appear in for four years. In the meanwhile, she married again, this time to Howland Sergeant, an Assistant Secretary of State for Public Affairs. This marriage would be her longest lasting, nine years. Of her four failed marriages Myrna would say in 1980, "I suppose if I were doing that today, I wouldn't get married so many times. But in those days we still had this thing that we had to get married. Not that I didn't love each of the men I married, but I might not have felt the need to make it official."

She returned to the big screen in 1956 this time playing a supporting role to Olivia de Havilland in *The Ambassador's Daughter*. She followed this by giving a strong dramatic performance as an alcoholic in Dore Schary's production of *Lonelyhearts*, playing the unhappily married wife of newspaper editor Robert Ryan and opening her heart to advice columnist Montgomery Clift. Following *Lonelyhearts*, Myrna was cast as yet another alcoholic, playing Paul Newman's mother in *From the Terrace*. In 1960 she would make her last movie for nine years, in the Doris Day–Rex Harrison thriller *Midnight Lace.*

During the '60s she began appearing on the stage. In 1961 she appeared in summer stock in *Marriage-Go-Round* and *Good Housekeeping.* But her biggest success on stage came in the mid-'60s when she starred in the national touring company of the Neil Simon hit *Barefoot in the Park. Coronet*, a popular monthly magazine, would write, "Beginning in Central City, Colorado, and starring in the comedy in large cities throughout the United States, again Miss Loy played to standing-room audiences. Then, on May 10, 1965, *Barefoot* opened in Chicago, a city which invites long runs to musical comedies, but which is notorious for rejecting within six or eight weeks the most celebrated straight plays or non-musical comedies, no matter how triumphant a run they may have had on Broadway. *Barefoo*t, a non-musical comedy, lasted incredibly for almost a solid year in Chicago — and to packed houses."

Writer Scott O'Brien, then a college freshman, got a chance to meet Myrna Loy when *Barefoot in the Park* came to San Francisco. "My parents said they would drive from our home in Stockton to San Francisco so I could see the play and they would meet me afterwards. I wrote Myrna a letter in care of the Curran, or Geary Theatre (I can't remember which) and asked if I could please meet her before the matinee. When I didn't hear from her, I decided to go backstage afterwards. The house was packed, and she absolutely sparkled on stage. Following the play I found the stage door and was told I could wait to meet Miss Loy. Standing in the same area was Richard Benjamin and Paula Prentiss. They were very friendly, asking if I had seen the play and what I thought about it. They probably knew I was a little star-struck about Myrna — and Benjamin began to rave on what a wonderful experience it was to work with her. I could really sense his admiration . . . Finally, someone said I could see Miss Loy and I walked down this large-open hallway and greeted her. 'Hello, Miss Loy. I am Scott O'Brien.' 'Scott O'Brien!' she exclaimed. 'Why, I expected you earlier — before the play!' I could have died on the spot. She had received my letter and had arrived early in order to talk with me. Before I could explain, she asked how I liked the play, etc.; very cheerful and sweet with me.

I had her sign the program, and she apologized for being in a hurry. Two very handsome and distinguished-looking gentlemen approached asking if she was ready to leave. I excused myself and left. I walked out the stage backdoor, up the street for a ways, turned around and stopped. Maybe I'd catch another glimpse of her. Sure enough, she and the now three good-looking gents exited the theatre. She caught my eye and turned and waved. 'Goodbye, Scott!' I overheard one of the men say, 'Myrna! He's so young!' They walked away at a clip, laughing and in good spirits. I walked away on cloud nine!"

In the early '70s Myrna was back in San Francisco with the play **Dear Love**, and O'Brien, no less a fan than ever, saw an evening performance and was able to see Loy again, in her dressing room. O'Brien recalled her as friendly as their earlier meeting and genuinely interested in his opinions. At one point he handed her a couple of stills to sign, one of which has her in a USO uniform from World War II. O'Brien would recall Myrna shaking her head and sighing, "Those times were different than today. I would never don such an outfit in support for the current conflict in Vietnam." She mourned the incredible loss of young people in the then-current war which had divided the country. She was very much a part of the present rather than one of those aging stars who spent all their time looking back on their past glories. She cared what the younger generation thought and only wanted them to have a better world to live in. Some people called her a do-gooder. "That do-gooder expression," she once said, "was created by people who simply don't want a change in the status quo, people who are convinced that the world is made up of haves and have mores. They don't care if slums can be replaced by decent housing or if the lot of deprived kids can be improved. The expression 'do-gooder' doesn't disturb those who care deeply about improvement. All it does is to make those who use the expression downgrade themselves."

She made only a handful more films. She was coaxed back by Jack Lemmon to play Charles Boyer's wife in **The April Fools**. She did a few television movies, including being reunited with old friend Melvyn Douglas in **Death Takes a Holiday**. She made the most of her few scenes in the all-star disaster flick **Airport '75**. She and Pat O'Brien played Burt Reynolds' parents in the enjoyable black comedy *The End*. She played Alan King's secretary and stole the show in *Just Tell Me What You Want*.

But she had one last great performance left in her, playing opposite a dying Henry Fonda, in *Summer Solstice*. It was Fonda who asked her to join him, in what would be his swan-song as an actor. He told Loy, "It's a mature love story which ought to be told." It was filmed on Cape Cod in the autumn of 1980, only shortly after Fonda had filmed his final feature film, *On Golden Pond*. Loy would later say of working with Fonda, "We have the same approach to acting — to be as real as possible." They are a married couple; it only is right that in her final performance, Loy is yet another wife — and truly "the good wife." The last scene was of Fonda holding his wife's lifeless body on the beach with a large hat covering her face. Fonda suggested that Loy's stand-in do it since her face wouldn't show on camera. "All I need's a sack of flour," Fonda said. "Well, here's your sack of flour," said Myrna, who insisted on doing the scene herself. "The scene was too intimate. It would not have been fair to Hank or the script."

Shortly thereafter, Loy retired and wrote her memoirs, *Myrna Loy — Being and Becoming*, one of the best and most revealing books written by a Hollywood celebrity. Hollywood finally began to accord her the honors it should have done years before. She received the National Board of Reviews Life Achievement Award, The Los Angeles Film Critics Career Achievement Award and then her career *and* service to her country were honored with The Kennedy Center Honors in 1988. Her health was slipping when she was awarded an honorary career Academy Award in 1991. She couldn't appear in person, but lights and cameras were set up in the living room of her New York townhouse and she graciously accepted the award in her final public appearance. "You've made me very happy. Thank you very much," she said.

She lived on another two-and-half years, dying of an undisclosed illness on December 14, 1993 at the age of 88. Nearly every obituary stated that she was best known as Nora in *The Thin Man* films — something she probably realized would happen, but they didn't shirk the fact that she was also a humanitarian who gave of herself tirelessly for others.

Growing older gracefully. Myrna with Dinah Shore, mid-'70s.

She ended her autobiography by quoting United States Senator Howard Metzenbaum reading an article into the Congressional Record which describes Myrna as "a woman who has the courage to stand up for her convictions." She wrote, "Well, I was raised to do that by pioneers who valued such attributes. I could ask for no greater tribute. Whenever I bemoan the current fate of those convictions, I am comforted by the knowledge that others will perpetuate them. After all, according to Robert Browning, whose consort I once played . . . 'a man's reach should exceed his grasp, or what's a heaven for?'"

CHAPTER THREE

THE THIN MAN

CAST: William Powell (Nick Charles), Myrna Loy (Nora Charles), Maureen O'Sullivan (Dorothy Wynant), Nat Pendleton (Detective Guild), Minna Gombell (Mimi Wynant Jorgenson), Porter Hall (MacCaulay), Henry Wadsworth (Tommy), William Henry (Gilbert Wynant), Harold Huber (Nunheim), Cesar Romero (Chris Jorgenson), Natalie Moorhead (Julia Wolf), Edward Brophy (Morelli), Edward Ellis (Clyde Wynant), Cyril Thornton (Tanner) Asta (himself).

COMPANY CREDITS: A Metro-Goldwyn-Mayer (MGM) film. W.S. (Woody) Van Dyke (Director), Hunt Stromberg (Producer), Albert Hackett and Frances Goodrich, from original novel by Dashiell Hammett (Writers), James Wong Howe (Cinematography), Robert J. Kern (Editing), Cedric Gibbons (Art Direction), William Axt (Original music).

PRODUCTION DATES: April 9-April 27 1934 with retakes in mid-May 1934. Released: May 25, 1934.

SYNOPSIS:
The film opens with the familiar MGM lion making its roar — and roar he might for this is the beginning of one of the thirties' classic films and one of films that defined the MGM of that period. It is also one of the great comedies of thirties cinema. For make no mistake about it; while there is plenty of mystery and suspense in *The Thin Man*, it is one of the funniest films of the screwball age. The credits are shown over a book cover depicting an illustration that many movie-goers thought was William Powell on the cover.

Movie Poster for *The Thin Man.* COURTESY OF LAURA WAGNER.

The depiction is of a man who is dapper, sophisticated, wears a well-tailored suit, sports a hat and wears a mustache. Some people have assumed that William Powell was the model for Nick Charles, but, in reality, Hammett based Nick Charles on himself. Over the years the "Thin Man" of the story became associated with William Powell's Nick Charles, but the "Thin Man" is Edward Ellis' skeletal, balding and white-haired Clyde Wynant. But MGM certainly understood the reality of movie-goer thinking and how to package a sequel to tie in with a well-known product, so every subsequent film title refers to William Powell as "The Thin Man." Over the backdrop of the book cover depicting this "Thin Man" the credits are spelled out. William Powell and Myrna Loy are given prominent billing above the title.

As the credits fade, we enter into the dark and grimy laboratory of inventor Clyde Wynant (played by the gaunt Edward Ellis). One gets the idea that Wynant is an impatient man who is quick to temper. An assistant enters the room to announce to Wynant that his daughter is here, but Wynant won't let the poor man get in one word edgewise because he is so upset that he is once again being disturbed while trying to work on an experiment. Wynant goes so far as to tell the man to pack up his things and get out — he's fired. At this point, Wynant's daughter, Dorothy (Maureen O'Sullivan), excitedly enters the room along with a man, her fiancé Tommy (Henry Wadsworth). It seems that old man Wynant has a heart under his blustery exterior after all as he brightens up with the appearance of his Dorothy. He even forgets that he has just fired his assistant! Dorothy has come to tell him that she and Tommy (who have only been together for three months) are going to marry and the wedding date is set for December 30, about two months in the future, and she wants to make sure that her father will be there to give her away. He intends to, but he wants her to know that he will be away for some time. Dorothy asks him where. The mysterious Wynant tells her that even she cannot be privy to that information. He just has to get away so he can concentrate on his experiments without interruptions. He promises her that he will be home before Christmas.

As Dorothy and Tommy are leaving, they run into Wynant's lawyer, MacCaulay (Porter Hall), who comes to deliver $1,000 in cash to Wynant, money he will need to finance his journey. The cagey MacCaulay is also in the dark about where Wynant is going and offers to buy the old man a train ticket in hopes of finding out the destination, but Wynant doesn't fall for it. Absolutely nobody is to know where he is going — not his daughter and not even his lawyer.

After receiving the money from MacCaulay, Wynant goes upstairs to a small office he shares with his accountant, Tanner (Cyril Thornton). Tanner is seated at his small desk going over the books when Wynant enters the room and heads to his safe. He tells Tanner that his daughter is getting married and he wants to make sure that he can convert $50,000 in bonds as a wedding present to her before going into hiding. It is of interest that as Wynant is opening the safe the camera pans to a suspicious-looking Tanner. We soon find out that Wynant can't find the bonds and initially he accuses Tanner of taking the money, which Tanner denies and suggests that instead the culprit could be Wynant's long-time mistress, Julia Wolf, the woman who broke up his marriage to Dorothy's mother.

The next scene has Wynant visiting Julia (Natalie Moorhead) and finding her in the company of her former gangster-boyfriend Morelli (Edward Brophy). Wynant tells Morelli to leave and not to see Julia again. Julia tells him that nothing was going on; they are just two old friends, in effect, getting together for a few laughs. Wynant accuses Julia of taking the $50,000 in bonds, which she initially denies doing. She then tries to tell him that he told her to "sell them" and he counters that she has been stealing from him for sometime and he's been letting her get away with it, but won't allow it any longer. Finally, she admits, "Certainly I took them" because he was always throwing money away on his deadbeat family, without thinking about her. Wynant demands the money back and is about to call the cops when Julia tells him that all she can come up with for the time being is $25,000. As this exchange is going on, we are introduced to another character when the phone rings; it is a man with a scar, later identified as Nunheim (Harold Huber). When it's Wynant who answers the phone and not Julia, Nunheim says nothing — and hangs up. Wynant deduces that Julia is involved with somebody else and split the money with him and threatens her that she better get the rest of it back — or else.

At this point we know a few things for sure: 1) Wynant is going away on a mysterious trip to a place nobody knows about, 2) His daughter is getting married and the bonds that Wynant wants to give her as a wedding present have disappeared from his safe, and 3) He encounters his mistress with another man and she admits that she took the bonds and he threatens her that she better get the entire amount back or else.

We are now ten minutes and thirty-seven seconds into the film and the plot advances two months forward to December 23. It is snowing outside a club where revelers are inside dancing the night away. Two of the dancers are Dorothy and Tommy. Dorothy is lamenting that it is almost Christmas and she hasn't seen nor heard anything from her father since he left. She is worried. Tommy tries to reassure her. She then recognizes a figure over at the bar. It is now eleven minutes and twenty-four seconds into the film when William Powell makes his first appearance as Nick Charles. It is a classic introduction for the character. Nick, with his back to the camera, is demonstrating to the assembled bartenders and others the proper way to mix a dry martini. "The important thing," Nick says, "is the rhythm," as he shakes the martini. We get the idea almost instantly that Nick Charles is a man who likes to drink. He already seems slightly cockeyed — and remains so throughout the film; not falling-down drunk, but certainly a little high.

Dorothy comes over to Nick and introduces herself. We become acquainted with the fact that Nick is a former private detective who did work some years back for her father and that Nick knew Dorothy when she was a little girl. Dorothy explains the situation to Nick: her father is missing and she has no idea where he is and she is to be married shortly. She tries to enlist Nick's help. He explains that he is no longer in the detective racket and tries to reassure Dorothy that her father is fine and is just preoccupied with his work.

At thirteen minutes and thirteen seconds into the film we get our first introduction to Myrna Loy's Nora Charles. Well, actually, we see her being led by the Charleses' terrier, Asta. She is carrying packages as Asta is leading her through the bar. She takes a spill on some steps and makes a slapstick entrance into the film. The maitre d' comes over to tell Nick and Nora that dogs are not allowed in the bar:

NICK: This is my dog . . . oh, and my wife.

NORA: You may have mentioned me first in the billing.

This exchange proves that Nora is more than Nick's match. Nick tells the maitre d' that Asta is "exceptionally well-trained," not so Nora. Nick and Nora sit down at a table and Nora can't resist mentioning the attractive young woman she just saw Nick talking with. Nick can't resist replying that the girl Nora saw him with is his long-lost daughter. Nora has ordered one martini and asks Nick how many he has had. "Six," Nick proudly proclaims. Nora asks the waiter to line up five more for her! She will prove to Nick that she can keep up with him in the booze department, too.

On Christmas Eve, Wynart's lawyer, MacCaulay, comes to visit Nick at the Charleses' Park Avenue apartment. It is made clear that Nick hasn't been a detective for four years. In that time he has met and married Nora and has been tending to her investments, including a lumber mill. They are only visiting New York for the holidays; otherwise, they live in California. MacCaulay, like Dorothy, is concerned about the whereabouts of Wynant. While they are discussing things, a call comes in from Wynant. When MacCaulay gets off the phone, he announces that Wynant is "alive and he's all right." Nick phones Dorothy to let her know the good news.

At this point in the film we are introduced to rest of Dorothy's rather eccentric family. We meet her mother Mimi (Minna Gombell), who is a flighty-looking woman who is constantly worrying about having enough money. She has remarried to a handsome younger man, Chris (Cesar Romero), who is no help in the finance department since he apparently has no job and has been living off of Mimi since their marriage. Then there is Dorothy's egghead brother, the bespeckled pseudo-intellectual, Gilbert (William Henry), who apparently does nothing except walk around carrying a book and trying to engage people in intellectual discussions. It is clear that this family is dependent on Wynant's money. Mimi is desperate for money because the money is running dry. She decides to encounter Julia to see if she has any information on where Wynant is.

Mimi arrives at Julia's apartment and knocks; getting no response, she opens the door and begins to look around the apartment. Entering the bedroom, she lets out a scream: Mimi is lying on the floor — dead. Something else catches Mimi's eye: the camera angle is such that the audience doesn't know what it is but we can tell that Mimi is taking whatever it is out of Mimi's dead hand. While all of this is going on, we are made aware that Nunheim, the man with the scar, is hovering outside. What is he doing there? And did he have anything to do with the murder? After pocketing what she found clutched in Julia's hand, Mimi calls the police.

The police come to a conclusion that the missing Wynant may have been the one who bumped off his mistress Julia. MacCaulay lets them know that while he hasn't actually seen Wynant in about three months he had heard from him earlier in the day, but he has no idea where he is. The police, led by Detective Guild (Nat Pendleton), pay a visit to Mimi. It appears that the coroner has deduced that something was taken out of Julia's hand after she was dead and they want to know if Mimi knows anything about it. Apparently, Julia had received $1,000 the previous night and they wonder if this was something that Mimi knew about. Mimi convinces the police that she was aware of nothing and they leave. Mimi enters her bedroom and begins opening a safe hidden behind a picture. Dorothy, who knows her mother and is suspicious, enters the room and confronts Mimi. She accuses Mimi of taking the money out of Julia's dead hand. Mimi counters that what she really took out of Julia's hand is "an important piece of evidence" — evidence which would seem to implicate Wynant: his watch chain.

It's Christmas Eve night and there is a sparkling party going on at Nick and Nora's apartment. The room is filled with Nora's friends (socialites) and Nick's (ex-cons, even those who Nick sent up the river). Reporters show up at the party and question Nick if he is on the case. Quick-witted Nora replies, "Yes, and a case of scotch — why don't you pitch in and help him out?" Nick assures them he isn't. It doesn't help matters when Dorothy shows up — obviously upset. Nick takes her into his bedroom so that they can speak privately. Dorothy takes a gun out of her bag which Nick quickly takes away from her. He sits her down and she explains that she's the one who killed Julia (obviously she is trying to cover for her father). Nick asks her a series of questions and gets the wrong responses which prove to him that Dorothy is lying. "Who are you trying to protect?" he asks her. Dorothy is disconsolate and Nick hugs her — enter Nora; unlike other wives who might be upset to find another attractive woman embracing her husband, the sophisticated Nora understands and puts an embarrassed Dorothy, who pulls away from Nick, at ease. Nick takes the gun that Dorothy showed up with (Dorothy explains that she got it earlier in the day at a pawnshop) and hides it in the bureau drawer and instructs Nora to try and help Dorothy calm down by getting her to have a drink.

At this point Nick leaves the bedroom and who appears next at his door, but Mimi. He takes Mimi into the bathroom, the only other place where they can have some privacy. Mimi pleads with Nick to help her find Clyde. Nick then spills the beans that Dorothy is also there and next thing we know Mimi is busting into the bedroom where she confronts her daughter. "What did you tell them!?" she demands to know, slapping Dorothy hard across the face. Nora is protective of the vulnerable Dorothy and says, "Too bad you didn't bring your whip!" Nick points out to Mimi that Dorothy didn't tell them anything, but obviously Mimi made a bad impression and makes both Nick and Nora suspicious of her. At this point, Nora is fully on Dorothy's side and she herself is urging Nick to take on the case to help "that little girl."

It is the middle of the night, early Christmas morning, Nora can't sleep — Nick wants to. Suddenly, there is a knock at the front door. Is it Nick who jumps out of bed to answer it? No! Of course, it's Nora. It's Morelli, the gangster ex-boyfriend of Julia's. She says she will go and get Nick, but he follows her into the bedroom with gun drawn. He wants to know from Nick if the cops think that he did it. If he doesn't get a straight answer, he will do some damage. Suddenly, the cops arrive at the Charleses' front door; Morelli thinks he has been double crossed by Nick and takes a shot, but just before Nick knocks Nora out of the way causing her to blackout. Nick jumps Morelli and gets the gun out of his hand as the cops come into the bedroom. Nick brings Nora to and she discovers he has been hit — but it's only a flesh wound. Nora is concerned:

NORA: Do you want a drink?

NICK: What do *you* think?

Of course he does. The police find the gun that Dorothy had brought earlier which Nick had hid in the dresser drawer. Detective Guild has lots of questions about Nick's involvement in the case. Nick now has no real choice; he has to take on the case because the cops think he might be involved in some way.

On Christmas morning attorney MacCaulay comes to visit Nick, telling Nick that he received a telegram from Wynant. Nick informs him that he too received a telegram from Wynant requesting that he take on the case to find out who murdered Julia. Then MacCaulay gets a phone call. He is told that Wynant committed suicide and he is needed to come to identify the body; he needs to take a train to Allentown, Pennsylvania. Later, Detective Guild tells Nick that the suicide was a phony and that they are convinced that Wynant is hiding because he is the murderer of Julia. Nick says, "Cops will think that every thin man with white hair is Wynant." It is the one and only time in the film that Wynant is referred to as "The Thin Man." It seems that everybody does have an airtight alibi and it's Wynant who must be the murderer.

Nick decides to do some investigation, but doesn't want the eager Nora accompanying him on a potentially dangerous situation. He hails a cab, opens the door, locks Nora in and tells the cabbie to take her to Grant's Tomb. With Nora out of the way, Nick and Detective Guild go and pay a visit to the man with the scar — Nunheim — at his apartment. They arrive as Nunheim and his mistress are having a quarrel. Nunheim's mistress leaves him and he wants to take off after her, pleading with Guild and Nick to let him go, but they won't let him — they want answers. Nunheim tells them he had nothing to do with this business and finally after repeated threats from Detective Guild he asks to be excused and goes into his bedroom to retrieve some vital information. Incredibly, Guild allows him to do this and Nunheim goes into the bedroom and closes the door! Nick knows better and after a few seconds he picks up the phone. Guild asks him what he is doing; he informs the detective that he is calling the station to get some police officers to help trail the escaped Nunheim.

We now cut to Nunheim calling somebody that the audience doesn't see. "If you want me to act dumb" and not squeal on him/her he needs "$5,000 more." Nunheim has just signed his death warrant. He goes to retrieve the money, opens a door and is shot dead. The police deduce that the bullets came from the same gun which also shot Julia Wolf dead.

Nora is back from Grant's Tomb, which allows this terrific exchange:

NICK: How did you like Grant's Tomb?

NORA: It's lovely — I'm having a copy made for you.

Dorothy breaks off her engagement with Tommy because she is convinced that mental illness runs in her family and doesn't want to marry Tommy and have children who may be affected. She decides she is going to run off and do as she pleases. Mimi confesses to the police that, yes, she had found something in Julia's hand and taken it — Wynant's watch band. It implicates him even more.

Nick decides to investigate. He is going to take Asta with him to Wynant's laboratory. He has a hunch about something. Nora is apprehensive about the danger that Nick may encounter, but, once again, Nick is not going to allow Nora to come with him. Nora, concerned for Nick's well-being, tells Nick that she doesn't want to become a widow:

NICK: You wouldn't be a widow long.

NORA: You bet I wouldn't.

NICK (*getting the upper hand*): Not with your money.

At the laboratory Asta takes particular attention to what seems to be a concrete slab which appears to be in better condition than the rest of the floor. Nick gets suspicious and begins digging the floor up. He finds skeletal remains. He goes upstairs to use the phone to call the police when who should come in but the accountant Tanner. Tanner tells Nick he used his own key to get in and just wanted to return some money that he had taken from Wynant — but insists that he didn't kill anybody.

When the police arrive with the medical examiner the concrete floor is dug up and the skeletal remains are taken out. There is nothing left to the body but surprisingly the clothes are in relatively good shape and they seem to indicate that a large man, approximately 250 pounds, was buried under the concrete floor and the police are convinced that this is yet another Wynant murder. With Julia, Nunheim, and now this, the police pin three murders on Wynant.

The police are again hounding Nick for information:

REPORTER: Can't you tell us anything about this case?

NICK: Yes, it's putting me way behind in my drinking.

Nick has a hunch who the skeletal remains belong to due to a bit of shrapnel found in the leg. Nick decides to try and crack the case by inviting all the suspects to a dinner party at Nick and Nora's apartment. He isn't sure who the murderer is, but believes if everybody gets together and they go over all the facts it would lead to the real murderer being apprehended.

All the suspects arrive (with the help of the police to make sure they do come) at the Charleses' apartment and are seated at an elegant table. The suspects are: Dorothy (who is found at a train station with another man, ready to go on her wayward ways), Tommy, Mimi, MacCaulay, Gilbert, Chris, Morelli, and Tanner.

With all the suspects seated, Nick begins to go over the details of the murder and makes the startling revelation that he had seen Wynant the previous night (which is true in a way). Mimi then adds that she too had seen him and so does Gilbert. Gilbert, however, allows that he saw Wynant in his crystal ball, not in the flesh. This leads to one of the funniest lines in the entire film:

NORA: Waiter, will you serve the nuts. I mean the nuts to the guests.

Nick explains to Mimi that she could not have seen Wynant in the flesh and slowly works his way up to revealing that the murderer is . . . (You'll have to see the movie to find that piece of information.)

The film ends with Nick and Nora in their cabin on a train making its way to California. Their cabin has two bunks and Nora asks Nick to let Asta sleep with her that night. To which Nick takes Asta and puts him up on Nick's upper berth and tells Nora: "Oh, yeah!" If anybody sleeps with Nora, it will be Nick.

Fade out — THE END.

FUNNIEST DIALOG:

NORA: Is that my drink over there?

NICK: What are you drinking?

NORA: Rye.

NICK (*picks up glass and slugs down its contents.*) Yes. That's yours.

THE SOURCE MATERIAL:

The Thin Man is the fifth and final novel that Samuel Dashiell Hammett (1894-1961) wrote. Hammett belonged to the so-called "hard-boiled" school of mystery and crime writers which, unlike the writings of Agatha Christie and Dorothy Sayers (among others), emphasized graphic violence, occasional profanity and sexual imagery. Other members of this "hard-boiled" school include Raymond Chandler and James M. Cain.

Hammett was born in southern Maryland on May 27, 1894 and his early education was in Baltimore and Philadelphia. He left school at age 14 to help support his family. Between 1915 and 1921 he was a Pinkerton detective, in between serving as an ambulance driver during the First World War (however, he never served overseas in this capacity). After his ambulance corp. service Hammett returned to the Pinkerton organization where he was sent west and he ended up in Spokane, Washington where he was assigned as a union buster (a duty he didn't enjoy). In the fall of 1920 Hammett's health broke and he was diagnosed with Tuberculosis and was sent to a public health hospital in Tacoma. According to Hammett's biographer, Diane Johnson, "He was declared completely disabled, his health ruined beyond repair." It was while he was hospitalized that he met the woman who would become his wife, Josephine (Jose) Annis Dolan, who served as a Red Cross nurse at the hospital. Again, according to biographer Johnson, Jose thought Hammett, "very clever and handsome and admired his neatness and the tidy military way he made his bed . . ." Gradually, Hammett's health improved, but he would never be in robust health for the remainder of his life. On July 7, 1921, Hammett and Jose married and settled in San Francisco. Eventually, the couple had two daughters.

Due to the fragile nature of his health he could no longer continue with the Pinkerton organization, so he took up writing and, using some of his experiences as a detective, began writing crime fiction for a magazine called *Black Mask*. For a time he used the nickname "Peter Collinson" but eventually he used his own name, dropping his first name and being published as Dashiell Hammett. It was in writing his short stories for *Black Mask* that he developed what would become his signature private eye, Sam Spade, and another more exotic detective called "The Continental Ot." The Continental Ot was the focus of Hammett's first novel, *The Red Harvest*, in 1929. The book became an immediate bestseller and later that same year appeared again in a second and even more successful novel, *The Dain Curse*. Meanwhile, Hammett's marriage to Jose was struggling by this time due to Hammett's frequent absences and infidelities.

In 1930 Hammett scored his biggest hit yet with the publication of *The Maltese Falcon*, which introduced Sam Spade in novel form. Spade was essentially a loner and a man who followed his own code of honor, which sometimes skirted the law. The next year he followed up with yet another solid bestseller, *The Glass Key*. Hammett was acclaimed by the literary critics. "There is an absolute distinction of art in his books," said the *New Republic*. "Anybody who doesn't read him misses much of modern America," proclaimed Dorothy Parker. By 1931, Hollywood was beckoning and Hammett essentially left his wife and went to Hollywood.

It was also the year that Hammett met the brilliant playwright Lillian Hellman, with whom he would spend much of the rest of his life with.

While he was helping to adapt his novels, *The Maltese Falcon* and *The Glass Key*, for the cinema, Hammett was also working on what would be his fifth, and, as would turn out, final novel, *The Thin Man*. Interestingly, in the early stages of the novel, the hero wasn't Nick Charles but Detective John Guild, who more resembled one of Hammett's typical hard-boiled detectives. The plot was much the same, but there were no Nick and Nora. Apparently, Hammett had a change of heart about the hero and decided to spice up this novel by introducing the married sleuths. It is said that he based the hard-drinking Nick Charles on himself while the resourceful Nora was based on his lover, Lillian Hellman. Lillian Hellman would later write, "It was a happy day when I was given half the manuscript to read and was told that I was Nora. It was nice to be Nora, married to Nick Charles, maybe one of the few marriages in modern literature where the man and woman like each other and have a fine time together. But I was soon put back in place — Hammett said I was also the silly girl in the book (Dorothy) and the villainess (Mimi). I don't know now if he was joking, but in those days it worried me; I was very anxious that he think well of me. Most people wanted that from him." When the book was released, it was an immediate smash, with over 20,000 copies sold in the first three weeks alone, and 30,000 copies in the first year. The reviews were probably the strongest for any Hammett book. "The best detective novel yet written in America," stated the critic Alexander Woollcott. "Dashiell Hammett is undoubtedly the best of American detective story writers, and *The Thin Man* is certainly the most breathless of all his stories," was the uninhibited view of Sinclair Lewis.

The novel is darker than the film version. The film has been called by some a "screwball comedy." The humor was emphasized because the director, Woodridge Strong Van Dyke, wanted it that way. He also downplayed the mystery and had his writers highlight the relationship between the two main characters. Among the most apparent differences between the novel and the movie is the character of the daughter of the inventor, Dorothy Wynant. In the novel Dorothy is manipulative, neurotic and even a bit of a bitch. Not so the celluloid Dorothy, who is the classic sweet-natured ingénue. The novel's Dorothy is not attached while in the film she is engaged. In the novel the relationship between Dorothy and Mimi is even more extreme than in the film. The novel makes it clear that Mimi often savagely beats her daughter. There is only a hint of this in the film when Mimi enters the Charleses' bedroom and finds Dorothy confiding in Nora and attempts to slap her — drawing the ire of Nora. The novel has a darker tone and the characters of Nick and Nora are not nearly as likable as in the film, though in both book and film they enjoy boozing and present a picture of a modern marriage where the wife is more of an equal. The film is pure and uninhibited escapism for a country still deep in the Depression.

The publishing house, Knopf, didn't hesitate to pander to the lowest common denominator if it meant increased sales. Case in point was a *New York Times* ad by the publisher which said, "I don't believe the question on page 192 . . . has had the slightest influence upon the sale of the book. It takes more than that to make a best seller these days. Twenty-thousand people don't buy a book within three weeks to read a five-word question." This certainly must have intrigued some people to find out what the five-word question was. (For the record, the passage in question has Nora asking Nick, "Tell me something, Nick. Tell me the truth: When you were wrestling with Mimi, didn't you have an erection?" Nick's reply: "Oh, a little.")

Hollywood soon beckoned again for Hammett and this time it was MGM offering $21,000 to buy the film rights to the book. Hammett took it, even though it was $4,000 less than what Paramount had paid him for *The Glass Key*. He felt with the country still in a depression he shouldn't complain.

The Thin Man, published in 1934, is Hammett's last book (though he did put out occasional collections of short stories and write a few magazine articles). There has been much speculation as to why Hammett never completed another book; apparently, he would start but never finish. Part of the reason may have been psychological. "He [Hammett] spoke to a psychiatrist about his inability to write and offered them his own explanation for his block: that he had nothing to write about, that his real life had ended when he became famous and was lifted out of the social class to which he belonged but in which he no longer fit." For the last twenty-seven years of his life he devoted himself (along with Hellman) to left-wing politics and was strongly anti-fascist — and even briefly joined the Communist party. When the United States entered the Second World War, Hammett enlisted. He had to pull strings to do so due to his disabilities from his service in the First World War. He spent the war on the Aleutian Islands where he helped put out an Army newspaper. After the war, Hammett joined the New York Civil Rights Congress. When four men with ties to this organization were arrested, Hammett raised money for their defense. In turn, he was investigated and, when he refused to provide information, he was imprisoned for five months for contempt of court. He, himself, was a victim of McCarthyism during the 1950s. He testified about his own activities but refused to speak about others and for this he was blacklisted. The IRS also garnished his income to pay back taxes. He was ill for much of the later part of the 1950s and died of lung cancer at New York's Lenox Hill Hospital on January 10, 1961. Fellow hard-boiled crime writer Raymond Chandler, the creator of Philip Marlowe, summed Hammett up this way: "Hammett took murder out of the Venetian vase and dropped it in into the alley . . . He gave murder back to the kind of people who do it for a reason, not just to provide a corpse; and with means at hand, not with hand wrought dueling pistols, curare and tropical fish."

THE DIRECTOR:

Woodbridge (Woody) Strong Van Dyke II directed the first four of the popular *Thin Man* series. He was considered one of MGM's most efficient and dependable directors. Film historian David Thomson, in his ***Biographical Dictionary of Film***, describes Van Dyke as "a trusted servant of MGM, able to turn his hand to most of the studio's idioms." He became known as "One-Shot" Woody because he allegedly allowed few retakes and believed that what you got on the first take showed the actors at their freshest and least mannered. Despite this (or maybe because of it) he directed several above-average films and a couple which have evolved into classics of the American cinema such as *Tarzan the Ape Man* (1932), *The Thin Man* (1934) and *San Francisco* (1936). He was a versatile director who excelled in several genres, including musicals (he directed most of the Jeanette MacDonald-Nelson Eddy films), comedies, dramas, melodramas and even Westerns.

Van Dyke was born in San Diego, California, on March 21, 1889. Van Dyke never got to know his father, who died of organic heart trouble the day after he was born. He was educated in Seattle and, as a youngster, he helped support his family. He got his first taste of show business by appearing on the vaudeville stage along with his mother, actress Laura Winston. As a youngster he traveled across the country with his mother and later said, "I think I've been to school in every state in the union." As he got older, he labored as a logger, gold miner and roadhouse call boy. He never lost the capacity for doing hard work as witnessed by his Hollywood output: directing ninety films in twenty-five years. Several sources say that when Van Dyke came to Hollywood in 1915 he was an assistant director to the legendary D.W. Griffith on his film master-piece *Intolerance*, but Van Dyke himself said that was a stretch and described himself instead as Griffith's "water boy" or "messenger." Nevertheless, he did observe the great director at length and came away star struck. "It was a case of hero worship, pure and simple, on my part." In addition to being an errand boy for Griffith, the director cast Van Dyke as an extra, playing a Roman soldier driving a chariot in the film.

Van Dyke made his directorial debut in 1917 in a film he also wrote, *The Land of Long Shadows*. During the silent era Van Dyke directed forty-four films, including several Westerns starring Buck Jones (*Winner Take All, Trail Rider, Hearts and Spurs, Timber Wolf*) and Tim McCoy (*War Paint, Winners of the Wilderness, California, Spoilers of the West*). In 1928 Van Dyke took over the production of MGM's *White Shadows on the South Seas* from director Robert J. Flaherty, a very talented documentarian, but over his head with a feature film. Van Dyke had been assigned to the film originally as a technical director. The long location shoot was making tempers flair and Van Dyke wrote in his journal, "Everybody hates everybody else's guts. They are fighting like mad. Flaherty doesn't know a thing." When the crew turned on their director, Flaherty quit the film in disgust and MGM replaced him with Van Dyke and gave him a mandate to speed up production and efficiently complete the film — which he did. This film was Van Dyke's first for producer Hunt Stromberg who would be the unit supervisor for many of Van Dyke's MGM films, including *The Thin Man*. As it turned out, *White Shadows on the South Seas* became a major success and Van Dyke's professionalism and speed made him a valuable member of the MGM family. His final silent film was *The Pagan*, with Ramon Novarro, which was released in 1929.

In March 1929, Van Dyke left for Africa to begin location work on *Trader Horn*, one of the most treacherous and legendary location shoots in Hollywood history. The film was based on a best-selling novel about an African trader who finds a dying missionary and decides to carry on the missionary's work of finding her missing daughter, now the queen of a savage African tribe. The picture was originally planned as a silent film but with the advent of sound, MGM decided to make it a talkie. Van Dyke was chosen to direct this film because of his efficiency in directing other exotic made-on-location films like *White Shadows in the South Seas* and *The Pagan*. (Interestingly, according to the *Oakland Tribune* on 1/25/42, Van Dyke was quoted as saying he "detest[ed] travel.") According to legend, when the script of *Trader Horn* was submitted to Van Dyke, he read it, decided to do the film and sent a note to MGM head Louis B. Mayer stating, "Only a goof would try it." The film was befallen by several calamities during the production, including the truck which carried the sound film falling into the river, *real* threatening native tribes, and the usual location problems of insects, snakes and crocodile-infested waters. The leading actors, Harry Carey and Edwina Booth, both suffered serious health problems due to the dangerous shoot. (Booth later sued MGM due to complications from being forced to sunbathe in the nude under the hot African sun, which caused a serious reaction, and won an undisclosed amount of money.) Van Dyke himself began falling behind schedule and began drinking heavily. The company spent more than a year shooting in Africa and returned to the United States in the spring of 1930 and later additional scenes were shot in Mexico. When the film was released in May 1931 *Trader Horn* was a huge success, in part because it was the one of the first sound films to contain extensive location shots, but in all likelihood it lost money overall due to its long production schedule, which spanned from March 1929 until December of 1930 — most unusual for a Van Dyke film. (The film cost over $1.3 million, making it one of the most expensive films made up to that time.)

Van Dyke's next notable film was *Tarzan the Ape Man*, which went into production in the fall of 1931. MGM had a lot of leftover location footage from the *Trader Horn* shoot and decided to utilize it once again, bringing Edgar Rice Burroughs's classic story of a man who was brought up by apes in the African jungles to the screen. It only made sense to hire Van Dyke to direct this one too. Unlike the long location shoot for *Trader Horn*, *Tarzan* was shot and completed over a two-month period, between October and November of 1931, with much of the film shot on MGM soundstages and in nearby Toluca Lake. When the film was released in August of 1932, it was an immediate smash hit. Part of the reason for this could be the provocative shots of Maureen O'Sullivan (as Jane) and Johnny Weissmuller wearing very skimpy costumes. This was pre-Code and in future *Tarzan* films (not directed by Van Dyke) they would not bare nearly as much skin.

Van Dyke then directed his first murder mystery, **Guilty Hands**, which starred Kay Francis and Lionel Barrymore. Actor William Blackwell had a supporting role in the film and recalled in his memoir *Hollywood Be Thy Name* that Van Dyke "shot so fast that the actors couldn't be sure whether they were doing a rehearsal or a take until they were surprised to hear his rugged voice shout: PRINT IT!" One day a script girl told Van Dyke that Barrymore was wearing the wrong tie in a continuity shot. That he should be wearing a polka-dot tie. Van Dyke reviewed the rushes from the previous day and determined that this was true and sent the disgruntled Barrymore to his dressing room to change ties. When it was taking Barrymore longer than it should have to return to the set, the time-conscious Van Dyke sent an assistant to find out what was keeping the actor. The assistant knocked on Barrymore's door and getting no answer he peered through the window to discover Barrymore "painstakingly painting tiny white polka dots on the solid navy-blue necktie, rather than admit that he had, in actuality, lost the original.

In 1933 Van Dyke worked for the first time with Myrna Loy in the crime-mystery *Penthouse*, which was written by Frances Goodrich and Albert Hackett, who would later adapt Hammett's novel of *The Thin Man* for the screen. Interestingly, this film also featured character actor Nat Pendleton, who would also have a featured role in *The Thin Man* a year later. Indeed, the success of *Penthouse* and the assembled talent behind it caught MGM's eye when developing *The Thin Man* and, according to Louella Parsons, "because *Penthouse* directed by W.S. Van Dyke, brought in the merry, merry shekels, *The Thin Man* will have the same director, same producer, Hunt Stromberg, and the same personnel. Frances Goodrich and Albert Hackett are adapting it."

Manhattan Melodrama, released in 1934, is another key film because it was, of course, the film which introduced to moviegoers that immortal team of William Powell and Myrna Loy. The story of two boyhood friends (Powell and top-billed Clark Gable) who go in different directions as adults; Gable becomes a gambler and crook and Powell is elected District Attorney, with Loy the woman who comes between them. Loy worked well with both Gable and Powell, but it's clear that from the first scene they shot together, of Powell stumbling into the backseat of Loy's limo, that something very special was occurring. *Manhattan Melodrama* was shot in eighteen days (mid-March thru early April of 1934) for producer David O Selznick, during the relatively short period of time that Selznick operated his own unit at MGM. Selznick was more concerned with his big-budget adaptation of the Dickens's novel *David Copperfield* than he was with *Manhattan Melodrama* and trusted Van Dyke to bring the film in on budget and on time. The film cost about $300,000 and then went on to gross over a million dollars. A film that grossed a million or more during the early '30s, especially during the Depression when average ticket prices were twenty-five cents, was considered a blockbuster. The film is also recalled as the movie which led to the downfall (indeed shooting death) of notorious gangster John Dillinger, who just couldn't resist going to the movies to see his favorite actress, Myrna Loy, with police getting a tip and waiting for him as he came out of the Biograph Theater. (Note, too, that Nat Pendleton is also cast in this film.)

Almost immediately after the filming of *Manhattan Melodrama*, Powell and Loy went into Van Dyke's *The Thin Man*. Van Dyke was a huge fan of detective novels and particularly enjoyed the hard-boiled novels of Hammett. When he found out that MGM owned the rights to the novel of *The Thin Man*, Van Dyke eagerly went to studio head L.B. Mayer and requested to be put on the picture. Mayer was more than willing since he saw the film as the type of low-budget quickie that Van Dyke excelled so at. But Van Dyke was also adamant that he wanted both Powell and Loy to play the sophisticated detectives, Nick and Nora Charles. Loy, often portraying exotic, oriental-type vamps, and Powell, who just left Warner Brothers for MGM, was considered, at best, an aging leading man, were not the studio's ideas of who should be cast as Nick and Nora. But perhaps because the film wasn't seen by the studio at the time as one of its major releases, MGM relented and gave Van Dyke the stars he wanted and one of the classics of the American cinema was born. For his part Van Dyke was nominated for the first of two times for the Academy Award for his direction of this film. He lost to Frank Capra for *It Happened One Night*.

Van Dyke directed several of the Jeanette McDonald-Nelson Eddy operatic musicals of the time, which were quite popular with the public. One of the biggest was *Naughty Marietta*. The British actress Elsa Lanchester had a part in the film and later, in her autobiography, recalled her impression of Van Dyke: "W.S. Van Dyke was the director, and working with him was about the best experience I could have had then. Van Dyke was very famous, not so much for directing great movies, but for directing big movies in record time. He never went over budget — a kind of sainthood to Louis B. Mayer — because he insisted on printing the first and only takes of a scene. It seemed to work because the first take did have a freshness no other take ever achieved. At least, it seemed to work for Van Dyke. And it helped me to think fast on my feet and get it right the first time."

San Francisco (1936) is another of Van Dyke's screen highlights. With the stellar cast of Clark Gable, Jeanette MacDonald and Spencer Tracy, it tells the story of good and bad in a city known for its sinfulness leading up to the epic 1905 earthquake. The highlight of the film is the incredible and superbly filmed twenty-minute earthquake sequence. Van Dyke's mentor, D.W. Griffith, was by then largely forgotten by the industry, but not by Van Dyke. He called upon his friend, who he credited with teaching him the fundamentals of filmmaking, for help in filming this sequence. The film was a major studio production and not one of Van Dyke's quickies. It was shot over a three-month period (mid-February to mid-May of 1936), which compares to the 18-day schedule that *The Thin Man* enjoyed. It became one of MGM's major film successes of 1936 — a year which also included the Van Dyke-directed second *Thin Man* film, *After the Thin Man*. 1936 was a banner year for Van Dyke, in which he directed five major films. Van Dyke was also nominated for his second and final Academy Award for his direction of *San Francisco*.

Van Dyke worked on nine films between the completion of his second *Thin Man* film and the third installment in 1939, *Another Thin Man*. They included *Personal Property* (with Jean Harlow), *Rosalie* (with Nelson Eddy, *sans* Jeanette MacDonald), *Stand Up and Fight* (with Robert Taylor), and even an Andy Hardy film. The two most important ones were directing the former first lady of MGM, Norma Shearer, in one of her most ambitious films and performances, *Marie Antoinette*, a costume period drama; and a charming screwball comedy, *It's a Wonderful World*, teaming Claudette Colbert and James Stewart. How many other directors could have produced such varied and quality products over such a short period of time? "Woody was the speed king," veteran MGM director George Sidney would recall. "His mottos were 'Don't waste time' and 'Don't take any Bullshit.' He was an amazing guy. He would get up at four in the morning and work out his day."

Between the third *Thin Man* film and the fourth and final adaptation that Van Dyke would direct, *Shadow of the Thin Man*, Van Dyke worked on seven more films, the best being yet another Powell-Loy delight, *I Love You, Again*, which cast Powell as an amnesiac who realizes that he is actually a con-man and falls in love with his soon-to-be ex-wife (Loy). It was during these years that Van Dyke worked with editor Harold Kress on three films: *It's a Wonderful World*, *Bitter Sweet*, and *Rage in Heaven*. Kress recalled his memories of Van Dyke in the book *First Cuts*: "Van Dyke directed just like the marines. He was in every morning at five o' clock. He laid out work he wanted to do that day. If he finished at three, wrap. If he finished at five, wrap. But he got that work done. He camera-cut, only shot up to a certain line in the script and cut. He knew he would go to a close up, pick up the end of the scene, another two-shot, wrap, and that's it. So you could only cut it one way. He never ran the film himself. We had to be on the set at eight in the morning to tell him whether the dailies were good or bad."

Van Dyke was intensely patriotic and a card-carrying Democrat and FDR partisan (he even attended the 1940 Democratic convention as a delegate). In the mid-'30s Van Dyke received a commission as a Captain in the Marine Corps Reserves. As the war clouds in Europe were gathering he was promoted to Major and began a recruiting program. In fact, in his last few films, Van Dyke's billing was "Major W.S. Van Dyke II. He strongly advocated US involvement in the European war and went so far as to urge such friends as Robert Taylor, Clark Gable and Robert Montgomery to enlist. Unfortunately for Van Dyke, his health would not permit him to actively serve in the military and he was bitterly disappointed when he was placed on inactive status. Van Dyke's final two films had a wartime feel to them, *Cairo*, with Robert Young and Jeanette MacDonald, and especially the Dore Schary-produced and very popular *Journey for Margaret* (also with Young and introducing a major new child star, Margaret O'Brien). Young played an American reporter in London during the blitz who tries to adopt two orphans. Van Dyke, then 53, was very ill during the shooting of this film suffering from cancer and heart problems. The film was shot from mid-June to late July of 1942 and Van Dyke, a committed Christian Scientist, endured his pain without pain killers. His final months were ones of suffering which he ultimately couldn't bear any longer, committing suicide on February 5, 1943. He left behind his widow, Ruth, the niece of infamous MGM executive Eddie Mannix (a clear indication that at MGM Van Dyke clearly was family). He also left three young children, Barbara, 7, Woodbridge III, 5, and Winston, 3. Van Dyke managed to put away quite a bit of money in his years at MGM and at the time of his death he left an estate worth more than $500,000, a considerable amount especially for those days. His funeral was a star-studded affair with many of the actors he directed attending, including William Powell, Myrna Loy and Joan Crawford. Per Van Dyke's request, Nelson Eddy and Jeanette MacDonald sang. Of his passing, Van Dyke's secretary would later say, "There was a huge group of men who worked on his pictures, and they were all hysterical when they found out Woody was dead. He was a wonderful man and a gentleman."

Van Dyke is not recalled by film scholars the same way contemporaries like John Ford and Howard Hawks are. He was a better-than-competent house director who, unlike many of the great directors, didn't infuse his films with his own unique vision. He was a reliable workhorse. Andrew Sarris, in his book *The American Cinema*, wrote, "Woody Van Dyke made more good movies than his reputation for carelessness and haste would indicate. Perhaps carelessness and haste are precisely the qualities responsible for the breezy charm of *Trader Horn*, *Tarzan the Ape Man* and *The Thin Man* . . ." He was a capable and interesting director, at a studio primarily known for its strong unit supervisors (Thalberg, Selznick, Stromberg), who liked to dominate their directors, as well as their actors. In addition to the two Best Director Academy Award nominations which Van Dyke received, four of his pictures were nominated for the Best Picture Oscar: *Trader Horn*, *The Thin Man*, *Naughty Marietta*, and *San Francisco*. He also guided such actors as William Powell, Spencer Tracy, Norma Shearer and Robert Morley to Oscar nominations. Not a bad track record for a director not well remembered today.

Henri Agel, in his book *Romance Americaine* (Du Cerf, 1963), wrote of Van Dyke, "This former assistant to Griffith has had great historical importance. He pioneered all the paths of escape and adventure: The South Seas (*White Shadows*), the horror of the pole (*Eskimo*, 1931), *Trader Horn* which is to black Africa what *Stagecoach* is to the western, the imagery of the jungle dominated by the superman (*Tarzan*). It is often said that Van Dyke was the artisan-type of MGM, the good (or good enough) craftsman who furnished a not too spicy diet, comfortable suspense for everybody."

It could be, too, that Van Dyke's greatest legacy was bringing together William Powell and Myrna Loy first in *Manhattan Melodrama* but more significantly in *The Thin Man* films. For this feat alone film audiences owe him a great debt. Myrna Loy deserves the final word on "Woody" Van Dyke, writing in her autobiography years after the final Thin Man film, "He seems to be neglected now, which puzzles me; he was one of Hollywood's best, most versatile directors. Perhaps that very versatility is the reason they haven't started honoring him yet. Critics and commentators, whoever makes those judgments, seem to go for genre directors — it's easier. But they'll get around to Woody one of these days." (Sources include: LA Examiner, 2/10/34, Modesto Bee, 1/26/34 & 2/5/43, Galveston News, 2/17/43.)

THE CAMERA MAN:
JAMES WONG HOWE (August 28, 1899-July 12, 1976)

Van Dyke had a great appreciation for cinematographers once saying, "A good camera man is a director's right hand." And on *The Thin Man*, Van Dyke had one of the best in James Wong Howe. Howe is considered one of the greatest of his craft and the stats demonstrate how appreciated he was. He photographed some 130 films and was nominated ten times for an Academy Award — winning the award twice (*The Rose Tattoo* in 1955 and *Hud* in 1963).

Howe was born Wong Tung Jim in Canton, China on August 28, 1899. The year that Howe was born his father came to the United States to work on the Northern Pacific Railroad and, saving up enough money, he sent for his family to join him in Pasco, Washington in 1904. Howe moved to Los Angeles in his late teens and took on many odd jobs and eventually found his way into meeting director Cecil B. DeMille at the Lasky Studios. DeMille took a shine to the young man, now known as "Jimmy" Howe (a name given to him by a school teacher) and gave him a job as a "slate boy." He recalled in an interview how working with DeMille helped prepare him for the future role of cameraman: "I held the slate on *Male and Female* (1919), and when Mr. DeMille rehearsed a scene, I had to crank a little counter . . . and I would have to grind 16 frames per second. And when he stopped, I would have to give him the footage. He wanted to know how long the scene ran. So besides writing the slate numbers down and keeping a report, I had to turn this crank. That was the beginning of learning how to turn 16 frames." He also took photographic stills during the production of films and one of them made actress Mary Miles Minters eyes look darker than they were and she requested that he be her official photographer. It was on the Minter film *Drums of Fate* in 1923 that Howe became head cameraman. Among the notable silent films that Howe served on as cinematographer are *The Trail of the Lonesome Pine* (1923) and *Laugh, Clown, Laugh* (1928). In the late '20s, when sound was making a revolutionary change in Hollywood, Howe was back in his native China filming backdrops for a film he hoped to one day film. When he returned, he found general lack of work because of his inexperience in working in sound film. Howe finally got his opportunity to work in sound films when he was requested by director William K. Howard to photograph *Transatlantic* (1931).

Howe was a freelancing cameraman until 1933, when he joined MGM. Howe worked well with Van Dyke on two of the director's very best films, *Manhattan Melodrama* and *The Thin Man*, both released in 1934. Howe became known in the industry for his use of "low-key" lighting which throws visible shadows on the set — and was commonly used in the '40s in the genre known as *film noir* (for a time Howe was referred to as "Low Key" Howe). Among Howe's MGM films were *Stamboul Quest* (again with Myrna Loy), *Mark of the Vampire* (with Bela Lugosi) and *Whipsaw*. He was loaned out to David O Selznick for *The Prisoner of Zenda* (1937) and *The Adventures of Tom Sawyer* (1938). In 1938 he left MGM and became associated with Warner Brothers and was given his first Academy Award nomination (on loan out) for his work on *Algiers*. He would stay with Warner's until 1947.

In his private life Howe experienced discrimination. He and writer Sanora Babb had a long relationship, and wanted to marry, but because she was Caucasian, it was not allowed because of anti-miscegenation laws. The law was finally repealed and they were allowed to marry in 1949 (though it took considerable time to find a judge who would perform the ceremony). Among the notable films that Wong photographed during the '40s were *Abe Lincoln in Illinois* (1940, on loan out to RKO), *Kings Row* (1942), *Yankee Doodle Dandy* (1942), *Air Force* (1943), *The Hard Way* (1943), *Objective, Burma!* (1945), and especially *Body and Soul* (1947), where he filmed the climactic fight scene while holding a hand-held camera (another of his innovations) while wearing roller skates and being moved around by an assistant!

After leaving Warner Brothers, Howe freelanced and made films for most of the major studios. His best work of the '50s and '60s include *Come Back, Little Sheba, The Rose Tattoo, The Sweet Smell of Success* (one of the best photographed black-and-white films ever made), *The Old Man and the Sea, Hud, Hombre, Seconds* (again utilizing the hand-held camera to great effect in tight, compact environments), and *The Heart Is a Lonely Hunter*.

In the early '70s Howe's output declined as ill health took over. However, in 1974, producer Ray Stark fired Vilmos Zsigmond as cameraman on the film *Funny Lady* and asked Howe to take over as director of photography. He collapsed on the set and was replaced temporarily by Ernest Laszlo, but after a hospitalization, Howe returned and completed the film (his last) and was nominated for his tenth and final Oscar nomination for his work. He died on July 12, 1976, at his Hollywood home, a little more than a month before his 77th birthday. Despite his innovations, Howe had little regard for what he considered "camera gymnastics." "Camera gymnastics and strange angles are not what I would call the stock of a 'brilliant cameraman,'" Howe wrote in 1945. "A man of limitations, director or cameraman may use these mechanics to cover his thinness of understanding. Some of the most well-known writers possess technical skill and slickness and very little else. A limited writer can do far more harm, or lack of good, than a limited cameraman, because of the power of word and thought. I believe that the best cameraman is one who recognizes the source, the story, as the basis of his work." (**The Cameraman Talks Back**, *American Cinematographer*, March 1945.) (Other sources: *Movie Maker Magazine*, **James Wong Howe: A Relative's Perspective**, Obit, *Van Nuys* (CA) *Valley News*, 7/16/76.)

THE BACK STORY:

The story that is most commonly told regarding the casting of William Powell and Myrna Loy as Nick and Nora Charles is that they were forced on Louis B. Mayer by Woody Van Dyke. After all, Bill Powell was a Warner Brothers contract star who was loaned by the studio to appear opposite Clark Gable in *Manhattan*

Melodrama, and, besides, his box office appeal had declined in recent years. As for Myrna Loy, she was typically seen playing vamps. Yet Louella Parsons, that mouthpiece of studio publicity, announced as early as February 10, 1934 that Powell had signed for the lead in *The Thin Man*. "You can well imagine how well pleased E.B. Hatrick, in charge of Cosmopolitan productions," Parsons wrote in her daily column, "when William Powell was signed for the lead in *The Thin Man*. You can also imagine that Metro Goldwyn Mayer, who will release this picture, felt a little elated in being able to borrow Bill Powell, for whom the Dashiell Hammett story might well have been written." Not only that but Louella also announced that "Myrna Loy plays the girl, Nat Pendelton, expert wrestler, one of the leading roles with William Van Dyke sitting in the saddle as director and Hunt Stromberg as producer." This news on *The Thin Man* was released even before production on *Manhattan Melodrama* (which wouldn't go before the cameras until mid-March) began.

This is significant because Hollywood myth leads us to believe that it was the chemistry that Powell and Loy exhibited together in *Manhattan Melodrama* which led MGM to cast them in *The Thin Man*. The record shows that they were actually signed for *The Thin Man* even before shooting began on *Manhattan Melodrama*. Powell was always considered acceptable for Nick Charles because he processed the urbanity that the role called for, and had more than a passing resemblance to the Nick Charles of the novel. As for Loy, her big break wasn't really Van Dyke's *Manhattan Melodrama*, but Van Dyke's 1933 film *Penthouse* which convinced MGM that she was capable of playing other roles than vamps and exotic femme fatales. *Penthouse* also had the same creative team that would make *The Thin Man* — producer Hunt Stromberg, director Woody Van Dyke, screenwriters Frances Goodrich and Albert Hackett. *Penthouse* turned in a tidy profit for MGM as well, and so the studio brass trusted this team with *The Thin Man*, and, knowing how much Van Dyke *and* Stromberg felt about Loy, it wasn't really that much of a stretch that she was cast as Nora Charles.

In many ways it made perfect sense for producer Hunt Stromberg to assign *The Thin Man* to married screenwriters Frances Goodrich and Albert Hackett. After all, this film was not designed to focus on the mystery element, but to demonstrate the playfulness and sexiness of a modern married couple. There are those who believe that Frances and Albert invested a good deal of themselves into the characters of Nick and Nora Charles (and certainly the characters in the movie are much more playful with each other than in Hammett's novel). Of course, Hammett is said to have written the novel with himself as Nick and his lover Lillian Hellman as Nora, but, as Frances Goodrich's nephew and biographer would later write, "The bond between the Hacketts was much more Charles-like than that between Hammett and Hellman." When they were assigned to write *The Thin Man*, Goodrich and Hackett didn't really think they would be up to the task because, "neither of us had ever read a mystery story, so we didn't know what to do." Van Dyke made it easy for them. "I don't care anything about the mystery stuff," he told his writers, "just give me five scenes between Nick and Nora . . . forget about the mystery." But the writers still found it tough sailing. "We're in a stew as usual," Frances wrote in late January 1934. "Trying to get a story out of *The Thin Man*. I doubt whether it will come through. I think that Stromberg will decide not to do it. I hope so. It strikes me as pretty run-of-the-mill . . . It stinks." It's clear that even as late as January 1934 there was no complete script and the screenwriters were so pessimistic about the project that they actually thought that Hunt Stromberg would ultimately decide not to make the picture. Yet, it's their script for *The Thin Man* which emphasizes the relationship between Nick and Nora which people remember so well today — much more so than the novel. The Hacketts would ultimately be nominated for an Academy Award for their screenplay of *The Thin Man*.

The first day of shooting on *The Thin Man* was April 9, 1934. The first scene shot is the one which introduces William Powell as Nick Charles. It's the scene where Nick is demonstrating the proper way to mix a martini. Van Dyke said, "Bill, take these cocktail shakers . . . go behind the bar . . . and just walk through the opening scene. I want to check sound and lights before we make the take." Powell did as he was directed, and stepped behind the bar. The other cast members took their places. Powell began performing the scene. Van Dyke called out, "That's it!" and snapped his finger and said, "Print it." Powell was surprised.

"What did you say?" asked Bill.

"Print it," responded Van Dyke.

"Do you mean to tell me you shot that scene?"

"I sure did, and it was the best take you ever made, you big stiff."

Similarly, on that first day, Van Dyke shot Myrna Loy's slapstick entrance into the picture, except Loy didn't realize that her character would be introduced in such fashion. "Your arms are full of packages," he told Loy. "You can't see where you're going. Asta, your little dog, is leading the way. You start across the lobby like this," Van Dyke then walked across the stage. "Your husband sees you and says, 'Here she comes now.' You trip and sprawl on your face on the floor, bundles and all."

Now it was Myrna's turn to be shocked. "Now, really, Mr. Van Dyke," she told her director, "my Mack Sennett training has been brief, you know!" But Myrna had confidence in Van Dyke, her biggest booster at the studio. If he asked her to take a fall in the first scene, by God, she'd do it. "What other director would introduce his leading lady with a perfect three-point landing on a barroom floor," Loy later wrote. "I was supposed to stroll in looking very chic, loaded down with packages, and leading Asta on a leash . . . I would have done anything for Woody, because I was devoted to him. 'You just trip yourself,' he explained, 'and then go right down.' He put a camera on the floor, a mark where he wanted me to land, and we shot it without any rehearsal. I must have been crazy. I could have killed myself, but my dance training paid off . . ."

It was by accident that Van Dyke shot one of the most famous scenes in the picture. During a break in production Bill Powell picked up an air rifle and began shooting ornaments off the Christmas tree on the Charleses' apartment set. Van Dyke thought this was terribly funny and decided to add a scene depicting Nick Charles laying on the sofa shooting the air rifle (obviously a Christmas gift from Nora) demonstrating several different positions as he does so. The scene is one of the funniest and best remembered of the film.

The climax of the picture had the suspects, in typical mystery story fashion, gathered around the dinner table as Nick Charles reveals the murderer. It was a long and technically difficult scene to shoot because you have to get reaction shots from all the actors. The result turned out quite unappetizing. "Poor Bill complained loudly that he had to learn so many lines while I just gave him those knowing Nora Charles looks every now and then," Myrna Loy recalled. "Everybody sat down at a long dinner table, waiters served oysters on a half shell, and Bill began unraveling the plot. After a valiant try, he groaned, 'I don't know what I'm talking about.' But Woody didn't care as long as it kept moving. So we'd begin again and those oysters would reappear. They wouldn't bring fresh ones, and under the lights, as shooting wore on, they began to putrefy. By the time we finished that scene, nobody ever wanted to see another oyster."

The film was shot in 14 days with a couple of days of retakes in the middle of May 1934 before it was previewed at the Huntington Theater. Here is the recollection of Samuel Marx, the head of MGM's story department, on that preview: "We attended the first preview in fear and trembling. The executives went down to Huntington Park, including Hunt Stromberg, the producer, who was a nervous man anyway. I'd brought this sprightly detective story for fourteen thousand dollars, and we had no idea whether this kind of comedy would go. It had two unprecedented elements that scared the hell out of the whole studio: they were having fun with murder, and they were a married couple who acted with total sophistication. Myrna joins Bill at the bar, asking, 'Gus, how many has he had?' When the bartender reports, 'Seven,' she says, 'Set 'em up.' And matches her husband, drink for drink. That could have been a jolt to post-Prohibition audiences still uneasy about social drinking. The matrimonial combination of Powell and Loy — even that was a risk, because in those days you got married at the end of the movie, not at the beginning. Marriage wasn't supposed to be fun . . . I can only tell you that it was a night of great jubilation on the Huntington Park sidewalk after the preview. The whole thing broke with tradition in several ways, yet it looked like a smash. The first preview was a thermometer that told us how much heat this team was generating. They had a chemistry that came out of Myrna Loy and William Powell . . . It was automatic that you would now continue to put them together. The reaction was so great and it never stopped."

Surprisingly, the picture didn't have too many problems with the censors. The Hays Office did tell MGM that lines like Powell's, "He didn't come anywhere near my tabloids" and Loy's "What's that man doing in my drawers," were censurable but were allowed to stay in the final film.

The film, which cost under $500,000 to make, was a huge hit with Depression-era audiences and earned in excess of $2 million at the box office, providing MGM with huge profits and a determination to make a sequel. (By September 22, 1934 Louella Parsons was announcing that Hammett had been commissioned by MGM to begin work on a sequel.) William Powell was nominated for his first Academy Award. (In an oversight Myrna Loy wasn't nominated. However, in 1934, the Academy nominated only three actors for each category.) The film was also nominated for Best Picture, Director and Writing.

SUPPORTING PLAYER PROFILES:
ASTA (A.K.A. SKIPPY)

There was a time in the mid-1930s when the most popular animal in motion pictures was a Wire-Haired Fox Terrier named Skippy, who was better known by his screen name of "Asta." Asta sniffed out clues for Nick and Nora Charles, but when the action got thick would inevitably be found with his tail wagging out from under a bed. "Asta, you're not a terrier," Nick would tell him to bolster his confidence. "You're a police dog." Needless to say, a *Thin Man* film wouldn't have been complete if it didn't include Asta. So great was his popularity that MGM had to assign a secretary to respond to his fan mail. Of the six *Thin Man* films the one which uses Asta to his full potential is probably the second (and funniest), *After the Thin Man*, which includes a secondary plot where Asta returns home to find that Mrs. Asta may have been fooling around with the dog next door because one of his pups looks distinctly un-Asta like.

The Charleses do have a dog in the novel *The Thin Man*, but the Asta of the novel is a she and not a Fox Terrier at all, but a female Schnauzer. It was decided that for the movie "Asta" would have to demonstrate more energy than a Schnauzer, and they decided to make her a him and a terrier. Skippy belonged to Henry and Gale

East with Frank Weatherwax, his principal trainer. By the time of the second *Thin Man* film Skippy was earning $200 per week, which compared to the $60 per week his trainer received. Skippy proved not only to be popular but a highly intelligent Method actor. According to one contemporary article, his owner, Mrs. East, explained: "When Skippy has to drink water in a scene, the first time he does it he really drinks. If there are retakes and he's had all the water he can drink, he'll go through the scene just as enthusiastically as though his throat was parched, but he'll fake it. If you watch closely you'll see he's just going through the motions of lapping and isn't really picking up water at all."

His popularity through the *Thin Man* pictures made him a leading choice for other films as well; though his roles outside of playing "Asta" are limited, they are choice: fought over in divorce court between Irene Dunne and Cary Grant in *The Awful Truth*; memorable as "George," Katharine Hepburn's bone-loving dog (Mr. Smith) in *Bringing Up Baby*, and as Mr. Atlas, Cosmo Topper's dog, in *Topper Takes a Trip*.

It is now widely believed that the original Skippy made the first two *Thin Man* films, but in subsequent films he was aided by doubles and by the final *Song of the Thin Man* the original Skippy was either put out to pasture or was in doggy heaven. Needless to say, his contribution to the popularity of the *Thin Man* films was wide and to this day the name "Asta" is as identifiable with canine stars as those of Rin-Tin-Tin and Lassie.

EDWARD BROPHY (February 27, 1895-May 27, 1960)

Edward Brophy played not-so-bright gangsters or Damon Runyon types so often, and so well, that he came to specialize in (as Leonard Maltin called them), "dese-dem-dose" characters. Physically, Brophy was a good fit for those parts with his short stature, rotund build, balding plate and pop-eyes. He was born in New York City, on February 27, 1895, and later was educated at the University of Virginia. He entered movies in the late teens and found occasional work in small bits on screen, but most of his early work was on the production end of films often serving as a prop man. It was in that capacity that he got to know Buster Keaton and was asked by Keaton to work with him in one of the most memorable sequences in *The Cameraman* (1928) in which he and Keaton attempt to undress in a small closet. This was one of Keaton's last silent comedies and he later cast Brophy in three of his sound films, as the sergeant in *Doughboys* (1930), one of Keaton's best sound films, and as the detective in *Parlor, Bedroom and Bath* (1931) and the somewhat underrated *What! No Beer?* (1933).

He appeared in many films during the '30s (for most of the major studios), including the part of Wallace Beery's manager in *The Champ* (1931), and one of the *Freaks* (1932) of Tod Browning's camp classic. Then came his gangster who wrestles with Nick Charles in the middle of the night in *The Thin Man*. Brophy would be one of the few actors, other than William Powell and Myrna Loy, of course, to appear in more than one *Thin Man* film — also appearing in *The Thin Man Comes Home* (1944), but in a different part. One of his most memorable roles was Rollo, the knife thrower, who is executed as a murderer and whose hands are grafted onto Colin Clive's concert pianist (whose hands were crushed in a train accident) and can't control the murderous hands he's inherited in Tod Browning's classic *Mad Love* (1935). Other memorable films during the '30s include *China Seas, The Case Against Mrs. Ames, The Last Gangster, A Slight Case of Murder, Golden Boy* and *You Can't Cheat an Honest Man* (opposite W.C. Fields).

It may be that Brophy's most memorable film was one in which he didn't appear physically, but his voice is heard to great effect — Walt Disney's classic *Dumbo* (1941). Brophy voices Dumbo's friend Timothy Q. Mouse, who convinces Dumbo that he can fly. (He is also, according to some sources, credited with voicing Mickey Mouse's high-pitched vocals in the 1952 Disney cartoon *Pluto's Christmas Tree.*) During the '40s he played the dim-witted flatfoot in *The Gay Falcon* (opposite George Sanders) and then the Falcon's dim-witted reformed hood friend "Goldie" in a series of *Falcon* films for RKO starring Sanders real-life brother, Tom Conway. In the '50s Brophy appeared increasingly on television, but did appear memorably in John Ford's *The Last Hurrah* (1958), opposite Spencer Tracy.

The Last Hurrah proved to be Brophy's final film, though there are some reports that he died while filming John Ford's 1961

Western *Two Rode Together* (though his name is not included in the credits). But contemporary reports indicate that the married, but childless, Brophy died on May 27, 1960, at age 65, of a heart attack while watching the fights on television in his Los Angeles home. One of his final roles was on a March 28, 1960 edition of *The Ann Sothern Show*, in which the newspaper listing describes his appearance thus: "Edward Brophy, whose face you'll remember from countless movies, is in this one, too." The name might not be recognizable, but the face sure was. (Sources: *Indiana Evening Gazette*, March 28, 1960; Obit, *Charleston Gazette*, 5/31/60.)

EDWARD ELLIS (November 12, 1870-July 26, 1952)
Edward Ellis' character of Wynant in *The Thin Man* is the talk of the movie even though he is only in it for the first ten minutes or so of the film, yet the character as played by Ellis makes an indelible impression. During the '30s Ellis proved himself such a capable character actor that it seemed that at an age when other actors were getting ready to retire, he was actually being groomed as the next Lionel Barrymore — even starring in some films for RKO.

Ellis was born in Coldwater, Michigan on November 12, 1870 and began appearing on the stage when he was nine years old. At age seventeen he took on the role of Simon Legree in the touring company of *Uncle Tom's Cabin*. Ellis had a long career on the stage before entering motion pictures. He made his Broadway debut in 1905 (at age 35) in the comedy *Mary and John*. Over the next quarter of a century Ellis would appear in over twenty Broadway shows, including *The Dummy, The Bat, Chicago* and *Cock Robin*.

Though Ellis appeared in some silent films, his first substantial film and breakaway role was in the 1932 classic *I Am a Fugitive from a Chain Gang* playing Bomber Wells. After *The Thin Man* other memorable roles included playing the sheriff in *Fury* (with Spencer Tracy); the stern elder of the church in *Maid of Salem* (with Claudette Colbert); the head of the Texas Rangers in *The Texas Rangers* (with Fred MacMurray); in one of his finest performances, as the alcoholic judge in *Winterset*; playing "Pop," the owner of the vaudeville hotel, in Shirley Temple's *Little Miss Broadway*; and President Andrew Jackson in *Man of Conquest*.

In 1938 RKO gave Ellis the leading role of the kindly small-town doctor in *Man of Conquest*, a generally satisfying piece of Americana that also marked Garson Kanin's directorial debut. The film won good reviews and Ellis was singled out. "Now in his middle 60's, Ellis is just beginning to go places," wrote a review in the *Oakland Tribune* (6/25/39). In fact, by this time, Ellis was actually nearing seventy years of age. The commercial success of that film led to several other minor pieces of Americana starring Ellis: playing a wise old Iowa storekeeper in *Career*; a small business owner who is able to build his store into a major player while maintaining his integrity in *Three Sons*; and a cagy crusading D.A. named "Abraham Lincoln" Boggs in *Main Street Lawyer*. In 1942 he retired from acting after working in the MGM Western, *The Omaha Trail*, which starred James Craig. He was 72, and, by this time, despite good performances, it was clear he wasn't going to be another Lionel Barrymore. Ellis lived on another decade, dying on July 26, 1952 in his home in Beverly Hills, California at age 81. (Source includes *Oakland (CA) Times* 6/25/39.)

MINNA GOMBELL (May 28, 1893-April 14, 1973)

Mina Gombell made a career out of playing tough-talking "broads" who were, shall we say, experienced in the ways of life, in a career which spanned fifty years. Gombell was born on May 28, 1893 in Baltimore, Maryland. Not much is known about her early life, but she did begin acting with touring companies around 1911, when she would be about 18 years of age, which makes it seem likely that she didn't attend college.

She made her film debut in 1929, but her career didn't really take off until the early '30s. Like Maureen O'Sullivan, Gombell made her first significant film under the direction of Frank Borzage, in *Doctor's Wives*, playing Joan Bennett's disillusioned mother. Borzage liked Gombell so much he used her in quick succession in two more films, *Bad Girl* (1931) and *After Tomorrow* (1932). She did a succession of quickie, mostly "B" films up until *The Thin Man*, a film which seemed to enhance her reputation and gave her the opportunity for roles in better films. She followed up with *The Lemon Drop Kid* (1934), *Miss Pacific Fleet* (1935), *Banjo on My Knee* (1936), and perhaps her best-remembered film today, if for anything because of the legions of fans Laurel and Hardy still inspire, *Blockheads* (1938), playing Mrs. Oliver Hardy, and demonstrating who really wears the pants in their home. That same year she gave a strong performance as a burlesque queen in *Comet over Broadway* and ended the decade playing the Queen of Beggars in the classic *Hunchback of Notre Dame* (1939). She was not tied down to any one studio; in fact, she made the rounds to all the majors.

In the '40s she stood out in *Boom Town* (1940), playing Spanish Eva, and *High Sierra* (1941), starring Humphrey Bogart and Ida Lupino, as Joan Leslie's mother. The films which followed over the next few years were mostly average, though she never was. Her next big film was the 1946 William Wyler-directed *The Best Years of Our Lives* (1946), in a standout performance playing Harold Russell's mother, heartbroken over her son having lost his hands in the war. She was equally good as the hard-hearted asylum nurse in *The Snake Pit* (1948). Her last film role was playing Doris Day's mother in *I'll See You in My Dreams* (1952). She made a short-lived comeback in 1961, playing one of the three witches in a television production of *Macbeth* which starred Sean Connery. (The other two witches were played by Jane Darwell and Mary Sinclair.)

It is said that she married three times, but her obituary didn't mention a current spouse and listed no children. She spent her final years at her Los Angeles home and died on April 14, 1973 at the age of 81. According to news reports, her body was flown back to Baltimore where she was buried in the family plot. (Source includes obit, *Nevada State Journal*, 4/18/73.)

PORTER HALL (September 19, 1888-October 6, 1953)

Porter Hall had his first major film role in *The Thin Man* at age 45 and soon became one of the most recognizable faces of '30s and '40s cinema, often cast in unattractive character parts — not always out-and-out villains, but certainly people who seem to get a kick out of being mean spirited. The perfect example is the 1947 classic *Miracle on 34th Street*. It's Hall's store psychiatrist who insists that Edmund Gwenn's kindly Kris Kringle is not sane for believing himself to be Santa Claus.

Hall was born in Cincinnati, Ohio, on September 19, 1888, and was educated in the Cincinnati public school system. He later attended the University of Cincinnati. His early work history resembled that of many Ohio men — working in a steel mill. In his spare time he enjoyed performing in plays and worked in many repertory companies, often performing works of Shakespeare. His weak chin and receding hairline marked him for supporting roles; often cast as the villain, rather than playing the lead. By the mid-'20s Hall became a fixture on the Broadway stage appearing in such plays as *The Great Gatsby, Naked* and *It's a Wise Child*. Hall played uncredited roles in two 1931 films and then returned to New York and the Broadway stage, appearing opposite a young Katharine Hepburn in the 1932 production of *The Warrior's Husband*.

He came out west in early 1934 when he was offered the plum supporting role of the attorney in *The Thin Man*. His performance and his shifty looks were enough and he stayed on in Hollywood appearing in many outstanding films. He appeared in two prestigious films for Warner Brothers, *The Story of Louis Pasteur* (1935, with Paul Muni) and *The Petrified Forest* (1936, with Leslie Howard and Bette Davis). Also in 1936, he played opposite Davis again in *Satan Met a Lady*, the second screen adaptation of Hammett's *The Maltese Falcon*, playing the role of the unlucky partner of the hard-boiled private eye (in this film named Ted Shayne, rather than Sam Spade) who is knocked off early in the film. Soon afterward, Hall went to Paramount, where he would spend much of the rest of his career. He worked in back-to-back films with Gary Cooper, *The General Died at Dawn* and *The Plainsman* (memorably playing the cowardly Jack McCall who shoots Wild Bill Hickok in the back, winning a Screen Actors Guild Award for his performance). He would work again in a Cooper film in 1937 with *Souls at Sea*. Hall ended the '30s on a high note appearing in yet another classic of the American cinema in Frank Capra's *Mr. Smith Goes to Washington*, playing a corrupt senator.

His '40s career began strongly by playing one of the hoards of cynical reporters in Howard Hawks' *His Girl Friday* opposite Cary Grant and Rosalind Russell. In 1941 Hall became a member of Preston Sturges' stock company, appearing in four memorable roles in Sturges' films during the decade: *Sullivan's Travels, The Miracle of Morgan's Creek* (1944, giving a fine comedic performance as the justice of the peace), *The Great Moment* (1944) and *The Beautiful Blonde from Bashful Bend* (1949, also featuring fellow *Thin Man* alumnus Cesar Romero). He had small, but choice, roles in two outstanding 1944 films. In *Double Indemnity*, he played Mr. Jackson from Oregon who helps arouse Edward G. Robinson's suspicions when he says that Barbara Stanwyck's dead husband doesn't look anything like the man he saw on the train prior to the murder (but he keeps suspiciously eyeing Fred MacMurray's Walter Neff). In the same year's Oscar-winning Best Picture, *Going My Way*, he played the crotchety atheist Mr. Belknap.

While Hall often played "meanies" on screen, he was anything but off. Happily married in 1927, he and his wife Geraldine had two children. He was active in his Presbyterian Church as a deacon, and generously gave of his time to charitable endeavors. He died of a heart attack at age 65 on October 6, 1953, prior to the release of what would be his final film, *Return to Treasure Island* (1954). (Source includes *San Mateo Times*, 10/8/53.)

MAUREEN O'SULLIVAN (May 17, 1911-June 23, 1998)

The beautiful and talented Maureen O'Sullivan appeared in many outstanding films for MGM throughout the 1930s and into the 1940s, without really becoming a major film star. Most of her roles, while substantial, were in support of the film leads. However, she is most fondly remembered today as Jane to Johnny Weissmuller's Tarzan in the first six films of that very popular MGM series (1932-1942).

She was born Maureen Paula O'Sullivan on May 17, 1911 in Boyle, Ireland, the daughter of a British military officer and his Irish wife. She was educated in parochial schools first in Dublin and then in London, where one of her classmates was Vivien Leigh, with whom she would later work with in the film *A Yank at Oxford* (1938), at MGM's London studios, just prior to Miss Leigh's coming to the United States and zooming to fame as Scarlett O'Hara in *Gone With the Wind*. After attending finishing school in Paris the cultured and extremely beautiful O'Sullivan returned to Dublin where she planned to work as a social worker. She was discovered by the American director Frank Borzage at a Dublin horse show in 1930 (at age 18) and cast in his film *Song o' My Heart* in the ingénue role — the type of part she would play for the next few years. She was signed by Fox and appeared in several films, including *A Connecticut Yankee* (1931) opposite Will Rogers, but her career didn't really begin to take off until she arrived at MGM in 1932.

It was upon being cast as Jane Parker in *Tarzan the Ape Man* (1932) that O'Sullivan met the director W. S. Van Dyke, who championed the young actress for this film. To play the part the director knew he needed an actress who could project both sophistication and naivety. The young and well-educated O'Sullivan could do both. Film audiences were also captivated by the sight of the physically beautiful O'Sullivan and Weissmuller swimming in the nude in one of the most remembered sequences in the film. O'Sullivan later recalled the outcry those scenes caused. "Letters started coming in. It added up to thousands of women objecting to my (scanty) costume. In those days, they took those things seriously." The film went on to be a huge grosser for MGM, making more than a million dollars in profits, and was the first of three films that she would make with "Woody" Van Dyke, the other two being *The Thin Man* and *Hide-Out*, both 1934.

When O'Sullivan wasn't playing Jane, she was lending her intelligence and beauty to other top MGM releases, supporting Norma Shearer and Clark Gable in *Strange Interlude* (1932) and Marie Dressler and Wallace Beery in *Tugboat Annie* (1933, as the love interest of Robert Young). Then came three top literary adaptations: *The Barretts of Wimpole Street* (1934, one of her warmest performances as Henrietta); Selznick's adaptation of Dickens' *David Copperfield* (1935); and *Anna Karenina* (1935) starring Greta Garbo. In 1936, after filming *Tarzan Escapes*, O'Sullivan was cast as the young love interest (along with Allan Jones) in the Marx Brothers' *A Day at the Races*. While she enjoyed working with the Marxes it was confirmation of her status at the studio that despite many excellent films she was still a second-tier leading lady. Would a major MGM leading lady be cast as the love interest in a Marx Brothers picture? Also in 1936 O'Sullivan married her first husband, director John Farrow.

O'Sullivan was reunited with William Powell in the 1937 comedy *The Emperor's Candlesticks*, and then played opposite Robert Taylor in both *The Crowd Roars* and *A Yank at Oxford* before being assigned to the fourth Tarzan film, *Tarzan Finds a Son!* (1939). By this time O'Sullivan had tired of the part of Jane. She enjoyed working with Weissmuller but despised the chimp, Cheeta, who apparently bite or spit at her one too many times. She balked at doing this film, until MGM told her that they would kill the Jane character off at the end. She made the film, pregnant with her first child, and was indeed killed off at the end, but test audiences complained so much that MGM had to re-shoot the ending with Jane alive and well. The studio threw her a bone in 1940 when they cast her with Laurence Olivier and Greer Garson in *Pride and Prejudice*. After that her career suffered a slump, with yet another Tarzan film (*Tarzan's Secret Treasure*) and then what must have been a bit of a letdown for her, playing second fiddle to Ann Sothern in *Maisie Was a Lady*. She consented to do a final *Tarzan* film (getting to dress up in contemporary clothing for *Tarzan's New York Adventure*) before announcing her retirement from the screen in 1942 to devote her time to bringing up her children. She and Farrow eventually had seven children, which included actress Mia Farrow.

After six years of relative inactivity (though she was a frequent presence on radio dramas during those years), O'Sullivan returned to films in 1948 appearing in her husband's superb crime melodrama *The Big Clock* opposite Ray Milland and Charles Laughton. It was a fine return for her, but the films she did thereafter were not of the same quality and included *Bonzo Goes to College* (1952). However, she did have a good part in Budd Boetticher's psychological Western *The Tall T* (1957) opposite Randolph Scott. Tragedy struck the following year, in her private life, when her firstborn child, Michael, died in a plane crash. Following the death of her husband in 1963, O'Sullivan, with most of her children now old enough and out on their own, resurrected her career. She appeared in several Broadway productions during the '60s, including two very successful runs in the comedy *Never Too Late* (1963-1965) and the very dramatic *The Subject Was Roses* (1965-1966). But she was more likely by the late sixties to be referred to as "the mother of Mia Farrow" and "mother-in-law of Frank Sinatra."

During the '70s she did more stage work and increasingly appeared on television, including a season on the ABC soap opera *All My*

Children. In the '80s she did more soap operas, including stints on *The Guiding Light* and *Search for Tomorrow.* In 1985, Woody Allen wrote one of his finest screenplays, *Hannah and Her Sisters*, starring his lover, Mia Farrow. The script called for a strong actress to play the part of Hannah's mother — who better than Farrow's real mother, Maureen O'Sullivan? O'Sullivan took on the role and she reveled in her combat with Lloyd Nolan, playing Farrow's father.

By the early '90s, O'Sullivan was slowing down and was enjoying life with her second husband, businessman James Cushing, whom she married in 1983. She was in Scottsdale, Arizona on June 23, 1998 when the end came at age 87. Mia Farrow said she felt her mother simply died of "old age." Bob Hope recalled her as "a lovely leading lady." (Sources include *Oakland Tribune*, 6/25/34, obit, *Syracuse Post Standard*, 6/24/98.)

NATHANIEL (NAT) PENDLETON (August 9, 1895-October 12, 1967)
The burly Nat Pendleton played Lt. John Guild, who was always two steps behind Nick Charles, in two *Thin Man* films — the first and the third installment, *Another Thin Man.* Pendleton's face was a recognizable one to '30s and '40s movie-goers and classic movie lovers to this day. He excelled at playing "dim" types, whether they are mugs, hoodlums, athletes or befuddled cops.

Pendleton was born in Davenport, Iowa and was a descendant of Revolutionary War hero Nathaniel Greene, for whom he was named after. He later attended Columbia University where he attained a place on the wrestling team in the heavyweight division. He was the Eastern Intercollegiate Wrestling Association champion two years in a row (1914 and 1915) and in 1920 he competed at the summer Olympics in Antwerp, Belgium as part of the American team, winning a silver medal. He used this success to pursue wrestling as a career when he returned to the United States and made a few random films during the 1920s without making any real impression. During the mid- to late 1920s Pendleton appeared in three Broadway shows, *Naughty Cinderella* (1925-1926), *Grey Fox* (1928-1929, starring Edward Arnold) and *My Girl Friday* (1929, which also featured Robert Benchley).

That all changed with the advent of the new decade. During the

1930s alone Pendleton appeared in more than 80 films; not always credited and not always in large parts, but by mid-decade he was a more than welcome sight with his parts increasing in length. Many of his early films were at Warner Brothers, but he generally made the rounds to the major and some of the minor studios. He played with Walter Huston in *The Star Witness* (1931); James Cagney in *Blonde Crazy* (1931) and *Taxi!* (1932); and was the Notre Dame assistant coach in *The Spirit of Notre Dame* (1931) starring Lew Ayes. He began his run of befuddled cops in *Girl Crazy* (1932) with Wheeler and Woolsey. He played a boxer in the John Barrymore film *State's Attorney* (1932); he worked for Cecil B. DeMille in the biblical drama *The Sign of the Cross*; and played a motorcycle cop in one of Bette Davis' early Warner Brothers epics, *Parachute Jumper* (1933). He twice worked with the Marx Brothers, in *Horse Feathers* (1932) and *At the Circus* (1939). Frank Capra used him as one of the Damon Runyon types who come to the assistance of "Apple Annie" in *Lady for a Day* (1933). That same year he worked with "Woody" Van Dyke for the first time in *Penthouse*, which also starred Myrna Loy. It would be the first of five films he would make for Van Dyke (the others being *Manhattan Melodrama*, *The Thin Man*, *It's a Wonderful World* and *Another Thin Man*). His muscular build again worked well for him in one of his best remembered and praised performances, playing "The Great Sandow" in *The Great Ziegfeld* (1936), which starred William Powell and Myrna Loy and was produced by Hunt Stromberg, the producer of the early *Thin Man* films.

In 1938, Pendleton began one of his most fondly remembered runs as part of the *Dr. Kildare* series playing the none-too-bright, but helpful ambulance driver, Joe Wayman in *Young Dr. Kildare*. He played Wayman in nine films up to 1943, even after Lew Ayres left and Lionel Barrymore's Dr. Gillespie became the series' focus. Another of Pendleton's signature roles, for which he is well recalled to this day, is playing the tough drill sergeant who inevitably gives Abbott and Costello (particularly Costello) a hard time in *Buck Privates* (1941) and its sequel *Buck Privates Come Home* (1947). This later film would be Pendleton's 114th and last. He did some television work during the 1950s before retiring to the San Diego suburb of Pacific Beach with his second wife, Barbara.

They had no children. Pendleton died of a heart attack at age 72. (Sources include obituary *Pacific Stars and Stripes*, 10/14/67.)

CESAR ROMERO (February 15, 1907-January 1, 1994)
Cesar Romero's grandfather was the liberator of Cuba, Jose Marti ("The Cuban war of independence was planned in my grandmother's house," Romero later said), but he, himself, was born in New York City on February 15, 1907 to a concert singer, Maria Maniela, and her Italian-born husband, Senor Romero, who also happened to be a wealthy import-exporter of sugar refinery machinery. When the sugar market collapsed the elder Romero lost his fortune. After being educated in New York City the handsome 6'2" Romero decided he wasn't cut out to be the banker his father wanted him to be and decide to follow his passion and become a dancer. He teamed up with a young dancer named Elizabeth Higgins, and played exclusive clubs in New York City, including the St. Regis Roof and Montmartre Café. They eventually were hired for a Broadway revue called *Lady Do* in which Romero did it all; according to film historian James Robert Parish, "Cesar waltzed, tangoed, and did a fast foxtrot and a bit of Apache dancing for fifty-six performances after the show opened on April 18, 1927." For the next few years Romero continued on as a nightclub dancer and Broadway actor (including a 232-performance run in the Kaufman-Ferber hit *Dinner at Eight*) before giving Hollywood a try.

The Thin Man was Romero's second film and he made a good impression as the handsome gigolo Chris. When he came to Hollywood, Romero was told that he would be the second coming of Valentino. "When I started in motion pictures in 1934 they said I was going to be the next Valentino. I was never a leading man, and very seldom did I ever get the girl, but I was saddled with the label ("The Latin Lover") because I had a Latin name. My background is Cuban, but I'm from New York City. I'm a Latin from Manhattan." Romero went from MGM to Universal where he made the Preston Sturges-scribed comedy *The Good Fairy* (starring Margaret Sullavan). He was then signed by Twentieth Century-Fox, where he would spend eighteen years as a contract player working in all kinds of genres including the Kipling action adventure of *Wee Willie Winkie* (as an Afghan leader) opposite Shirley Temple for director

John Ford. He worked with Temple again a couple of years later in *The Little Princess*. He proved adept in comedy, usually as the other man, supporting Carole Lombard in *Love Before Breakfast*, Sonja Henie in My Lucky Star and Loretta Young in *Wife, Husband and Friend*. One of his most interesting roles came in 1939 in Allan Dwan's cult Western *Frontier Marshal*, which featured Romero in the key role of Doc Holliday opposite Randolph Scott's Wyatt Earp. That same year Romero played opposite Warner Baxter in *Return of the Cisco Kid* and by the next year he took over the part, playing the Cisco Kid in six popular "B" films released by 20th over the next two years.

His background in musical comedy aided him well during the 1940s when he appeared in several of Fox's best musicals alternating between Alice Faye vehicles (*Weekend in Havana, The Great American Broadcast*) and Betty Grable vehicles (the excellent *Springtime in the Rockies* and *Coney Island*). After completing the Sonja Henie musical *Wintertime* in 1943, Romero enlisted into the U.S. Coast Guard at San Pedro, California, where he served with distinction, eventually reaching the rank of lieutenant. After leaving the service in 1946, he bought his family out to live with him in a large Brentwood, California house he bought for $15,000 (and would sell thirty-seven years later for $400,000).

1947 brought him one of his best roles, playing the Spanish conqueror Cortes in *Captain from Castile* opposite good friend Tyrone Power. He was loaned to MGM for the Greer Garson-Walter Pidgeon change-of-pace comedy *Julia Misbehaves* (showing a flair for slapstick comedy) and returned to Fox to work opposite frequent leading lady Betty Grable in *That Lady in Ermine*, which had the advantage of director Ernst Lubitsch's famous touch. In 1949, he again worked with Grable, this time in the less-than-ideal Preston Sturges comedy *The Beautiful Blonde from Bashful Bend*. His final film as a Fox contract player was *Love that Brute* in 1950.

During the 1950s Romero appeared more frequently on television, including the first *Lucy-Desi Comedy Hour* in 1957. He also headlined a moderately successful television series, *Passport to Danger*, which proved lucrative for him since he owned a piece of it. Most of the films he made during these years were disappointing. By the end of the decade he was headlining Las Vegas in a Latin Mardi Gras-type revue. Of his film career Romero would point to his best films as being *Show Them No Mercy!*, *Captain from Castile* and "any of the musicals" as his favorites. During the early '60s Romero's best roles were in the popular Rat Pack comedy *Ocean's Eleven* and the John Ford-directed John Wayne action-comedy set in Hawaii, *Donovan's Reef.*

In 1966, Romero, still devilishly handsome with steel-white hair, hid his good looks behind a clown's façade to play the "Joker" in the campy television series *Batman*, winning a new generation of fans. Afterwards, he kept busy working well into the '80s with stage productions, television programs and occasional movies. One of his last films was the cult classic *Lust in the Dust* in 1985 playing Father Garcia. He described his enthusiasm for the film this way: "I play a Catholic priest who used to be a rabbi. No explanation is given. I think it's going to be a very funny picture — not campy but funny." The film, starring Tab Hunter and the transvestite Divine, was funny *and* a camp classic. He appeared opposite Jane Wyman for two seasons on *Falcon's Crest.*

Romero never married, explaining, "How could I? When I had so many family responsibilities." He was often described in that very veiled way as a "confirmed bachelor." Several books have alleged that Romero was gay but almost to the end he kept up appearances. In 1984, at age 77, he said, "I have no regrets (about not marrying). Right now I'm seeing a lady quite a bit younger, and we have a good relationship." He hosted a vintage film show on cable television almost up to the very end, enjoying the responsibility of introducing a favorite film with one of his many Hollywood anecdotes — from a man who knew them all. When he died (complications from a blood clot), on January 1, 1994, he was nearly 87 years young. Jane Wyman remembered him as "a dream. A very, very gentle man and a very giving person." (Sources include: *Syracuse Herald Journal*, 6/20/84, Obit, *Chicago Daily News*, 1/3/94.)

REVIEWS:

"Out of Dashiell Hammett's popular novel, *The Thin Man*, W.S. Van Dyke, one of Hollywood's most versatile directors, has made an excellent combination of comedy and excitement . . . Myrna Loy as Nora . . . aids considerably in making this film an enjoyable entertainment. She speaks her lines effectively, frowns charmingly, and is constantly wondering what her husband's next move will be . . . Mr. Powell's performance is even better than his portrayals of Philo Vance in the S.S. Van Dine stories. He has good lines and makes the most of them . . ."

New York Times, 6/30/34

"A picture you simply cannot afford to miss unless you want to cheat yourself."

New York World Telegram, 6/34

"A new screen team which certainly sticks is that of William Powell and Myrna Loy. When they are provided with a story like Dashiell Hammett's 'The Thin Man,' then you have something. A preview of this show last night was a thrill. It was smoothly directed and expertly acted and was absolutely 100 percent entertainment."

South Dakota Evening Huronite, 6/6/34

"*The Thin Man* . . . is one of the most unusual pictures to come out of Hollywood in a long time. A detective mystery, it presents William Powell in the most amusing sleuthing role of his career, assisted by charming Myrna Loy as his wife, Nora . . . The picture never lags in interest, keeps the audience on the edge of their seats every minute and furnishes respite from the tension . . . by a liberal sprinkling of humorous situations and dialog."

Oakland (CA) Tribune, 6/25/34

"Changes made in the Dashiell Hammett mystery novel, which enjoyed a best seller rep, in its transfer from the printed page to the screen haven't lessened its literary value at all. To the contrary, here is one instance where any material that it was found necessary to add more than makes up for all that was deleted. *The Thin Man* was an entertaining novel, and now it's an entertaining picture; as a picture should do as well comparatively as the book in the way of coin . . . The comedy as inserted, and also as directed by W.S. Van Dyke and played by William Powell and Myrna Loy, carries the picture along during its early moments and gives it an impetus which sweeps the meat of the mystery story through to a fast finish . . . For the leads the studio couldn't have done better than to pick Powell and Miss Loy, both of whom handle their semi-comic roles beautifully. Most of the support playing consists of character studies, all well done by a cast of vets."

Variety, 7/3/34

"Dashiell Hammett's story of the same name has been highly praised. The new version of it must rate as high. It has three murders in it, a good round number for even the most thrilling of out and out thrillers, but the solution is worked out with such jauntiness by the ex detective Nick Charles (William Powell), that one hasn't the usual feeling of being hammered over the head with situations guaranteed to keep one swallowing his heart. The free and easy relations between Charles and his wife Nora (Myrna Loy) give the picture a humorous pitch which we have never seen approached in a detective movie."

Wisconsin State Journal, 7/9/34

"An amusing, exciting and generally satisfying motion picture has been made out of the popular Dashiell Hammett's febrile detective story, *The Thin Man*. Altho the screen usually is at its best in the manipulation of mystery narratives, its propensity for mixing comedy with murder frequently has unfortunate results . . . It might, therefore, seem less than enthusiastic praise to say of *The Thin Man* that its mood essentially is one of gaiety. Yet so skilful is the amalgamation of the qualities of comedy and melodrama that the possibly warring elements fit together beautifully. Thanks to some excellent direction by the expert W. S. Van Dyke, and two striking performances by William Powell and Myrna Loy, the new film is excellent entertainment . . ."

Literary Digest, 7/14/34

"You'll like Nick and Nora better than any two movies characters you've met in a long time. They are crack-brained but exciting and are acted with perfection by Bill Powell and Myrna Loy."

Los Angeles Evening Herald Express, 7/16/34

". . . on the whole it was thoroughly well conceived and carried out — a strange mixture of excitement, quips and hard-boiled (but clear and touching) sentiment. It is a good movie and should not be missed."

Otis Ferguson, *The New Republic*

"A way above the average murder mystery story — *The Thin Man* grips the interest right at the start, gains impetus from William Powell and Myrna Loy and travels at a fast pace to a surprise climax."

Winnipeg Free Press, 10/12/34

". . . *The Thin Man* (1934), directed by W. S. Van Dyke, set a high mark in realism with the ease, spontaneity, and intimacy of the actors' speeches and the flow of images and talk generally. The camera did not wait on the sound, and the conversation did not seem to be aware of the microphones presence."

Lewis Jacobs, *The Rise of the American Film*
(Teachers College, 1968)

"Directed by the whirlwind W.S. Van Dyke, the Dashiell Hammett detective novel took only 16 days to film, and the result was one of the most popular pictures of its era. New audiences aren't likely to find it as sparkling as the public did then, because new audiences aren't fed up, as that public was, with what the picture broke away from. It started a new cycle in screen entertainment by demonstrating that a murder mystery could also be a sophisticated screwball comedy. And it turned several decades of movies upside down by showing a suave man of the world (William Powell) who made love to his own rich, funny, and good humored wife (Myrna Loy); as Nick and Nora Charles, Powell and Loy startled and delighted the country by their heavy drinking (without remorse) and unconventional diversions . . . The cast includes the lovely Maureen O'Sullivan (not wildly talented here), the thoroughly depressing Minna Gombell (her nagging voice always hangs in the air), and Cesar Romero, Harold Huber, Edward Brophy, Nat Pendleton, Edward Ellis (in the title role), and a famous wirehaired terrier, called

Asta here. Warning: There's a lot of plot exposition and by modern standards the storytelling is very leisurely."

Pauline Kael, *5001 Nights at the Movies*, 1982

". . . Today the film is just another murder mystery, but Powell and Loy are nonchalant, debonair, take-it-or-leave-it and it is startling to realize that their chief interests are sex, money and booze . . ."

David Shipman, *The Story of Cinema*

"Myrna Loy was a delightful foil to Powell, but in this film she is essentially just his playmate; Powell dominates the picture with his deep, rich voice, his gliding, subtly unsteady physical movements, and his little mustache that he hopes makes him look more grownup than he feels. For audiences in the middle of the Depression, 'The Thin Man,' like the Astaire and Rogers musicals it visually resembles, was pure escapism: Beautiful people in expensive surroundings make small talk all day long, without a care in the world, and even murder is only an amusing diversion."

Roger Ebert, 12/22/02

"Classic blend of laughs and suspense . . . delightfully unpretentious blend of screwball comedy and murder mystery."

Leonard Maltin, *Movie and Video Guide*, 1992

"The delight of this film is the banter between its stars."

Mick Martin and Marsha Porter, *Video Movie Guide*, 2001

"*The Thin Man* is, in its way, a piece of social history, a sweet and soft image of the 1930's with a hero who is almost always drunk, shoots the ornaments off the Christmas tree with a toy air gun, and never goes without his trusty but spectacularly cowardly dog Asta . . ."

Nick Rodd, *Magill's Survey of Cinema IV*

Thin Man Photo Gallery

Bill, as Nick Charles, trying to get some sleep while Myrna, as Nora Charles, wants him on the case in *The Thin Man*, 1934. COURTESY OF SCOTT O'BRIEN.

From the Christmas Party Scene in *The Thin Man*. COURTESY OF SCOTT O'BRIEN.

Bill with Maureen O'Sullivan and Nat Pendleton in *The Thin Man*.

The Lovely Maureen O'Sullivan with Bill in *The Thin Man*.

Bill, Myrna and Maureen O'Sullivan in *The Thin Man*.

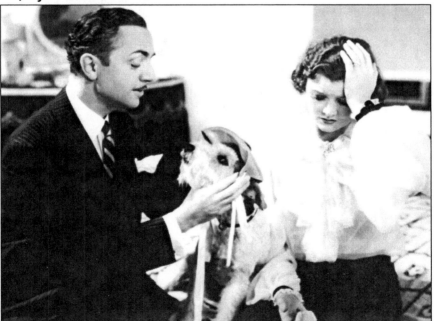

Nora and Asta have hangovers while it's just another day for Nick in *The Thin Man*.

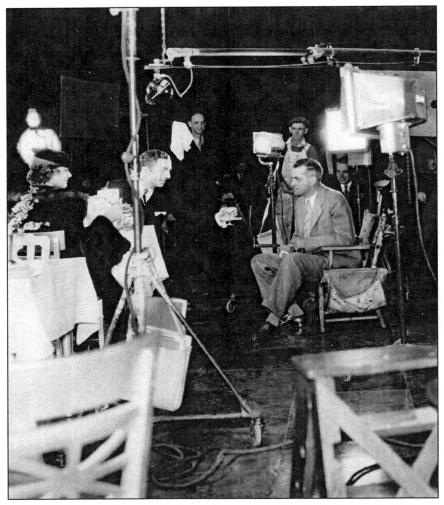

Myrna, with Bill, offering a drink to director Woody Van Dyke, on the *Thin Man* set.

CHAPTER FOUR

AFTER THE THIN MAN

CAST: William Powell (Nick Charles), Myrna Loy (Nora Charles), James Stewart (David), Elissa Landi (Selma), Joseph Calleia (Dancer), Jessie Ralph (Aunt Katherine), Alan Marshall (Robert), Sam Levene (Lt. Abrams), Dorothy McNulty [Penny Singleton] (Polly), William Law (Lum Kee), Paul Fix (Phil), Teddy Hart (Casper), George Zucco (Dr. Kammer), Asta (himself).

COMPANY CREDITS: A Metro-Goldwyn-Mayer (MGM) film. W. S. (Woody) Van Dyke II (Director), Hunt Stromberg (Producer), Albert Hackett and Frances Goodrich with a story by Dashiell Hammett (Writers), Oliver T. Marsh (Cinematographer), Robert J. Kern (Editing), Cedric Gibbons (Art Direction), Herbert Strothart and Edward Ward (Original Music).

PRODUCTION DATES: late September-October 31, 1936. Released: December 25, 1936.

SYNOPSIS:
Unlike the first film, which began by establishing the mystery plot and introducing key suspects with little or no humor in its first thirteen or so minutes, the first twenty minutes of the sequel, *After the Thin Man*, are pure and unadulterated comedy. The film picks up on the train heading toward California where the first film ended. It is quite possibly a day or two later (in actuality, these scenes were filmed nearly two and a half *years* after the end of the original film) and the train is fast approaching its destination in San Francisco.

Poster for the first sequel, *After the Thin Man*, **1936.**

Nick Charles is no different from we last remembered seeing him — still slightly cockeyed. Nick and Nora are in their drawing room and Nora is packing and calls out to Nick, "Are you packing, dear?" To which the tipsy Nick replies nonchalantly, "I'm just putting away this liquor," as he takes a swig.

Reporters greet Nick outside the train platform as they disembark. Word of the **Thin Man** murder case, which Nick just solved back in New York during the Christmas holidays, has been headline news on the coast as well. They are wondering if this means that Nick has come out of retirement and is going to pursue detective work full time again. "I'm retired," Nick tells them. "I'm just going to take care of my wife's money, so I'll have something for my old age." An amused Nora is in the background. Nick adds that he will only take on a case again to provide excitement for Nora, to which Nora emphatically replies, "He will *not* take up another case — and you can print that."

As they stroll through the station to meet their car and driver, Nora has a run-in with an old friend of Nick's, "Fingers," who, unbeknownst to Nora, swipes her purse; Nick realizes it and stops him. Nick and "Fingers" greet each other like long-lost friends and Nick makes a point of letting "Fingers" know that Nora is his wife. "Fingers" slips the handbag to Nick. When Nora finally notices it missing, Nick hands it over to her. This allows Nora to once again say, "Dear, you know the *nicest* people."

As Nick and Nora are driving thru town on their way home, Nick is greeted by many of his other "friends," including a liquor supplier passing by in his truck. Nick yells out that he can "start delivering again," adding, "No, the big kegs." Finally, Nora is recognized by a stuffy-looking, obviously wealthy couple with the man in top hat and woman in fur. "Oh, hello, Nora!" the woman calls out. Nora greets them back and this time it's Nick who asks, "Who are they?"

NORA: Oh, you wouldn't know them, darling. They are respectable.

When they arrive home, they want nothing more than to spend a nice quiet New Year's Eve home alone with each other. "So peaceful, so quiet," says Nora. Asta, too, is excited to be home because he has been away from his Mrs. — and their pups. As Asta is proudly looking over his family, he notices one pup that looks out of place — a black Scotty — who looks suspiciously like the Scotty who lives next door. What has Mrs. Asta been up to while he has been away? Asta makes sure to bury the entrance way his competitor has been coming thru to see Mrs. Asta.

As Nick and Nora enter their front door they are confronted with a loud, boisterous, drunken party going on inside. It's supposed to be their "Welcome Home" party, but none of the guests recognize Nick or Nora. When they finally make their way to the kitchen, they are recognized by the domestics.

MAID: What do you think of the surprise party that they are giving you?

NORA: It looks like we're giving it.

At this point, we get some kind of vague idea of the mystery to come when Nora is told that her Aunt Katherine has been calling the house repeatedly asking for her. There is a call again, but this time it's from Nora's cousin, Selma (Elissa Landi), who sounds clearly distressed about something. Suddenly, old Aunt Katherine (Jessie Ralph) takes the phone away from Selma, to which Nora says, "Oh, hello, Aunt Katherine" and Nick, in the background, calls out, "The old battle axe." It's clear they don't get along. Aunt Katherine wants to play down Selma's emotionalism, but clearly wants Nora *and* Nick (who she doesn't think is suitable as a husband for Nora) to come to dinner that night. To Nora, it is uncharacteristic of Aunt Katherine to want Nick's attendance and so, intrigued, she says, "All right, we'll come." Nick almost drops his drink. He begins to make another drink when Nora, who, so far, has been drink-less, calls out, "Pour me one, too."

We know something is up as the family gathers for dinner. Aunt Katherine has a big announcement for the assembled brood: "Nora and her husband are coming." The rest of the mostly elderly and stuffy-looking family is aghast that Nick will be welcomed back, "after what happened last time!" But Katherine tells them to treat

Nick respectfully — even though she acknowledges that it will take "an effort" on their part.

The door bell rings and Nick and Nora have arrived. Nora looks as glamorous as ever and Nick is even decked out in tie and tails and wearing a top hat, but under his breath he is making incomprehensible sounds.

NORA: What are you muttering to yourself?

NICK: I'm trying to get all the bad words out of my system.

The doddering old butler, who looks as if he has been with the family for fifty years, answers the door and Nick says to Nora, "Is this the waxworks?" Of course, the poor old guy can't hear a word of what Nick has said. Nick throws his coat to the butler, almost causing the old fellow to topple over, and then in a sight gag which is as old as the hills, but still works when being performed by the incomparable William Powell, the old butler says, "Please walk this way, sir."

NICK: Okay, I'll try.

Nick then copies the old man's decrepit movements behind him. Nora calls out to him, "Nicky, *please* pull yourself together."

NICK: One squint of Aunt Katherine will sober anybody up.

Selma enters the room, still looking distressed. Nora rushes over and hugs her and asks, "Selma, what's wrong?" Nora is very empathetic to her cousin, much in the way she was to Maureen O'Sullivan's Dorothy Wynant in the first film. But Aunt Katherine won't have any of it, telling Nora that "any discussion will be postponed until after dinner." Nick and Nora do ask where Selma's husband Robert is. It's clear that his absence has caused Selma much pain.

After dinner the men are assembled in the dining room while the women have gathered in Aunt Katherine's parlor. Selma is quietly playing the piano with a faraway look on her face. Nora, seated nearby, decides to find out what is wrong. Selma tells her that "Robert has disappeared." Katherine observes this and calls out, "Selma! Keep playing." Selma tries, but can't; she suddenly stops, gets up and yells, "I can't . . . I just can't. Are you trying to torture me?" She runs off. Nora confronts Katherine and asks, "How can you treat her this way?" Katherine tells Nora to get Nick, who is seated with the other men around the dining room table. Nick is the only one who is still awake and is carrying on a conversation with his sleeping tablemates.

At this point we find out that Robert has been missing for three days. Aunt Katherine thinks that Selma is "overreacting" and doesn't want Selma to call in the police. She wants to avert any hint of scandal involving the family. That is why Nick is there — she would like him to quietly look into this and see if he can find Robert because of his past experience as a "flat foot." Selma thinks that Robert has run off with another woman, "Oh, you know that he only married me for my money — sometimes I wish he were dead."

NICK: I'm confused — do you want him back or don't you?

Selma collapses and Katherine says, "Of course she wants him back." Now we are introduced to another pivotal character, Selma's former fiancé, David (James Stewart). It seems that David still carries a flame for Selma, and has come over to see if she (and Nick and Nora) will go out on the town with him — hopefully to take Selma's mind off of her missing husband. Selma doesn't think so; she wants to be close to the phone — "just in case." Then, Selma changes her mind, and is willing to go out, but Aunt Katherine won't allow it. Nora urges Nick to help the family out.

NORA: You will try to find Robert — it will get you in good
           with Aunt Katherine.

NICK: That's what I'm afraid of.

David leaves the house with Nick and Nora, and reveals one more bit of vital information: Robert has contacted him. If David will give Robert $25,000, he would leave Selma for good. David asked for some time to think it over. Nick and Nora decide to go out on the town, with Nick telling his chauffeur that he wants to go some place which will "get the taste of respectability out of our mouths." David won't go with them because he has "too much to think about."

Nick and Nora go to a nightclub in Chinatown, where apparently Robert liked to hang out. The club is in full-fledged New Year's revelry and the floor show is on. The entertainer is a dark-haired singer named Polly (Dorothy McNulty). Later, we see Polly being slapped around by Phil (Paul Fix), who wants some information — but what is it he wants? Phil is apparently Polly's brother. When he comes out of Polly's dressing room we are introduced to Dancer (Joseph Calleia), who is the owner of the club and warns Phil not to shake Polly down. Phil is then thrown down the stairs by Dancer where he bumps into Nick. Phil calls out, "Get out of the way, you clown." Nick finally feels at home again.

As Nick and Nora enter the club, they see Selma's missing husband, Robert (Alan Marshal), sitting drunkenly at a table and they go over to find out what's up. Robert is less than thrilled to see them. "So she sent the great big detective after me." He tells Nick and Nora, "I'm having a swell time — and I'm not going back until I want to and I don't think I'll want to."

As Nick and Nora go to their own table, Dancer tells them that Robert has been hanging around drunk for three days. Nora tells Dancer that "his wife" is worried and Dancer tells her that he will try to get Robert's girlfriend, Polly, to tell him to go home.

DANCER: His relatives just flew in.

POLLY: What will we do?

It's clear that Dancer and Polly are involved in some kind of plot involving Robert.

Dancer comes back and informs Nick and Nora that "Polly will make sure that Robert gets home."

Polly goes over to Robert's table, where Robert tells her, "We can have a lot of fun on $25,000." (Remember, according to David,

Robert had asked him for $25,000 to give up Selma.)

POLLY: You don't have it yet.

ROBERT: I'll have no problem.

We next see Robert on the phone with David. "Okay, I'll give you the money," David tells Robert. They make plans to meet.

At this point Robert and Polly leave the club; Polly is being trailed by Phil. Next, we see Dancer and also Dancer's associate, Lum Kee (William Law), both leaving the club as well. The next thing we see is David paying Robert the $25,000. Robert tells David that he's going home — but only to pack.

Robert is at home packing his clothes when the sleeping Selma wakes up and puts on the light. He tells her that he is leaving her. "I won't have it," Selma tells Robert. She won't have him make a fool out of her. But Robert just laughs her off and leaves the room. Selma goes to a drawer, pulls out a gun and follows after him. Outside, in a fog-misted night with several suspects in close vicinity and forty-five minutes into the film, Robert is shot dead. Selma, close behind him, discovers him dead. David shows up behind her and assumes that Selma shot Robert. He takes the gun away from her and tells her to go back to the house and tell nobody that she left. The shell-shocked Selma does as he requests.

We now cut back to the club. It's midnight and the tipsy Nick kisses an unknown blonde who is seated next to him, thinking it's Nora. His face is full of lipstick when he finds Nora waiting to use a pay phone (she wanted to call Selma to see if Robert arrived home). Nora notices the lipstick on Nick's face.

NORA: Nicky, you're bleeding.

And, then, one of the best exchanges in the film follows between Nick and Nora. Nick asks Nora if she has made a New Year's Resolution.

NORA: No, not yet. Any complaints? Or suggestions?

NICK: Yes — complaints.

NORA: Shoot.

NICK: You don't scold, you don't complain, and you look far too pretty in the morning.

NORA: Okay, I must remember: must scold, must complain and must not be too pretty in the morning.

Nora complains that she has been waiting to use the pay phone. Nick takes her to Dancer's office where they can use his phone. Nick is on the phone when Dancer comes back to the club and enters the office. Dancer is taken aback by Nick and Nora's presence in his office and complains about Nick being a "gumshoe."

DANCER: I thought you'd given it up once you married a pot of money.

NORA: Did he call me a pot?

Nick tells Dancer that it looks suspicious when "you, your partner, your prima donna (Polly) and best customer (Robert) all leave at the same time." It's clear that Nick has been doing more than just drinking. Nick, on the phone, gets thru to Aunt Katherine, who informs him that Robert has been killed. At this point Nick calls up Police Lt. Abrams.

Abrams (Sam Levene) comes to Aunt Katherine's house and is interviewing the household staff. We are introduced to Dr. Krammer (George Zucco), who comes downstairs from attending to Selma. Abrams is less than taken with Krammer and makes mention that he has seen Krammer three times in his life — each time on the stand testifying for the defense against the person arrested by the police and being prosecuted, including one woman who "shot her husband, too." When Abrams says this, an outraged Aunt Katherine thinks he has prejudged the case.

ABRAMS: Anybody's tongue is bound to slip.

Nora, leaving Nick at the club with Dancer, arrives back at Aunt Katherine's to comfort Selma. Selma is convinced that she is going to be arrested for killing Robert. She tells Nora, "I didn't kill him," then, less definitely, "I'm sure I didn't." She adds that David, too, thinks she did it, but stops short of telling Nora that David had discovered her with a gun.

Nora now goes to visit David, who pretends not to know what happened. As Nora begins explaining to David that Robert had been killed, Nora suddenly notices a shadow outside on the fire escape — it's Phil, who turns and runs. Nora tells David to stop him and, as David is about to leave to pursue Phil, a gun-toting plain-clothed police officer stops him and takes both David and Nora down to police headquarters.

Dancer also confronts Phil and, approaching him in a menacing way, tells Phil, "I told you not to put the squeeze on us." The scene dissolves before we see what happens.

At police headquarters, David admits that he had paid $25,000 for Robert to leave Selma. Selma admits that she had been outside when the shooting took place and had a gun, but vehemently denies that she shot Robert. Abrams says only one thing will prove it — the gun, so that they can match it against the bullet in Robert's body. David admits that he threw the gun in the river, thinking that Selma had, indeed, shot Robert. He asks for her forgiveness, but Selma is arrested for Robert's murder.

After Nora is rescued from jail by Nick, they return home. Nick wants nothing more than to get some sleep. Nora wants nothing more than to discuss the case, saying over and over "poor Selma." She suggests that they have some scrambled eggs. Nick is less taken by the idea and Nora tells him, "Oh, I can make scrambled eggs," but they wouldn't be as good as Nick's. She then asks Nick if he "can reach the [pitcher of] water."

Nick is about to pour Nora a drink of water when Nora says, "Oh, no. I just wanted to make sure you could reach it." Nick gets the point and in a resigned voice says, "Come on, let's scramble those eggs."

As Nick and Nora are in the kitchen scrambling eggs and discussing the case, a rock suddenly comes busting through the kitchen window. Nora screams. Does Nick go running outside to find out who threw it? Nope.

Nick (yelling out the window): Hey, don't forget to shut the gate!

Before they can get the rock, which they discover has a note attached to it, Asta takes the rock and wants to play. This allows for a slapstick chase around the living room between Nick and Asta. Finally, Nora is able to get the note, which reveals a clue: "Phil Burns is an ex-con who was married to Polly." So we are now being told that Phil is not Polly's brother, but her husband.

The next day, Nick goes to Phil's apartment to investigate. While there, he discovers Phil's body — murdered. Was it Dancer? Later, Nick observes Dancer entering Polly's apartment; Nick follows him down to the basement where he discovers the body of the janitor. It turns out that the janitor, named Pedro, used to be Nora's father's gardener. Nick and Nora interrogate Dancer and Polly; both admit they had been in cahoots together to swindle the $25,000 that David was going to pay Robert, but they both deny that they had any part in any murders. With all the suspects gathered together, one of them makes a slip of the tongue which enables Nick to put two and two together. Nick announces that the murderer made a slip . . . and he can now reveal who done it.

Who killed Robert? Who killed Phil, and why? And why was Pedro the janitor murdered? And how do they all relate? Nick makes the surprising announcement.

Just as the first film ended on a train leaving New York, this film ends on a train leaving San Francisco. Nick discovers Nora crocheting a baby's bootie and when he inquires about it she says, "And you call yourself a detective."

THE END.

BEST LINE:

NICK: Come on, let's get something to eat. I'm thirsty.

TRIVIA:

The cinematographer on this picture was Oliver Marsh, the brother of silent screen star Mae Marsh. Marsh was the favorite cameraman of Jeanette MacDonald, who requested him for many of her pictures, including *The Merry Widow* (made in 1934 at Paramount), *San Francisco, Sweethearts, Maytime* and *Bitter Sweet*. He also worked frequently with director Woody Van Dyke. In addition to the MGM films that Van Dyke made with MacDonald, Marsh also was the cameraman on *His Brother's Wife, Love on the Run, It's a Wonderful World, Another Thin Man, I Love You, Again* and *Rage in Heaven.* Marsh was the cameraman for *Smilin' Through*, also starring Jeanette MacDonald, when he collapsed on the set of a heart attack and later died that day, May 5, 1941, at the age of 49. MacDonald volunteered to sing at his funeral. (Sources include *Charleston Daily Mail*, 5/19/41, and *Oakland Tribune*, 5/6/41.)

THE PRODUCER
HUNT STROMBERG (July 12, 1894-August 25, 1968)

Hunt Stromberg was one of the key figures at MGM from its very beginning, but didn't really come into his own until Louis B. Mayer's successful power ploy against Irving Thalberg in 1933, in which Mayer suppressed Thalberg's central producer system and created four individual "unit" supervisors (what the producer was called at that time). The other three units were supervised by Irving Thalberg, Walter Wanger and David Selznick, Mayer's son-in-law. Pandro Berman, who became a producer at MGM in the early '40s, would recall Stromberg as "a good-old fashioned roughneck producer. I liked Hunt's work very very much."

Stromberg was born in Louisville, Kentucky, on July 12, 1894. His early career was spent in St. Louis, Missouri, as a sportswriter for the *St. Louis Times*. A friend with connections got Stromberg a job as publicity director for the Samuel Goldwyn Company in New York in 1916. In 1918, the Goldwyn Company sent Stromberg to California, where he developed a strong interest in filmmaking. He left Goldwyn soon after and became an assistant to silent film director Thomas Ince. In 1922 Stromberg became an independent producer, forming Hunt Stromberg Productions, where he produced several moderately budgeted and generally successful film comedies starring a popular matinee idol of the time, Bull Montana, and directed by Malcolm St. Clair, who had helmed several shorts for Mack Sennett and Buster Keaton. Stromberg gave up his own company in 1924 to join the newly-merged Metro-Goldwyn-Mayer studios. He would spend the next 18 years at the studio and was responsible for more than one hundred of its films.

Stromberg didn't seem to fit the mold of the average film producer, according to author David Goodrich. "Tall and lanky, with untidy hair, wearing round-lensed glasses, three-piece suits, and sometimes unlaced shoes, he looked more like an eccentric professor than a Hollywood producer, and his story conferences were held in clouds of pipe smoke. A workaholic, he was interested in all kinds of story material; one of his colleagues called him 'truly phenomenal, with a quick and prodigious intellect . . . Everyone around him likes him so well that they can refuse him nothing.'"

It was in the 1928 *White Shadows in the South Seas* that Stromberg became associated with director W. S. Van Dyke II. They would form a close producer-director bond over the next several years and Stromberg utilized Van Dyke as director in twelve films, among the most famous being *Penthouse, The Thin Man* (all four *Thin Man* films that Stromberg produced were directed by Van Dyke), *Hide-Out, Marie Antoinette* and *I Married an Angel*. Van Dyke also directed several of the Stromberg-produced Nelson Eddy-Jeanette MacDonald films, such as *Naughty Marietta* and *Rose Marie*. Several of his early successes featured Jean Harlow (*Red Dust, Bombshell, Wife vs. Secretary*) and Joan Crawford (*Our Dancing Maidens, Letty Lynton, Chained*). Stromberg also produced the Greta Garbo film *The Painted Veil*. Perhaps the crowning film achievement of Stromberg's association with MGM was his 1936 production of the musical-biography extravaganza *The Great Ziegfeld*, which starred William Powell as Ziegfeld and Myrna Loy, once again playing Powell's onscreen wife, as the actress Billie Burke. It was the studio's biggest budgeted film since its 1925 epic *Ben-Hur*, costing $2 million, becoming one of the studio's biggest hits. The picture won the Best Picture of 1936.

In 1937, after Irving Thalberg's sudden death from pneumonia, Stromberg's status at the studio increased. He became part of the management circle which received a percentage of Metro profits: 1.5 percent, in addition to a weekly salary of $8,000. Stromberg was not only one of the most powerful producers in Hollywood, but one of the wealthiest. In fact, the Treasury Department named him as one of the ten highest paid executives in the United States several times during the 1930s.

Hunt Stromberg had the allegiance of many people, including the writers Albert Hackett and Frances Goodrich. "So strong was Frances and Albert's attachment to Hunt Stromberg," wrote their nephew in his biography of the Hacketts, "that when their contract came up for renewal in March 1935, they signed for less than their Hollywood agent thought they should, just to keep working for him." Frances wrote a friend, "And we feel that our confidence and trust in Hunt, and our friendship, and our perfect relationship and ease and comfort with him, are worth the sacrifice of immediate money . . . we cannot work if we are not happy."

Other key films produced by the "Stromberg Unit" include *Maytime, Night Must Fall, Idiot's Delight, The Women, Northwest Passage, Pride and Prejudice* and *Susan and God.* After producing I Married an Angel in 1942, Stromberg walked away from his MGM contract, which still had three years to run, after Mayer refused to allow him to set up an independent production unit within MGM. By this time Stromberg was fighting an addiction to the painkiller morphine, used to ease the pain from a ruptured disc in his back. According to the Hacketts, during story conferences, Stromberg would be "waiting for the doctor to come with the shot . . . we couldn't work with him when he was on drugs." It's also speculated that the main reason Mayer willingly let Stromberg leave MGM before his contract expired was due more to his drug addiction than anything else.

Stromberg became an independent producer and signed the distribution rights to release his films thru United Artists, which also had deals with Charles Chaplin, Mary Pickford, Walt Disney and David Selznick. Stromberg's first foray as an independent producer was *Lady of Burlesque* starring Barbara Stanwyck and based on a mystery novel by Gypsy Rose Lee called *The G-String Murders.* However, the subsequent films he produced didn't equal the success of his first production. These films include *Young Widow* (1946) and *Lured* (1947), which was an interesting psychological suspense film about a serial killer, starring George Sanders and Lucille Ball, and included two alumni of *After the Thin Man*, Joseph Calleia and George Zucco. The last film produced by Stromberg was a potboiler starring John Derek (and directed by Phil Karlson) called *Mask of the Avenger* in 1951. This same year, his wife Katharine died and Stromberg seemed to lose interest in filmmaking, perhaps due to the mixture of losing his spouse and his string of failures as an independent producer. Stromberg went into quiet retirement for the remainder of his life — seventeen years.

Money was never a problem for Stromberg in retirement. Along with his savings and a generous MGM pension, Stromberg had amassed millions by investing in various racetracks. He died at the age of 74 of a stroke on August 25, 1968, and was survived by his son, also a producer, Hunt Stromberg, Jr. Stromberg was buried at Calvary Cemetery in Whittier, California. (Sources include: obits from *The Fresno Bee*, 8/25/68, and *The Valley* (**Van Nuys**) *News*, 8/27/68.)

THE BACK STORY:

Following the overwhelming response of the *Thin Man* motion picture there was no doubt at all that MGM would make a second film. The public loved the characters as played by William Powell and Myrna Loy and wanted to see more of the Charleses' byplay.

The Thin Man was released in late May of 1934 and by October of that year MGM was asking Dashiell Hammett to write a sequel. On October 27, 1934, Hammett sent Lillian Hellman a telegram in which he signed off as "Nicky": SO FAR SO GOOD ONLY AM MISSING YOU PLENTY=NICKY. Two days later he sent a letter to Hellman: "We're going make the picture with all the surviving members of the first cast — which won't be silly if I can devise a murder that grows with same logic out of the set-up we left everybody in at the end of 'The Thin Man,' and I think I can. We may title it 'After the Thin Man.'" What is interesting is that Hammett says he will devise a screenplay using "all the surviving members of the first cast," which would mean supporting characters, too — such as Maureen O'Sullivan's Dorothy Wynant, daughter of the murder victim of the first film. The other problem is that Nick and Nora were heading west to San Francisco at the end of the first film and most of the rest of the cast would still be in New York, including Nat Pendleton's Lt. Guild. It must have eventually dawned on Hammett that the only characters which counted in the sequel would be Nick, Nora and Asta, all the rest were disposable, and rather than have the characters return to New York, why not set a whole new mystery in San Francisco just after the Charleses arrive home?

Hammett's correspondence to Hellman is illuminating in that it demonstrates that the author was not somebody MGM could depend on — primarily due to his drinking.

Here is what he writes Hellman on November 5, 1934: "I haven't written to you for a few days because I've been too ashamed of myself. I've been faithful enough to you, but I went back on the booze pretty heavily until Saturday night — neglecting studio, dignity, and so on. And I was sick Sunday and today! This morning I showed up at MGM for the first time since last Tuesday and squared myself, but didn't get much work done, since the publicity department took up most of my time, what with photographs, interviews and the like."

Eventually, Hammett did work out a story which the Hacketts, Frances and Albert, fleshed out into another engagingly funny screenplay. But they wanted *After the Thin Man* to be the final Nick and Nora adventure — at least the final one written by them. According to the Hacketts' biographer, their nephew David Goodrich, "Frances and Albert had a pressing reason for making Nora pregnant [at the end Nora reveals to Nick that she is pregnant]: they were afraid they might be asked to write yet another sequel (as, of course, they later *were*), which would be boring and difficult: they would have to mine still more interest and amusement out of two characters they were growing sick of. The Hacketts thought that giving the Charleses a baby to care for might put an end to their adventurous life." The studio may have imposed this ending on the Hacketts rather than allow what they initially proposed. "We wanted to kill both of them at the end (of the second picture) just to be sure," Frances wrote a friend, "but Hunt [Stromberg] wouldn't let us."

If the same producer and the same writers were involved, it made perfect sense that the same director would also be called upon, and there was never any doubt that the director Stromberg wanted for the second picture would also be W.S. Van Dyke. Van Dyke would later write, "The word 'sequel' is a bugaboo that frightens most directors, and I am no exception, for if the sequel fails to approach its parent picture in public favor or financial returns, it is the director who is left holding the bag."

Here were some of the pitfalls for the second picture that Van Dyke foresaw: "The return of Nick and Nora in a second mystery would not have such helpful allies as adaptation from a best-selling novel and universal ballyhoo through newspaper serialization. This time it must be an original story written solely for the screen, yet it must retain an interest equal to, if not greater than, that of the first story. Too, it must be as good, if not better than the first . . . Bill and Myrna had grown three years older [actually two] than the original Nick and Nora, and had alienated themselves from those characterizations by many successive screen roles of varied interpretation, so it was necessary for them also to step back three years into the amusing, delightful characters of Nick and Nora."

But Van Dyke was a huge booster of the original film and there was really no real doubt that he would return for the sequel.

In casting the pivotal roles in the sequel, the part of Elissa Landi's lovesick suitor, David, went to a young, gangling relative newcomer to films, James Stewart. Stewart had already worked with Van Dyke in *Rose Marie* and Van Dyke liked him and thought that the casting of Stewart as David would be a huge boost to how the film eventually evolves. Stewart had other supporters in Frances and Albert Hackett, the writers of *Rose Marie*. Frances wrote her friend Leah Salisbury, who was also Stewart's agent at the time, "I shall speak to Hunt about Stewart, as I have such faith in the boy that I would like Hunt to have a chance to have him." Stewart was screen-tested and hired for the film. Years later, Albert Hackett would proudly say, "We helped to start Jimmy Stewart's career." Stewart was happy to be in this film for another reason — the opportunity to work with Myrna Loy. "Jimmy Stewart, in one of his first film roles," wrote Myrna Loy in her memoirs, ". . . was very excited and enthusiastic about it all, rushing around with his camera taking pictures of everybody on the set, declaring, 'I'm going to marry Myrna Loy!'"

The film had several location shots filmed in San Francisco (most of which does not appear in the finished film). "Since *After the Thin Man* has San Francisco as its theatre," wrote Van Dyke, "I chose to capture the true atmosphere of the city so the picture might breathe its true life. Although confronted by many handicaps, such as overenthusiastic crowds, who interfered with the shooting, and low-hanging stubborn fogs, we did succeed in filming most of our exteriors up and down San Francisco's throbbing streets and around its historic landmarks, with the mighty Golden Gate and San Francisco-Oakland Bay bridges, symbols of the new and greater San Francisco, constantly in the background."

Myrna Loy later recalled that she and Bill Powell took the train together to San Francisco to film the exteriors. Along with them was Jean Harlow. "She wasn't in the picture," Myrna later recalled, "but he [Powell] had somehow managed to get her away from her mother. The grip she had on that girl was unbelievable. Bill and Jean were unofficially engaged, and he'd given her an enormous star-sapphire ring, which she proudly displayed on the train." When they arrived at their hotel, the St. Francis, the management had reserved the Flyshaker Suite for Bill and Myrna, "the management assumed we were married. Already they considered us a couple after only five pictures together! Well, of course, it was hysterical." To make matters worse, the hotel was booked solid due to a convention, except for one small hall bedroom downstairs. Everybody would assume that Bill Powell, ever the gentleman, would gallantly take the small room downstairs, but it was Jean Harlow who volunteered Bill for that room. "There's nothing for you to do," Harlow told Loy. "We'll just have to put Bill downstairs." So Myrna and Jean Harlow shared the suite while Bill moved downstairs. "I never saw his room," Myrna later wrote, "so I don't know how bad it was, but Bill complained bitterly; let me tell you, angling to get upstairs." Myrna would say that the experience of sharing the room at the St. Francis with Jean Harlow "brought me one of my most cherished friendships. You would have thought Jean and I were in boarding school we had so much fun."

After the Thin Man would be the third film that Powell and Loy would film in 1936; in fact, they had just completed shooting *Libeled Lady* on September 1 and reported to the *After the Thin Man* set only three weeks later — in that extraordinary time when the studio system could crank a movie out, complete with editing, scoring, and previews, in a matter of a few months. Retakes on the picture went into November of 1936. There is a note to Van Dyke from the Hacketts (in the Frances Goodrich and Albert Hackett papers, at the Wisconsin State Historical Society Archives) which says that a new opening to the final drawing room scene, where Nora announces that she is pregnant, was written and "intended to be faster and brighter than the original — with no reference to David, who has been properly disposed of in our preceding last episode. Following the above scene we go into the present end of the picture."

The Hacketts also punched up the scene in the nightclub where Nick and Nora confront the missing husband, Robert. In the original script the dialog is pretty cut and dried:

NORA: Robert! Robert!

ROBERT (without enthusiasm): Oh, hello.

NORA: We just saw Selma.

ROBERT: Yeah?

NORA: She's terribly worried about you. Don't you think you should go home?

The retake, also filmed in November, adds a bit more color and gives Nick some dialog which he doesn't have as the scene was originally filmed:

NORA: Oh, Robert, where have you been?

ROBERT: Well, fancy meeting you here!

NORA: Why haven't you sent any word to Selma? She's almost crazy with worry.

ROBERT: She ought to know better by now. Well, Nicholas!

NICK: Hello. How's it coming?

ROBERT: Fine . . . up to now.

The film is longer than the original by 22 minutes and cost over a million dollars, but when released it was a huge box-office hit — one of MGM's biggest of 1936.

SUPPORTING PLAYERS:
JOSEPH CALLEIA (August 4, 1897-October 31, 1975).
Joseph Calleia was yet another recognizable face to many movie-goers, without ever being a recognizable name. He was born Giuseppe Maria Spurrin-Calleja in Malta on August 4, 1897 and spent his first seventeen years there before beginning a career as a singer who appeared in music halls throughout Europe. In his native Malta, Calleia is a recognized name and the country and its people are proud of his Hollywood success. In July of 1997, almost twenty-two years after his death, and on his hundredth birthday, the government of Malta issued two stamps in his honor.

Calleia came to the United States in the mid-1920s and began a career on Broadway and over the next seven years he appeared frequently on the Great White Way in such prominent plays as *Broadway, The Front Page, The Last Mile, Grand Hotel* and *Honeymoon.* Like his later film career, his roles on the Broadway stage were never leads, but he always made the most of his character parts. In *Grand Hotel*, Calleia played the chauffer and also acted as the stage manager for the production.

In 1931, Calleia was brought to Hollywood by Paramount, appearing in his first film, opposite Fredric March and Tallulah Bankhead, *My Sin*, in a standard ethnic villain role — the type of which would define his career. He quickly followed that up with a role opposite Gary Cooper and Claudette Colbert in *His Woman*, but his early excursion to Hollywood didn't bring many dividends and Calleia returned to the New York stage.

He was then brought out to Hollywood again in 1935, this time by the biggest studio in town — MGM — and put under contract. In all, Calleia would be credited with appearing in some fifty-seven films, but in reality he appeared in many more than that, sometimes in just walk-ons or bits in which he wasn't even billed. He played an assortment of villainous/gangster types in his early

MGM films, including *Public Hero #1* (opposite Jean Arthur and Chester Morris) and *His Brother's Wife*, which was directed by "Woody" Van Dyke and released just prior to Calleia appearing as Dancer, the crooked nightclub owner, in Van Dyke's *After the Thin Man*. (He would make a third film for Van Dyke in 1938, *Marie Antoinette*.)

On occasion, Calleia played against type, such as his police inspector in *Algiers* and his Catholic priest in John Farrow's underrated *Full Confession*, where he attempts to save an innocent man from the electric chair. Farrow must have seen the humanity inside Calleia's villains because he used him well again as a condemned murderer who is the only one objective enough to decide who should live and who should die in Five Came Back. Then, it was back to his bread-and-butter villains, including a racketeer in *Golden Boy* (which also featured two other *Thin Man* alums, Sam Levene and Edward Brophy); the corrupt town boss opposite W.C. Fields and Mae West in *My Little Chickadee*; the corrupt mayor who frames an innocent Wallace Beery for murder in *Wyoming* and the gambling house proprietor in *The Glass Key* (another adaptation of a Dashiell Hammett novel).

In 1942, Calleia appeared in one of his favorite films, and best remembered roles, as the merchant and aged storyteller in *The Jungle Book* opposite Sabu. Other prominent '40s films include *For Whom the Bell Tolls, The Cross of Lorraine, Gilda* and *Lured*. During the '50s he appeared frequently, often in ethnic roles, in a variety of films, including playing Dean Martin's father in the Martin and Lewis film *The Caddy*; the padre who puts a horse in sanctuary in *The Littlest Outlaw* and, most memorably, as the loyal sergeant to Orson Welles's corrupt Captain Hank Quinlan in Welles's masterpiece *Touch of Evil*. His final significant role was as a Mexican leader in John Wayne's *The Alamo* in 1960.

After doing a bit in the 1963 cult film *Johnny Cool*, Calleia retired from acting and returned to Malta, where he quietly spent his final years in the adulation of his fellow Maltans. He died on Halloween, 1975, at the age of 78.

PAUL FIX (March 9, 1901-October 14, 1983)

Paul Fix was one of the busiest character actors in Hollywood with a career which spanned well over fifty years. Western fans have a special appreciation for Fix due to his role as Marshal Micah Torrance on the long-running television Western *The Rifleman* (1958-1963), and as a veteran of many films starring his good friend, John Wayne.

Fix was born Peter Paul Fix on March 9, 1901, in Dobbs Ferry, New York. He was the son of German immigrants who had arrived in New York during the 1870s. Fix was the product of a large family with two sisters and three brothers. He was the family runt. His father worked for the Manilla Acre Brewery as brew master. When Fix was 13, his mother died and two years after that his father passed away and Fix was sent to live with extended family members — married sisters in Yonkers, New York and Zaneville, Ohio.

In 1918, not long after the United States entry into the First World War, the patriotic Fix, just turned seventeen, joined the U.S. Navy. He spent much of the war stateside with stints in Newport, Rhode Island and Charleston, South Carolina. He also was assigned to the *U.S.S. Mount Vernon*, which was torpedoed by a German U-boat off the coast of France, but didn't sink because it was so close to land. It was while in the Navy that Fix got his first taste of acting, appearing in drag in a Navy relief show.

After leaving the Navy, Fix returned to Zaneville, and to his girlfriend, Frances Harvey. They were married in 1922 and, wanting to enjoy a warmer climate, moved shortly thereafter to California. As it turned out, they settled in Hollywood where he soon became friendly with another young man who moved to California from Ohio, Clark Gable. Gable and Fix later became part of a theater troupe which traveled up and down the west coast during the mid-'20s performing in stock productions. In the mid-'20s, Paul and Frances were blessed with their first child; in all they would have four children.

Fix recalled that his earliest film roles were in William S. Hart Westerns. He had parts in several silent films and by the early talkies was a recognizable face in many films. His more notable films of the '30s include *Scarface, The Last Mile, Back Street, Little Man, What Now?, The Count of Monte Cristo, The Prisoner of Shark Island* (the first film he would make for director John Ford), the two films he appeared in 1936 with William Powell (*The Ex-Mrs. Bradford* and *After the Thin Man*), as well as *Souls at Sea* and *Mannequin*. Fix kept busy appearing in more than 100 films during the 1930s, seventeen alone in 1936, the year of *After the Thin Man*. Most of the roles Fix specialized in were villains, often hoods and convicts.

Fix's first film with John Wayne was 1931's *Three Girls Lost*, and they cemented their friendship due to Fix helping the uneasy and gangly Wayne with acting lessons on the side — making him relax in front of the camera, something Wayne never forgot. (One bit of trivia is that it was Paul Fix who taught John Wayne his distinctive walk.) In all, Paul Fix would appear in 27 films with Wayne, including *Pittsburgh* (1942), *Tall in the Saddle* (1944, a film which Fix also wrote), *Back to Bataan* (1945), *Red River* (1948), *The Fighting Kentuckian* (1949), *She Wore a Yellow Ribbon* (1949), *Island in the Sky* (1952), *Hondo* (1953), *The High and the Mighty* (1954), *Blood Alley* (1955), *The Sons of Katie Elder* (1965), *El Dorado* (1967) and *Cahill, U.S. Marshal* (1973). Thanks to his association with Wayne, Fix was finally seen as more than the villain, increasingly playing sheriffs, military men, judges and kindly doctors.

Among Fix's better known films and roles include *Giant* (1956), playing Elizabeth Taylor's father; as the grandfather of Patty McCormick's evil little girl in *The Bad Seed* (1958); and the courtroom judge who seems sympathetic to Gregory Peck's client in *To Kill a Mockingbird* (1962). He increasingly appeared on television and in 1958 won the role of the town marshal who often needs the help of Chuck Connors' *The Rifleman* to keep law and order (on occasion, even resenting it). He had an opportunity to appear on another iconic television series which didn't pan out: he appeared in the second pilot of *Star Trek* in 1966, but was replaced by DeForest Kelley as the ship's doctor.

During the '70s Fix stayed active in the industry, appearing on such episodic television programs as *Mannix, Alias Smith and Jones, The FBI, The Streets of San Francisco, Barnaby Jones* and *The Rockford Files*. His final feature film was Wanda Nevada in 1979 and his last television role was on the Jack Klugman medical-mystery series *Quincy M.E.* in 1981.

Paul Fix died of kidney failure at St. John's Medical Center in Santa Monica, California on October 14, 1983 at the age of 81. When asked why he never had a dry period and was always in much demand, Fix said, "People around the business knew I would accept any kind of talking part and could deliver on the first take . . . I rarely made over $750 a week . . . but it was steady. My idea was to keep working — and I did." (Sources include obit, *Letherbridge Herald*, 10/17/83 and Paul Fix biography on www.rifleman-branded.com.)

ELISSA LANDI (December 6, 1904-October 21, 1948)

The beautiful Elissa Landi was born in Venice, Italy. (Her mother, who should know, says that Landi was born not in Venice but on a farm outside of Vienna, but Landi always insisted it was Venice.) She was the daughter of a Venice Count and Countess and rumor has it (even printed in her 1948 obituary) that she was the granddaughter of Empress Elizabeth of Austria. (For her part, Landi always refused to confirm or deny any royal connection.) Landi spent her early years in Austria but was mostly educated in England. Landi grew up with a very cultured background and had a wide variety of interests in the arts which included not only acting, but also writing and sketching. In fact, her first love was probably writing — it's what actually led her to the theater. Landi joined a repertory company with the intention of studying play structure and thru it found a fascination with acting.

She appeared on stage throughout Europe in local theatrical companies as a young girl and into her teenage years. She made her London stage debut in a production of *Storm* in 1925, winning enthusiastic reviews from the critics and running five months on the West End. She turned down an opportunity to take the play to the New York stage and instead stayed in London where she completed her first novel, *Neilsen.* Her film debut came opposite Dorothy Gish in *London* (1926). In the late '20s, she made a strong impression in the Swedish film *Synd* ("Sin," 1928). She also appeared in many English films and made a strong impact in the 1930 film *The Price of Things*.

Landi came to the United States in 1931, where she appeared in the stage version of *A Farewell to Arms* (directed by Rouben

Mamoulian). While it didn't conquer Broadway (closing after only 24 performances), her exotic beauty caught the attention of Hollywood. She was brought out to the coast, where she appeared as the leading lady in *Body and Soul*, a film featuring an early performance by Humphrey Bogart and, also in support, Myrna Loy. Landi had leads in several early '30s films, including *Always Goodbye, Yellow Ticket* and *Woman in Room 13*. But, probably, the film which caused her the most attention was playing opposite Fredric March and Claudette Colbert in Cecil B. DeMille's production of *The Sign of the Cross* (1932). While Landi was the leading lady, her role was overshadowed by that of the third-billed Colbert, who stole the film with her tempestuous performance. Still, DeMille was fascinated by Landi, later saying, "There is a depth of the ages in her eyes, today in her body and tomorrow in her spirit." She followed as leading lady in a variety of pictures, including comedies such as *By Candlelight, Enter Madame* (opposite Cary Grant) and *The Warrior's Husband*, soap operas like *Without Regrets* and the adventure classic *The Count of Monte Cristo* (with Robert Donat). She was signed by Irving Thalberg and taken to MGM in 1936, where she appeared in that witty satire of murder mysteries, *Mad Holiday*.

After being the leading lady in so many films, it might have been considered a letdown to play a supporting role in *After the Thin Man*, but Landi didn't let it get her down. By this time, her interests were moving in other directions, such as rediscovering her writing. In the last twelve years of her life, Landi would publish six novels and a book of poetry. She would appear in only two more films after *After the Thin Man* — the final one being the WWII drama *Corregidor* (1943) with Otto Kruger. In the late thirties and through the early forties Landi spent considerable time on the stage, returning to Broadway to appear with Vincent Price in The Lady Has a Heart. She also appeared on the summer stock circuit in productions of *Rebellion in Shadow* (which she wrote under the pseudonym of "Mady Francis"), *Romance, Candida* and *Tomorrow, the World!* Her final acting job may have been appearing during August of 1945 at Bass Rocks Theatre in Gloucester, Massachusetts in *Another Language*. In 1943, Landi married writer Curtiss Thomas, with whom she had one daughter, Caroline. (Her first marriage, to John Cecil Lawrence, a London barrister, lasted from 1928 to 1936.)

Landi was an accomplished pianist (the scene where she briefly plays the piano in *After the Thin Man* is not performed by anybody else), and she also had an active interest in many other subjects, including horses — she was an avid rider. She was very cosmopolitan in her interests (not surprising given her upbringing) and enjoyed ballet, and watercolors. In her final years, Landi renounced her British citizenship and became an American citizen and, with Thomas, she settled on a 123-acre farm, "Bright Acres," near Kingston, New York. Her death, on October 21, 1948, at age 43, from cancer, was surprising. The seriousness of the illness was kept from Landi and she was told by her physician only that she was suffering from a "chronic condition." According to the doctor, Landi's family had known of the seriousness of her condition and of her prognosis for nine months, but had decided to keep the news from her, so that she could lead as normal of a life as possible. The doctor said that Landi's husband "had done a wonderful job in keeping it from her." An Associated Press obituary summed Landi's many talents up this way: "Miss Landi was an artist of multiple facets, equally successful as a motion picture and stage star, as a novelist, as a linguist, as a pianist and as a singer. Her varied talents, combined with her subtle blonde beauty, won her praise from both dramatic and literary critics of a half dozen nations." (Sources include *Nashua* (NH) *Tribune*, 10/21/48.)

SAM LEVENE (August 28, 1905-December 28, 1980)

Sam Levene was first and foremost a Broadway actor, who also worked infrequently in Hollywood. His most famous Broadway role was that of Nathan Detroit in the 1950-1953 production of *Guys and Dolls*. Though he wasn't a strong singer, the producers made sure his one solo song, "Sue Me," was written in one octave so that he could effectively deliver it.

Levene was born on August 28, 1905 in Russia and his family immigrated to the United States two years later; he became a naturalized U.S. citizen in 1937. He made his Broadway debut in 1927 at age 22 in *Wall Street*. Among his other significant Broadway appearances were *Three Men on a Horse* and *Room Service*.

Levene came to Hollywood in 1936 to recreate his stage role of the superstitious gambler in *Three Men on a Horse* for Warner Brothers. His second film was as Abrams, the headstrong detective suspicious of William Powell's Nick Charles, in *After the Thin Man* (a part he would reprise in 1941's *Shadow of the Thin Man*). Over the next few years he alternated between playing cops and Damon Runyon-type hoods in such films as *The Mad Miss Manton, Grand Central Murder, The Big Street, Sunday Punch* and *Whistling in Brooklyn.*

In the postwar years Levene appeared in four outstanding American films: as the police lieutenant in director Robert Siodmak's *The Killers*, the reporter in Elia Kazan's *Boomerang!*, the tortured prisoner in *Brute Force*, and the murder victim of Edward Dmytryk's *Crossfire*. Then, in the late forties, he returned to the Broadway stage with a three-year run in *Guys and Dolls*. Between 1950 and 1956 Levene only made two films because of his stage work, but he returned to Hollywood to appear in five films in 1956-1957, most significantly the breezy MGM romp *Designing Woman* and the hard-bitten exposé of Broadway columnists, *Sweet Smell of Success*, playing the manager of the musician that Burt Lancaster's J.J. Hunsecker wants to destroy. After this, Levene would only appear in nine more films over the next twenty years as he again concentrated on the stage — most significantly winning a Tony nomination for *The Devil's Advocate* in 1961. Later in that decade he enjoyed a long run in the successful Broadway comedy *The Impossible Years*. One of his longest runs on the New York stage (and later on tour) was as Al Lewis in Neil Simon's *The Sunshine Boys* (playing the role that George Burns would win an Academy Award for in the 1975 movie version). His final film, released a year before he died, was Norman Jewison's . . . *And Justice for All*, which starred Al Pacino.

Levene's final Broadway play was *Horowitz and Mrs. Washington*, which opened in April of 1980 and closed after only four performances. He died of a heart attack on December 28, 1980 at his residence of many years, the Central Park South Hotel. He had just returned from appearing in a Canadian production of *Horowitz and Mrs. Washington* the day before and his body was discovered by his son, Joseph Levene, who was to meet his father for dinner. Levene, the ultimate New Yorker, derived most of his satisfaction from his career appearing on stage, once saying, "Being in the presence of an audience and hearing their applause is what keeps an actor going much more than appearing on some cold inhospitable soundstage in Hollywood." Despite this, Levene made an indelible mark in more than 30 films — several of them classics of the American cinema. (Sources include *New York Times* obit, Broadway Database.)

ALAN MARSHAL (January 29, 1909-July 13, 1961)

Alan Marshal was a sturdy, dependable light leading man in the tradition of George Brent, but without really ever attaining the level of even Brent's stardom. Marshal was born on January 29, 1909, in Sydney, Australia. He came to the United States in the 1920s and began working on stage in summer stock and eventually on Broadway. He appeared in several Broadway productions during the early 1930s, including *While Parents Sleep* (with Ilka Chase), *Lady Jane*, and *The Bishop Misbehaves.*

Marshal was brought to Hollywood in 1936 by David Selznick and cast in a supporting role in the Selznick film *The Garden of Allah*, which starred Marlene Dietrich and Charles Boyer. His second film was *After the Thin Man*, in a role which filled no more than ten minutes of celluloid, as the gigolo husband-cum-murder victim, but his good looks and rich voice got him noticed. His first real "meaty" role was as good guy Justin Laurie opposite Robert Montgomery's murderous psychopath in *Night Must Fall.* He had other good featured roles opposite Clark Gable and Myrna Loy in *Parnell* and Henry Fonda and Joan Bennett in *I Met My Love Again.* He was Ida Lupino's doubting fiancé in the second of Twentieth Century-Fox's Sherlock Holmes films starring Basil Rathbone, *The Adventures of Sherlock Holmes*, in 1939. He ended the decade in style opposite Charles Laughton in the classic *The Hunchback of Notre Dame*, playing Phoebus.

Marshal began the '40s as the romantic lead in *Married and in Love*, which was directed by John Farrow, who by this time was the husband of Maureen O'Sullivan. He followed that up with *Irene*, playing an also-ran to Ray Milland. He played other also-ran roles in *He Stayed for Breakfast*, losing Loretta Young to Melvyn

Douglas, and *Tom, Dick and Harry* with Ginger Rogers. He then played one of Merle Oberon's lost loves in *Lydia*. He was off the screen then for three years before coming back strongly in one of his best roles and performances as Irene Dunne's doomed lover in 1944's *The White Cliffs of Dover*. Marshal, surprisingly, only made a handful of films after this one, allegedly because of a nervous condition that prevented him from appearing on camera. He spent much of the subsequent years on the stage, but also was a frequent guest star on episodic television series during the 1950s in shows like *Perry Mason* and *Alfred Hitchcock Presents*. His final film appearance was in the 1959 horror cult classic *House on Haunted Hill*, playing one of five people invited by host Vincent Price to spend a night in an allegedly haunted house.

The end for Marshal came as he was appearing in Chicago with Mae West in her play *Sextet* on July 13, 1961. He was stricken with severe back and chest pains while appearing on stage during the final ten minutes of the play, but managed to finish the early show. A second performance was cancelled and Marshal retired to his room at the Edgewater Beach Hotel. He suffered another heart attack that night and was found dead the next day by his son Kit, who was also featured in the stage production. Marshal was only 52. (Sources include *Fresno Bee*, 7/10/61.)

DOROTHY McNULTY (A.K.A., PENNY SINGLETON)
(September 15, 1908-November 12, 2003)

You simply can't be blamed if you didn't realize that the part of Polly in *After the Thin Man* was played by the actress who would become internationally known in 28 films playing Chic Young's cartoon creation *Blondie*. After all, the actress playing Polly was a brunette and played a character that was a wanton woman — and, furthermore, went by the name of Dorothy McNulty. But Dorothy McNulty, within a few years of *After the Thin Man*, would dye her dark locks peroxide blonde and change her name to Penny Singleton and in 1938 zoomed to fame in the first *Blondie* film for Columbia Pictures.

She was born Mariana Dorothy Agnes Letitia McNulty on September 15, 1908, in Philadelphia, Pennsylvania. Her father, Barney, was a reporter of Irish stock and her mother, Maria, was from a German ancestry. Her father was also related to the famous Irish politician Jim Farley, who was Franklin Roosevelt's campaign manager in 1932 and 1936 and later served as Postmaster General of the United States.

Dorothy showed an avid interest in show business from an early age. While still attending elementary school, she appeared on the vaudeville circuit singing and dancing with the likes of a young Milton Berle and Gene Raymond. At age eight, she was billed as "Baby Dorothy" and entertained patrons between showings at a local silent movie theater. Her big break came in 1925, when she was still just 17 years old, landing the small role of a cloak room girl in the Broadway musical *Sky High*. She was noticed with five other girls singing "Trim Them All But the One You Love" and signed a contract with the Schubert Brothers. For the Schuberts she appeared in such revues as *Sweetheart Time* and *The Great Temptation*. In *The Great Temptation*, Dorothy got the opportunity to sing, dance and show her budding expertise at comedy, playing Jack Benny's "stooge" in a comedic routine. The act was a huge success and Dorothy and Benny received equal billing. In late 1927 Dorothy joined the road company of the popular college musical *Good News*, playing opposite Jack Haley. She and Haley then joined the cast of the successful musical *Follow Thru* where together they performed the hit novelty number "Button Up Your Overcoat." She also had a solo number in the show, "I Want to Be Bad!"

In 1930 Dorothy was brought out to Hollywood to recreate her stage role in the first movie version of *Good News* for MGM. She appeared in two other films for MGM during that year, *Love in the Rough*, starring Robert Montgomery, and in a comedy short with Frank Morgan called *Belle of the Night.* Her movie career wasn't going anywhere, however, and she ended up going back to New York and the stage where, over the next few years, she appeared in *Hey Nonny, Nonny!* and was well received singing the song "Wouldn't That Be Wonderful." She would appear in other plays and revues over the next few years before coming back out to the coast and returning to MGM to appear as Polly in *After the Thin Man*. With her fine singing voice, Dorothy was used to good advantage belting out two songs in *After the Thin Man* ("Smoke Dreams" and "Blow that Horn") and gave a strongly convincing performance playing a tough New York nightclub singer. Dorothy followed this up in 1937 with two mediocre films — getting to sing again in Walter Wanger's production of *Vogues of 1938* and then appearing in a programmer for Republic, *Sea Racketeers*.

At around this time, Dorothy married a dentist named Lawrence Singleton (they would have one child), and, deciding that she needed a change in her professional name (to bolster her career), she took on her husband's last name, Singleton, and added a new first name, Penny, which she came up with due to a passion for collecting pennies. It was as Penny Singleton that she made her next film for Warner Brothers, co-starring Humphrey Bogart, called *Swing Your Lady*. This film also featured another *Thin Man* alumnus, Nat Pendleton. In 1938, Penny, under contract to Warner Brothers, appeared in several films, including *Boy Meets Girl* (with Jimmy Cagney), *Secrets of an Actress* (starring Kay Francis), and had the leading female role in a college musical short called *Campus Cinderella*.

It was also in 1938 that Singleton was summoned to Columbia Pictures, where she tested for the title role in a movie version of the popular comic strip *Blondie*. The role was originally going to be played by actress Shirley Deane, but Deane was let go, allegedly because of illness (though other reports indicate that she didn't work comfortably with the child who played "Baby Dumpling" in the film). When Penny was selected to play the zany, but well-meaning Blondie opposite Arthur Lake's hapless Dagwood, she naturally had to dye her chestnut hair a bleached blonde. She never went back. The blonde hair became her trademark for the remainder of her life and career. With Lake, a new comedy team was born, and, with the exception of three films, she never played anything else on screen other than Blondie for the remainder of her movie career.

The *Blondie* films became hits for Columbia — efficiently and inexpensively made, they more than made back their investments. You could decipher the plot just by the title of each film: *Blondie Meets the Boss* (1939), *Blondie Takes a Vacation* (1939), *Blondie on a Budget* (1940), *Blondie Plays Cupid* (1940), *Blondie Goes Latin* (1941), *Blondie Goes to College* (1942), *Blondie's Blessed Event* (1942), *Blondie's Anniversary* (1947), *Blondie Hits the Jackpot* (1949) and 18 others over a twelve-year period.

During the *Blondie* run, Singleton became attracted to the series producer, Robert Sparks, and their affair became publicly known after Singleton was injured in a car accident in 1940 with Sparks. Singleton later confirmed the rumors to Hollywood columnist Louella Parsons, divorcing her dentist husband and marrying Sparks and eloping to Goldfield, Nevada. Singleton and Sparks later had a baby girl.

During the run of *Blondie*, Singleton also appeared, on occasion, playing Blondie on radio (also with Arthur Lake, though while Lake continued on as Dagwood, Singleton eventually left the series).

After making the final *Blondie* film in 1950, *Beware of Blondie*, the 42-year-old Singleton began to appear increasingly on television, but was not part of the *Blondie* television series which debuted in 1957. (Barbara Britton took on the role with Arthur Lake still playing Dagwood.) Singleton occupied her time back on the musical stage, appearing in tours of *Bells are Ringing* and *Call Me Madam*. In 1962, she leant her voice to another cartoon character, Judy Jetson, in the animated television series *The Jetsons* and would appear over the next twenty-odd years playing this character when the cartoon was revived. Singleton's final movie role was in the film *The Best Man* (1964), but her scenes were later deleted from the finished film.

With acting roles less frequent and desirable, Penny began another career as a union official. She was elected vice president of the American Guild of Variety Artists (AGVA). In this role she pushed to make sure that producers and club owners paid social security and unemployment compensation and devise pension plans, something they had never done before. She later led strikes against the New York nightclub The Latin Quarter, and on behalf of the Radio City Music Hall Rockettes. She also became an outspoken proponent for woman's equality. In 1974 she received an honorary degree as a Doctor of the Fine Arts from St. John's University.

In late October 1993, Singleton suffered a severe stroke and died two weeks later at Sherman Oaks Hospital on November 12, 2003, living to the ripe old age of 95. (Sources include: **www.cnn.com**, 11/14/2003.)

JESSIE RALPH (November 5, 1864-May 30, 1944)

Jessie Ralph came to motion pictures in 1933, when she was already in her late sixties (she had appeared in some early silent films but without much success), coming from a prominent background on the stage. Coming to movies at such an advanced age, Ralph often played domineering old ladies, such as the one she played in *After the Thin Man*, but within that framework she played maids, duchesses, countesses, grandmothers, and several variations of aunts.

Ralph was born on November 5, 1864, the thirteenth child of a sea captain who sailed vessels out of the Gloucester, Massachusetts port. She made her stage debut with a stock company out of Providence, Rhode Island at the age of seventeen. She appeared in many plays with stock companies traveling across the country. She made her New York stage debut in *The Kreutzer Sonata* in 1905 (when she was 39 years old) and would accumulate extensive Broadway credits. Over the next thirty years she would appear in all kinds of Broadway shows, including musicals with George M. Cohan (*A Prince There Was, Once Upon a Time*) as well as Shakespearian productions starring Jane Cowl, the most famous being Ralph's performance as the nurse in *Romeo and Juliet* in 1923. Other famous Broadway plays she was cast in include *Ruggles of Red Gap*, *The Road to Rome* and *The Good Earth*, which was her last Broadway show in 1932.

Her first film in 1933 was as the caustic aunt in *Child of Manhattan*, which starred Nancy Carroll. Her other important films of the '30s include *The Affairs of Cellini, Les Miserable, Captain Blood, David Copperfield* (as the nurse), *Little Lord Fauntleroy, Camille* (playing Garbo's maid), *The Last of Mrs. Cheyney, San Francisco, The Good Earth* and *Drums Along the Mohawk*. She made only a handful of films before retiring in 1941, due to circulation problems which led to an amputated leg. She remained in poor health in her last few years, dying while visiting a niece's home on May 30, 1944, at the age of 79. (Sources include obit, *Nebraska State Journal*, 5/31/44.)

JAMES STEWART (May 20, 1908-July 2, 1997)

James Stewart today is recognized as one of the great icons of the

American cinema and one of the best-loved actors this country has ever produced. With the exception of Powell and Loy, Stewart is the biggest star to appear in the Thin Man films, but at the time he was still a rising newcomer. *After the Thin Man* was only Stewart's ninth picture.

James Maitland Stewart was born on May 20, 1908, in Indiana, Pennsylvania. His father was Alex, a Scottish-Irish hardware store owner, and his mother, Bessie, the daughter of a Civil War general. James, or Jimmy, was the firstborn child of the young couple. In the next few years Jimmy would be joined by two sisters. One of Jimmy's sisters had talked her parents into buying her an accordion, but she eventually discarded it, and Jimmy took up the instrument, and it later became a Stewart trademark. A bright boy, Jimmy attended the Model School in Indiana, an institution associated with the State Teachers College. Upon graduating from the Model School, Jimmy attended the Mercersburg Academy.

After graduating from Mercersburg Academy, Stewart entered Princeton University. While at Princeton, Stewart joined the Princeton Triangle Club, where he met Joshua Logan, later a prominent theatrical director, and formed a lifelong friendship. In the spring of 1932 Jimmy graduated from Princeton with a B.S. in architecture. The Depression was now at its height and Jimmy took work wherever he could get it. Joshua Logan offered his friend a chance to act in summer stock with the University Players in West Falmouth, Massachusetts in the summer of 1932, and Jimmy leaped at the chance. Jimmy had a small part in a play which also featured such actors as Mildred Natwick, Myron McCormick and Bretaigne Windust (later a prominent theater and film director).

Jimmy then moved to New York, where he shared an apartment with Logan, McCormick and another veteran of the University players, Henry Fonda, who would soon become Stewart's best friend. Stewart was now working on the New York stage in such shows as *Carrie Nation, Goodbye Again* and *Spring in Autumn*. The early part which caused the most attention for the young Stewart was playing Sergeant O'Hara in the Sidney Kingsley play *Yellow Jack*. This was followed by a part in *Divided by Three*, which starred Judith Anderson.

In 1935 Hedda Hopper, not yet one of the queens of Hollywood gossip, was working as a talent scout, and saw something in Stewart, and recommended him to MGM, where he was tested and signed to a seven-year contract. Coincidentally, friend and roommate Fonda also was brought to Hollywood to recreate his Broadway role in *The Farmer Takes a Wife*, opposite Janet Gaynor. Like in New York, Stewart and Fonda became roommates. They also became known as eligible bachelors about town.

Jimmy's first film was playing "Shorty" opposite Spencer Tracy in *Murder Man*. Tracy offered Jimmy the sage advice to "forget about the camera" and concentrate on listening and reacting to the lines. He was next selected to play Jeanette MacDonald's brother in Rose Marie, which was produced by Hunt Stromberg and directed by W.S. Van Dyke. Jimmy's part in *Rose Marie* was originally slated to be no longer than a three-day job, but Van Dyke was so taken by Jimmy, that he kept adding bits of business for Jimmy to do and a three-day job turned into three weeks. Jimmy's first significant role was on loan-out from MGM to Universal to star opposite Margaret Sullavan, the ex-wife of Henry Fonda, in the film *Next Time We Love*. The chemistry between Jimmy and Sullavan was strong. Sullavan was fond of her co-star and she did a great deal to help him in his early Hollywood career. They would end up making three more pictures together over the next four years (*The Shopworn Angel*, the classic Ernst Lubitsch romantic comedy *The Shop Around the Corner* and *The Mortal Storm*). Jimmy returned to MGM and more routine films, and despite his starring role opposite Sullavan, he was back in supporting roles at his home studio. His final film of 1936 was *After the Thin Man*, in which his gangly, boy-next-door persona was used to good advantage.

Stewart's first picture of 1937 was against-type, on loan-out to Fox, *Seventh Heaven*, playing a French sewer worker. He came back to MGM, but was given sub-par roles. It was on loan-out again (this time to RKO) that Jimmy got his next really good film, the engaging George Stevens comedy *Vivacious Lady*, which teamed him with Ginger Rogers. It was at Columbia that Stewart first worked with director Frank Capra, in the adaptation of the George S. Kaufman-Moss Hart satiric play *You Can't Take it With You*. The film proved popular and was selected the Best Picture of 1938.

1939 would be the year that Jimmy Stewart emerged as a top Hollywood star. That year he appeared in five films — two of them among the classics of the American cinema. *Mr. Smith Goes to Washington*, directed by Frank Capra and made at Columbia, in the role of Jefferson Smith, is one of Stewart's career highlights, and is definitive of his pre-war screen persona. *The Nation* proclaimed, "James Stewart as Jefferson Smith takes first place among Hollywood actors." Jimmy was nominated for the first time for an Academy Award and won the prestigious New York Film Critics' Best Actor Award. His final film of 1939, the second undisputed classic, was opposite Marlene Dietrich in the western-comedy *Destry Rides Again.*

Stewart's momentum continued into 1940, working opposite Katharine Hepburn and Cary Grant in the MGM classic *The Philadelphia Story.* Stewart won the Academy Award for Best Actor for this performance; many people thinking it a consolation Oscar for having lost out in 1939.

After the spectacular run of 1939-1940 films, MGM inconceivably put Stewart into such films as *Come Live with Me, Ziegfeld Girl* and, on loaned out, *Pot O'Gold.* Who knows what would have been next, but Stewart became the first American motion picture star drafted into the military — eight months before Pearl Harbor. Stewart had already become a pilot as a civilian so it made sense to assign him to the Air Corp. He was a bombardier instructor until late 1943 at Moffett Field in California when he was assigned to the 445th Bombardment Group. Jimmy flew 25 combat missions. When he left the military in late 1945, he was ranked as a colonel and had won many decorations for this valor under fire.

MGM fully expected that Jimmy would be returning to the Culver City lot after the war, just as their other stars that had joined the war effort — including Clark Gable and Robert Taylor — had done. But Jimmy decided not to renew his MGM contract, but rather freelance. When Stewart returned to Hollywood, he stayed with Henry Fonda (just out of the Navy) and his wife and children at their Brentwood home.

It was Frank Capra who offered Jimmy his first post-war film role, playing George Bailey in *It's a Wonderful Life.* The part is important because early in the film we are presented with the

Stewart that audiences knew and loved, the small-town gangly wide-eyed innocent, who, as the film continues, morphs into the Stewart that filmgoers would ultimately see more of: a neurotic, angry and desperate man; one who, in this film, goes so far as to contemplate suicide. At 39 years old, having seen war, death and destruction, Jimmy Stewart was now presenting a new world-weary maturity to movie-goers. *It's a Wonderful Life* has become one of the most cherished films of all-time and a Christmas holiday perennial, but in its day it was only moderately successful at the box office. It was only through repeated viewings on television beginning in the '70s that the film's reputation grew. Nevertheless, Stewart's performance was nominated for an Academy Award; his third.

Meanwhile, Jimmy's personal life took a turn. Long one of Hollywood's most eligible bachelors, Stewart had dated such beautiful women as Ginger Rogers, Olivia de Havilland, Dinah Shore, and queen of the Metro lot Norma Shearer. But, on August 9, 1949, at age 41, Stewart married the attractive and sophisticated divorcee, Gloria Hatrick McLean, and became the stepfather to her two young sons. Within two years of their marriage, Jimmy and Gloria would become the proud parents of twin baby girls.

Stewart began the '50s with a Western at Fox, *Broken Arrow*; the actor's first time in a Western since *Destry Rides Again*. The film offered a sympathetic look at the American Indian, one of the few films of its era which would do so.

Stewart very much wanted to play inebriated Elwood P. Dowd, who may or may not be in possession of an invisible 6' rabbit, in the film version of Mary Chase's Pulitzer Prize-winning play *Harvey*, which Universal bought the film rights to for a considerable sum. To guarantee the success of the film, the studio wanted a star name in the lead role. Stewart fit the bill, but the studio also decided that they wanted Stewart for more than one picture. They said that to play Dowd they wanted Jimmy to also film a Western which had been sitting on their shelf for some time, *Winchester '73*. Stewart and his agent, Lou Wasserman, however, also decided to play hardball. Stewart became one of the few actors up to that time to ask for and get a percentage of the profits rather than being paid a straight salary. Universal accepted this and from this point forward this would be a standard contractual agreement for any studio which wanted Jimmy's services for a picture. The deal turned out well for both Jimmy and Universal. *Harvey* proved successful at the box office, and Jimmy was nominated for the fourth time for an Academy Award as Best Actor.

Winchester '73 also turned out well, becoming Universal's most profitable of the year. By collecting a portion of the profits, Jimmy made a whopping $600,000 — three times more than his straight salary of $200,000. It was also significant as the first Stewart film to be directed by Anthony Mann. The Westerns that Jimmy and Mann made together during the '50s (*Winchester '73, Bend of the River, The Naked Spur, Thunder Bay, The Far Country, The Man from Laramie*) presented Jimmy away from the "aw-shucks" persona of his youth. He was now a hardened man, often with revenge on his mind, easily provoked to violence. Jimmy was also entering the period of his greatest success at the box office and during the '50s would be one of the top ranked box-office stars in the United States. The Mann films (which also included the very popular *The Glenn Miller Story* and *Strategic Air Command*) went a long way toward solidifying the new popularity that Stewart acquired. So, too, did the films that Stewart did with his other significant director of the '50s — Alfred Hitchcock.

Stewart was the perfect Hitchcockian "every man" hero. Where Cary Grant was presented by Hitchcock as the man everybody wanted to be like, Jimmy was the man that most men could identify with. The first of three films that Stewart and Hitchcock collaborated on during the decade was *Rear Window*, which cast Jimmy as a wheelchair-bound photographer-turned-voyeur. The film became one of the blockbusters of 1954. Hitchcock and Stewart followed this up with the very profitable remake of Hitchcock's own 1934 suspense film, *The Man Who Knew Too Much*. Then, in 1958, they made what is now considered their masterpiece together, though at the time it was one of the few Hitchcock (or Stewart) pictures of the period to fail at the box office, *Vertigo*, with Kim Novak. Stewart hoped that he and Hitchcock would work together again, but *Vertigo* would be their final film together.

Jimmy ended the '50s with one of his best films, *Anatomy of a*

Murder, for director Otto Preminger, based on a best-selling novel about a small-town lawyer who defends a serviceman (Ben Gazzara) accused of killing a man he believed raped his wife (Lee Remick). The film, very adult for its time, generated a lot of talk and Jimmy delivered a superb performance as the cagy defense attorney. The critics agreed and Stewart, again, won the New York Film Critics Award as Best Actor of 1959. He was also nominated for the Academy Award, for the fifth and final time, but lost to Charlton Heston for *Ben-Hur*.

The '50s was the peak of Stewart's film career; beginning in the '60s, good opportunities in films became less frequent. He appeared in some Westerns (*How the West Was Won, The Rare Breed, Firecreek, Bandolero!*) and family comedies (the very popular *Mr. Hobbs Takes a Vacation, Take Her, She's Mine, Dear Brigitte*). His best films of the decade were two Westerns he made for director John Ford, *Two Rode Together* and *The Man Who Shot Liberty Valance*, which teamed Jimmy with John Wayne.

With good film roles drying up, Jimmy decided to give television a chance, starring in the 1971-72 half-hour sitcom *The Jimmy Stewart Show*, which presented Jimmy in all his stammering, aw-shucks glory. The series failed to find a big enough audience. He tried again the next season, playing a lawyer in *Hawkins*. But this show also left the air after a couple of seasons, not so much because of its ratings, but because the actor (now approaching his late 60s) was becoming increasingly deaf and it was becoming a trial for him to hear the other actors. He made few films during the '70s. He engagingly teamed with old friend Henry Fonda in the comedy-western *The Cheyenne Social Club*. The film, directed by Gene Kelly, has one very funny and realistic sequence, where the two saddle pals discuss their differing political views: Fonda's character is a dyed-in-wool Democrat while Stewart is a "respectable Republican businessman." In real-life Fonda and Stewart usually avoided discussions of politics due to their differing politics. Fonda was a liberal Democrat and Stewart a conservative Republican. They truly did attempt to avoid discussing politics during the shooting of this picture because, just prior to its filming, Stewart and Gloria lost their son, Ronald, who was killed while serving in Vietnam. The loss devastated both parents.

Stewart was now an American icon and treated as such. During the '80s he received many show business honors, including the prestigious Life Achievement Award from the American Film Institute. He was also awarded the Kennedy Center Honors in December 1983. He was awarded a second Academy Award, this time for lifetime achievement, in March of 1985, presented to him by his friend and one-time co-star, Cary Grant. He turned up frequently on television talk-shows, particularly on Johnny Carson's *Tonight Show*, where he treated the audiences to "Jimmy Stewart," the stammering, aw-shucks, elderly grand man of Hollywood. One of his most memorable appearances on Carson was to promote his bestselling book of poems, *Jimmy Stewart and His Poems*, in 1989, where he read a poem he had written about his dog Beau, which caused the audience to both laugh and cry by the end.

Stewart had pretty much retired and became a virtual recluse after his beloved wife Gloria died of lung cancer in February 1994. His own health deteriorating due to age and heart problems, Stewart died on July 2, 1997 of a pulmonary blood clot. He was 89. His death, as would be expected, made front page news around the world. In the end most people summed up the life of Jimmy Stewart by saying it was "wonderful."

GEORGE ZUCCO (January 11, 1886-May 28, 1960)

George Zucco specialized in villains but in his private life he was known to be a modest dog lover who enjoyed reading. He was born in Manchester, England, on January 11, 1886. His father was a Greek merchant and his mother was a former lady in waiting to Queen Victoria. Zucco began his career in his early '20s by appearing with acting companies in the Canadian provinces. He also appeared in American vaudeville in a comedy sketch called *The Suffragette* with the woman who would eventually become his first wife.

When the First World War broke out Zucco returned to England and enlisted into the army. He experienced combat and suffered a serious wound to his right arm. Eventually he lost the use of two fingers and a thumb on his right hand. After the war he continued on with his acting career on the English stage. His first film was in 1931 in a British film *Dreyfus* starring Cedric Hardwicke. He kept busy over the next several years appearing in 13 British films. In late 1935, Zucco returned to the United States to star opposite Helen Hayes in the legendary Broadway production of *Victoria Regina*, in which Zucco played Disraeli. He worked in that play for eight months into 1936, when he was summoned to MGM, where his first film was *Sinner Take All* (which also featured Joseph Calleia). He then did *After the Thin Man*. He was getting typed into roles where his hawk-like features and authoritarian bearing were used to villainous effect. He became a man that people loved to hate. He also played members of British society in such films as *Parnell* and *Suez*. He was an all-out villain in *Charlie Chan in Honolulu*, *Arrest Bulldog Drummond* and, especially, as Sherlock Holmes' arch-nemesis Professor Moriarty in *The Adventures of Sherlock Holmes* (opposite Basil Rathbone).

In the '40s he increasingly appeared in horror films, including several in the *Mummy* cycle (*The Mummy's Hand, The Mummy's Tomb, The Mummy's Ghost*), *The Monster and the Girl, House of Frankenstein* and *Voodoo Man*. One of the more interesting horror roles, which presented Zucco with a dual starring role, was in the film *Dead Men Walk*, playing a kindly doctor who is murdered by his sinister twin, who comes back from the grave to extract revenge. He worked opposite Rathbone again in one of the modern Universal *Sherlock Holmes* films, *Sherlock Holmes in Washington*, playing a German spy. Occasionally, Zucco was allowed out of the horror-villain cycle to play nicer guys, such as the detective in *Lured*, the kindly doctor of *The Secret Garden* (1949) and a judge in two Fred Astaire films, *The Barkleys of Broadway* and *Let's Dance*.

His final film, unbilled, was in the 1951 *David and Bathsheba*. He suffered a severe stroke while working on the film *The Desert Fox* and was never healthy again; in fact, he spent his last years at an assisted-living facility in South San Gabriel, California. He left behind him a widow, his second wife, Stella, and his daughter Frances (a prize-winning equestrian, who would die of throat cancer two years later). George Zucco was 74. (Sources include obit from *Modesto Bee,* 5/29/60.)

REVIEWS:

"*After the Thin Man* is a great feather in Metro-Goldwyn-Mayer's cap not only because it is another hilarious comedy but because they have followed their first smash hit with another equally good. In brief, I was particularly impressed with Myrna Loy, who has never looked prettier in any picture, and even if Bill Powell has put on considerable weight, it doesn't detract from his swell performance. If there is any criticism, it is that the story is a little slow getting into the exceptionally well motivated mystery and the honest-to-goodness surprise denouement. It isn't fair to give away the plot, but I know you'll agree with me, when you see the picture that they've done some daring casting here, especially with Jimmy Stewart."

Louella Parsons,
Los Angeles Examiner, 11/5/36

"If *After the Thin Man* is not quite the delight *The Thin Man* was, it is, at the very least, one of the most urbane comedies of the season and an enterprise so agreeable that we are convinced that the Capitol (where it begins its engagement today) is one of Santa Claus's favorite children. Sequels commonly are disappointing and Metro-Goldwyn-Mayer was borrowing trouble when it dared advance a companion piece to one of the best pictures of 1934. But Dashiell Hammett's sense of humor has endured, W.S. Van Dyke retains his directorial facility and William Powell and Myrna Loy still persuades us that Mr. and Mrs. Nick Charles are exactly the sort of people we should like to have on our calling list on New Year's Day and for the rest of the year."

New York Times, 12/25/36

"It is long and there are occasional lapses in action, but new interest is quickly generated and in the end the results are enjoyable, even though not outstanding."

Commonweal, 1/1/37

"*After the Thin Man* avoids the pitfall of most sequels that of seeming a weak copy of the original, by being so much like its original that only experts in Dashiell Hammett plots will be able to tell the difference. In this picture, Asta, Detective Nick Charles's wire-haired terrier, has a mate, and the scene of operations is San Francisco instead of New York. In other respects, Mr. and Mrs. Charles (William Powell and Myrna Loy) maintain unchanged the amiably frantic domesticity which, in *The Thin Man*, set the style for detective cinema in 1934."

Time, 1/4/37

"The air of married happiness which Mr. William Powell and Miss Myrna Loy contrive to convey . . . is of far more interest than the tracking down of the murderer. Too often cinematic love stories are stories of passions and improbabilities, quarrels and reconciliations, but here is the more genuine material of marriage — the private jokes shared together, the routine of daily life, the amused and affectionate tolerance each shows toward certain traits in the other . . . Nick and Nora play into each other's hands . . . and it is the gaiety, the proper but never exaggerated sophistication, the charm and the irresponsibility, within limits, they bring to their lives which more than justify this sequel."

London Times, 4/8/37

"These stars, director and the author of *The Thin Man* have together manufactured a new film of light-hearted murder and marital badinage, if anything rather superior to the first. Between them they attain a rather awful efficiency: not 30 seconds is left unfilled by an expert and amusing gag."

Graham Greene,
The Spectator, 4/9/37

"***1/2 — Slightly overlong but first rate, with a truly surprising culprit and a cute finale involving Asta."

Leonard Maltin,
Movie and Video Guide, 1992

"****1/2 — the dialogue is fast-paced and quite droll, and Powell and Loy demonstrate a chemistry that explains the dozen hits they had together. Not to be missed."

Mick Martin and Marsha Porter,
Video and Movie Guide, 2002

After the Thin Man PHOTO GALLERY

Bill, Myrna and Asta in a studio portrait. COURTESY OF LAURA WAGNER.

From Left to Right, William Law, Sam Levene, Dorothy McNulty, Bill, Joseph Calleia in *After the Thin Man*, 1936. PHOTO COURTESY OF LAURA WAGNER.

Bill, Myrna, Elissa Landi, Sam Levene and a young James Stewart in *After the Thin Man*.

Bill and Myrna with Asta facing a good friend.

CHAPTER FIVE

ANOTHER THIN MAN

CAST: William Powell (Nick Charles), Myrna Loy (Nora Charles), Otto Kruger (Van Slack), C. Audrey Smith (Col. MacFay), Virginia Grey (Lois MacFay), Ruth Hussey (Dorothy Waters), Nat Pendleton (Lt. Guild), Patric Knowles (Dudley Horn), Tom Neal (Freddie), Sheldon Leonard (Phil Church), Marjorie Main (Mrs. Dolley), William A. Poulsen (Nick, Jr.).

COMPANY CREDITS: A Metro-Goldwyn-Mayer (MGM) film. W. S. Van Dyke II (Director), Hunt Stromberg (Producer), Frances Goodrich and Albert Hackett (Screenwriters) based on a story by Dashiell Hammett. Fredrick Y. Smith (Editing), William Daniels and Oliver T. Marsh (Cinematography), Edwin B. Willis (Art Direction), Edward Ward (Musical Score).

PRODUCTION DATES: Mid-July-late August 1939 with retakes in October 1939. Released: November 17, 1939. 105 minutes. Black and White.

SYNOPSIS:
Nick and Nora Charles return to New York from yet another vacation (with numerous suitcases in tow) and have their little bundle of joy, Nick Charles, Jr. (not yet born at the end of the second film), now about a year old, along with them. Nora is giving directions to the men bringing their luggage into their suite as to where they should put things. "That goes there," she points. "And that goes there" and when one man comes in carrying a martini, she points to Nick and says, "And that goes over there." Nick gives the man a tip and says,

Poster for *Another Thin Man*.

"Don't forget to drop in often." They can barely unpack their bags before a call comes in and they are summoned by Col. MacFay (C. Aubrey Smith), an old associate of Nora's father, to his elegant Long Island estate — yes, Nick's services as an amateur sleuth are once again in demand. Not wanting to be drawn into another case, Nick tells Nora not to return the call! But motherhood hasn't reformed Nora from the thrill of the chase, and she tells the Colonel that they will be there. Meanwhile, Nick and Nora have engaged a nurse to accompany them and keep an eye on little Nicky. The nurse, Dorothy Waters (Ruth Hussey), appears to have a mysterious past. On the way up the road which leads to the estate (driven by a chauffer sent by the Colonel), Nick and the driver notice a body lying on the road with a knife in his back. They stop to investigate, but when they get out of the car, the body has mysteriously vanished. This is just one of several "pranks" that has been occurring at the Colonel's estate. The driver, shaken, runs away, and Nick has to finish the drive.

When they arrive at the mansion, they find the place a virtual prison with guards everywhere. One guard stops Nick at the gate.

The guard notices baby Nicky in the back seat:

GUARD (to Nick): What's the idea of the kid?

NICK: Well, you see, we had a dog and he was lonesome. (To Nora) That was the idea, wasn't it, Mom? (Nick refers to Nora as "Mom" many times in the film, as opposed to "Sugar" in the original film.)

It turns out that the old Colonel has been threatened by a former employee, Phil Church (Sheldon Leonard). But, as usual in a mystery story, there is a house full of suspects and this one is no exception. Among the guests are MacFay's adopted daughter, Lois (Virginia Grey), and her fiancé Dudley (Patric Knowles). Dudley explains to Nick and Nora that Church blames the Colonel for sending him to jail, which is why the Colonel is convinced that Church is out to kill him — it all comes down to revenge. They are also introduced to the Colonel's private secretary, Freddie (Tom Neal). Freddie (obviously Nick's kind of guy) offers Nick and Nora a drink when they arrive at the estate. The old Colonel will have none of that. "Mrs. Charles doesn't drink and I want Mr. Charles to have a clear head." So, no drink for Nick. As Freddie locks up the liquor cabinet, Nick has a look of pure agony on his face. (It is worth noting that, while Nick continues to have a strong urge for alcohol, Nora's character has almost been made into a teetotaler. As we recall in the first film, Nora could match Nick drink for drink, but now that she's a mother, the censors, and that apostle of all that is good, Louis B. Mayer, probably insisted that she put a lid on her drinking, but that doesn't mean she won't try and help Nick.) Later, the ever-resourceful Nora sneaks the key to the liquor cabinet and gives it to Nick.

NICK: You darling!

NORA: I haven't been married to you for nothing.

We are also introduced to the Colonel's efficient housekeeper, Mrs. Bellam (Phyllis Gordon), who may have had a secret past with the Colonel.

Strange things do happen during the course of the evening. For instance, during dinner, the housekeeper announces that the swimming pool (!) is on fire. When Nick investigates, he finds the Colonel's dog, dead, in the bushes. It turns out that Church wants money from the Colonel or he will spill the beans about past business malpractices by the Colonel and quite possibly Nora's father as well.

Nora (to Nick): You know my father wasn't in on this . . . if it was anything wrong. My father was just as honest as yours!

NICK: Someday you'll find out what a hot recommendation *that* is!

Nick is more "concerned" about more practical matters:

NICK: I'd hate to wake up some morning and find the fortune I'd married you for was gone.

NORA: Stop talking that way!

NICK: Of course I can always make a good salary as a detective. But what are you and Nicky going to live on? That's what worries me. (Nora gives him a nice, swift kick.)

During the night the Colonel is murdered and the lead investigator, Assistant District Attorney Van Slack (Otto Kruger), eventually comes to believe that Nick is involved in some way. Also, in the confusion after the murder, the Charleses discover that the Nick, Jr.'s nurse has disappeared; "personally, I think she's very wise" is Nick's wry comment on this turn of events. Assisting in the investigation is also Nick's old pal Lt. Guild (Nat Pendleton, returning to the role he had in the original film). During the course of the police investigation gun shots ring out and a second victim is claimed — Dudley Horn.

When the Charleses return to their New York apartment, Nora gets a mysterious call directing her to the Rio Club. There she runs into Nick who was following up on another lead; he finds out that Church had two girlfriends, one named Linda Mills. Meanwhile, another girlfriend of Church's turns up missing. Then Church himself comes out of hiding and threatens to kill Nick unless he abandons the case. Nick pursues him and Church winds up shot and dead (by who?) as the police arrive — yet a third killing. The deaths in this film are really piling up. The clues and suspects are also piling up. Freddie discloses that while Lois will inherit several million dollars of the Colonel's estate, the housekeeper, Mrs. Bellam, will get a cool $100,000. Not a bad sum to retire on and enjoy a few good years — if you speed things up a bit.

Nick then has a bombshell: he tells the police that Church was shot and killed by the same person who killed the Colonel and Dudley — and the killer is . . . No telling here . . .

The film's ending, after Nick has properly identified the murderer, has Nick approach Nora:

NICK: Mommy, let's sit down.

NORA: Sit down? What for?

NICK: Just to get a little rest after our quiet weekend in the country.

While that is a nice and quaintly funny ending to the film, the Hacketts had another, more elaborate and sexy ending in mind which, while it appears in script form, didn't make it to the final print; a real shame because it's so good. Nick and Nora are back home and they have plans to meet people for dinner/drinks. According to the book *The Real Nick and Nora*, married screen-writers Frances Goodrich and Albert Hackett "plagiarizing from themselves" in creating it. They are in their bedroom, changing into evening clothes and awaiting the arrival of their friends. Nora is seated at her dressing room table when Nick asks when their friends will be arriving:

NORA: They ought to be here now. They said they'd telephone up. (She rises) They're going to take us to all the new nightclubs. (She begins to fix Nick's tie) Here. I'm crazy to go, aren't you?

NICK: Huh huh. (Pause) Of course, it's the first time we've been alone in days.

NORA: I know. But we can always be alone.

NICK: Can we?

NORA: Of course.

NICK: (Looks over her dress) New dress?

NORA: Huh huh.

NICK: When did you find time to get a new dress?

NORA: I telephoned, between murders. Like it?

NICK: Huh huh. (Looking at her lips) And new lipstick?

NORA: Kiss proof.

NICK: Really?

NORA: It's not supposed to come off.

NICK: (Nick kisses her) Did it come off?

NORA: It did for me.

(The telephone rings. Neither of them makes a move to answer it.)

NICK: What time are they supposed to call?

NORA: At ten.

(Phone rings again. Nick looks at his watch)

NICK: It's five minutes after.

(Now the doorbell begins buzzing)

NORA: So it is.

(Now the telephone and doorbell are both ringing)

NICK: Do you suppose they've forgotten?

NORA: I'm sure they have.

(Nick takes Nora in his arms for the fade out.)
Now, *that's* an ending!

BEST DIALOG:

NORA: I got rid of all those reporters.

NICK: What did you tell them?

NORA: We're out of scotch.

NICK: What a gruesome idea.

NORA: How did you find me here?

NICK: I saw a great group of men standing around a table. I
           knew there was only one woman in the world that
           could attract men like that. A woman with a lot of
           money.

THE SCREENWRITERS:

FRANCES GOODRICH (December 21, 1890-January 29, 1984)
ALBERT HACKETT (February 16, 1900-March 16, 1995)

This husband-and-wife writing team wrote the screenplays for
the first three *Thin Man* films, and in the course of a 35-year career
they wrote scores of plays and motion pictures. They were considered
among the best in the business and highly valued by the studios
which employed them. Writer-director Garson Kanin (who often
wrote in tandem with his wife Ruth Gordon) said of Frances and

Albert, "They were the writers that producers used to kill to get." The pinnacle of their joint careers was in writing the play *The Diary of Anne Frank*, in 1954-1955, adapted from the real-life diaries of a courageous young girl hiding from the Nazis. This play, and the later motion picture, won the Hacketts many honors and citations.

Frances Goodrich was born in Belleville, New Jersey, of "American, Welsh, English, French and Dutch stock." Her father was a lawyer who belonged to a prominent New York law firm. Her mother was described as "never without a book and was passionate about the novels of Henry James." Frances' family was very prominent and was listed in the social register (according to her nephew, Frances "spoke with a faintly actressy accent, saying 'darling' and 'lovely' a lot"). But while her father may have been a prominent lawyer, he got his greatest satisfaction from directing amateur plays and reciting poetry. Frances attended private schools and became interested in dramatics while a student at Vassar College in Poughkeepsie, New York. She appeared in several student productions as an actress. She graduated with a BA in 1912 and then went on to New York City where she had plans of becoming a social worker, but by 1913 her interests were back to the theater and between 1913 and 1916 Frances worked at the Northampton (MA) Playhouse usually in ingénue roles. At one point during her time at Northampton Frances found herself playing opposite a young William Powell in an adaptation of *Hamlet*. Years later, when Powell was a leading Hollywood actor and Frances and Albert were writing the *Thin Man* pictures, Powell told Albert that "I was with her [Frances] in the Civil War." In 1917 she married the first of three husbands, actor Robert Ames; the marriage lasted six years and produced no children (Frances would never bear children). After her marriage, Frances kept busy in a string of stage roles (and even an occasional film role). Frances would recall, fondly, that the New York stage of the 1920s was a happy and productive time for actors because, "you could count on fifty-two weeks work out of the year."

Albert Hackett was born in New York City, almost a decade after Frances, on February 16, 1900. His father was a store clerk who later became tubercular and was sent to a sanitarium in Denver, Colorado. It was while in Denver that he died, leaving a young widow with three children. Albert would later recall that half of his mother's family felt that she should put the children up for adoption and the other half felt that she should put them on the stage. The stage won out, and Albert made his stage debut at the age of six. In 1907 Albert acted in the play *Rip Van Wrinkle* playing the part of a girl, while his sister was also cast in the play — as a boy. "It was years before we got our sexes straightened out!" Albert later joked. He attended the Professional Children's School and acted for three years with the Lubin Stock Company out of Philadelphia, Pennsylvania. He appeared in several Broadway shows, including *Whoopee!* (he also acted in the 1930 film which starred Eddie Cantor) and *Twelve Miles Out*. Albert was renowned for his sense of humor and good nature. His nephew would recall that Albert "delivered off-beat, self-mocking quips with many chuckles, a wide-eyed, innocent look, and precise pronunciation."

Frances and Albert first met in 1924 when she was appearing in the George Kelly play *The Show-Off* and Albert was appearing at the same time in *The Nervous Wreck*. Their paths went off in other directions after that but they were brought together again in 1927 when they both were members of a summer stock company in Denver, Colorado. Frances showed Albert a play she had written called *Such a Lady*. She felt it wasn't quite ready and so Albert offered to look it over and critique it. Frances later said that Albert "tore it to bits and destroyed it." It was also in 1927 that Frances married historian and author Henrik Willem Van Loon, a marriage which lasted until 1929.

Both Frances and Albert took turns rewriting *Such a Lady* and at some point in this collaboration they decided to just start from scratch on a new play, a comedy, titled *Western Union*, which was produced in Skowheagan, Maine in the summer of 1930. The play didn't bring in big dollars but by this time they decided that they worked well together and they were also forging a personal relationship and decided to remain as a writing team. Their next project — another comedy — *Up Pops the Devil* opened on Broadway at the Masque Theatre on September 1, 1930. It ran for 148 performances and was a moderate success. In addition to writing the play, Albert also appeared as an actor in the play.

Frances and Albert were married on February 7, 1931. They decided to give Hollywood a try, realizing that they could potentially make more money in Hollywood as writers than on Broadway (and they wanted to save as much money as possible so that they could eventually return to writing for the stage). Their first film as Hollywood screenwriters was adapting their own play *Up Pops the Devil* for the movies. It was released in 1931, by Paramount Pictures, and featured a young Carole Lombard. In 1933 they were signed by MGM, where they had a hit from their screenplay of *The Secret of Madame Blanche* which starred Irene Dunne. That same year the Hacketts did the screenplay for *Penthouse*, the first picture they would make with director Woody Van Dyke and producer Hunt Stromberg. The picture was a major success at the box office and, when the time came to adapt *The Thin Man*, Hunt Stromberg immediately thought of the Hacketts for the job. In fact, it was much the same team with Stromberg, the Hacketts, Van Dyke and Myrna Loy (whose part in *Penthouse* was one of her first major roles not playing some kind of oriental/exotic vamp) in the key role as Nora.

Frances and Albert would write five more films (total of seven) for the producing/ directing team of Hunt Stromberg and Woody Van Dyke. (The other five being *Hide-Out*, two Jeanette MacDonald and Nelson Eddy epics [*Naughty Marietta* and *Rose Marie*], and two more *Thin Mans* [*After the Thin Man* and *Another Thin Man*]. In fact, all but one (1939's *Society Lawyer*) of their '30s films for MGM were produced by Stromberg's unit and only three of them were not directed by Woody Van Dyke: *Ah, Wilderness!* (Clarence Brown), *Small Town Girl* (William Wellman) and *Firefly* (Robert Z. Leonard). Of the thirteen screenplays the Hacketts wrote during the seven years they spent at MGM during the '30s, two were nominated for Academy Awards: *The Thin Man* and *After the Thin Man*; however, they lost out both times.

By the time they had written the third Thin Man film both Frances and Albert were physically and mentally tired, "A lovely nervous breakdown," Frances later called it, "and we enjoyed it together. We just broke down at the typewriter and started crying and neither of us could stop crying. In a relationship like ours if one partner gets sick, he soon puts the other one in the same condition." They decided to leave Hollywood and go back to New York and writing for the stage.

Back in Manhattan they began revising a ten-year-old comedy play they wrote, **Western Union, Please**. There had been a performance of it at the Cape Playhouse in Dennis, Massachusetts in 1937. But while it was well-received, they didn't quite think it was right for the big time. Albert hadn't quite gotten the acting bug out of him yet, either. In 1941 he was offered the lead role in the mystery-comedy *Mr. and Mrs. North*, based on stories published in *The New Yorker* about a middle-class couple (unlike the wealthy Charleses) who solve murders. Albert accepted the part saying, "Frances felt it would be good for me to feel like an actor again, and I wouldn't have to worry about speeches and dialogue and things." The play opened in January of 1941 and ran until late May; overshadowed by the awesome success of *Arsenic and Old Lace*. Still, Albert garnered some good reviews: "His air of ineffectual politeness and well-bred surprise is wholly entertaining." Albert enjoyed it, but this would be his swansong as an actor.

In 1942 Frances and Albert adapted a novel, *The Great Big Doorstep*, for the stage. The play, presented at the Morosco Theater, starred Dorothy Gish and Louis Calhern, but, despite some decent reviews, the play closed after only 28 performances.

In 1943 the team was lured back to Hollywood, this time to Paramount Pictures, where they were hired to adapt the Broadway hit *Lady in the Dark* (which was written for the stage by Moss Hart). The film, released in 1944 and starring Ginger Rogers, cut many of the songs and was not considered as effective as the stage production which starred Gertrude Lawrence. Frances and Albert didn't even like the finished film, in part because the director, Mitchell Leisen, had another writer punch up their script; they virtually disowned the finished product.

As writers, Frances and Albert had a routine. "Each of us writes a version of a scene," Frances told the *New York Herald Tribune* in an article published on June 3, 1956. They would write in a room at separate desks facing in opposite directions. Exchanging drafts, they evaluated each other's work. "I never knew there could be so many battles over little words."

Following the bad experience on *Lady in the Dark*, the Hacketts collaborated on two more screenplays for Paramount, *The Hitler Gang* (about the rise of the Nazi party in Germany) and an opportunity to write a Western, *The Virginian*.

The Hacketts returned to MGM for several pictures, including a few musicals: *Summer Holiday* (a musical version of *Ah, Wilderness!*), *The Pirate*, *Easter Parade* and *In the Good Old Summertime*. They continued to make films for MGM in the '50s, including *Father of the Bride* (for which they would earn their third Oscar nomination) and its sequel, *Father's Little Dividend*, with Spencer Tracy and Elizabeth Taylor. Both were immense successes. There was talk of a third in the series, but the Hacketts definitely didn't want to get back to writing series films like they had with the *Thin Man*. They followed that up with *Too Young to Kiss* and *Give a Girl a Break*, then wrote two of MGM's biggest hits of the '50s, *The Long, Long Trailer*, which starred Lucille Ball and Desi Arnaz at the peak of their I Love Lucy television stardom, and *Seven Brides for Seven Brothers*. They enjoyed writing this film and were flattered to be nominated (for the fourth and final time) for an Oscar, but were under no illusion that they would actually win — and they didn't.

After this they left Hollywood again to devote their time to a labor of love — adapting the book *Anne Frank, Diary of a Young Girl* for the stage. It took them two years to complete.

When the play was presented, it was an immediate sensation on Broadway (with young Susan Strasberg in the role of Anne). In 1956 the New York Drama Critics Circle named *The Diary of Anne Frank* the best new American play of that season. On May 8, 1956, Frances and Albert were awarded the Pulitzer Prize for their writing of *The Diary of Anne Frank*. In 1958, they adapted their play for the motion picture screen for director George Stevens, and while the film version of *The Diary of Anne Frank* was generally successful the Hacketts didn't believe it was nearly as good as the stage play.

After the stage and movie productions of *Anne Frank* the Hacketts only made three more films: *Gaby* (a remake of *Waterloo Bridge*), *A Certain Smile* (based on a novel), and their last theatrical film, released in 1962, *Five Finger Exercise*, which starred Rosalind Russell.

By this time Frances was well into her seventies and Albert his sixties and both were slowing down, but they would live many more (lucrative) years. They both grew deaf and ended up with hearing aids, though Frances, vainer, tried to put off the inevitable as long as possible by learning to read lips. Over the years they hadn't completely given up on writing and worked for several years on a play, *Days in the Trees*, which they hoped Lynn Fontanne would perform, but she didn't, and Ingrid Bergman later turned it down as well. After that, they lost interest. Frances would live to be 93, dying of lung cancer in 1984. Albert would remarry the following year and live on another decade, dying in 1995 at the age of 95. Of their relationship Frances once said, "We do everything together. Poor Hackett. He never gets away from me. He never gets to take advantage of all the opportunities in Hollywood — and there are so many!" By all accounts, Albert wouldn't have wanted it any other way. (Sources include *NY Herald Tribune*, 6/3/56, *Current Biography*, October 1956.)

THE BACK STORY:

Frances Goodrich and Albert Hackett thought that they had come up with the ideal way to end the series with *After the Thin Man* by having Nora become pregnant. They believed that nobody would want to see any more films with a domesticated Nick and Nora having a baby to take care of. "We thought this finish would end the adventures of Nick and Nora," Albert later wrote. "But in the first review of the picture the critic said, 'It is obvious that they intend others as there is a promise of a baby!'" The second film also made too much money and profits for MGM to discontinue it. Like the *Tarzan* series, it was MGM's intent to present a new *Thin Man* film every two years, and so soon after the second film was released producer Hunt Stromberg requested that Dashiell Hammett come up with an original story for the third Nick and Nora adventure.

Meanwhile, in late 1936, William Powell, who had a banner year in five hugely popular films that year, was playing hard ball with MGM, demanding more money. "Powell, I hear, is fighting with MGM over a new contract," Dashiell Hammett wrote Lillian Hellman on December 3, 1936, "holding out for $200,000 a picture. MGM's recent statement that there would be no more sequels to 'The Thin Man,' no matter how well this one does, is, I suppose, just a piece of the iron pipe to slug him with." Soon the studio and Powell did come to terms, not at $200,000 per picture but at $8,000 per week over a 40-week period, still an extraordinary amount of money. The studio also signed Hammett to $2,000 per week to write an original scenario for a new *Thin Man* film. On February 11, 1937, Hammett granted MGM perpetual rights to the *Thin Man* characters for a quick infusion of $40,000. But Hammett by this time was unreliable and while he took the money he did little work — spending too much time boozing. As late as September 9, 1937 he received a cable from the Hacketts, who were vacationing in Stockholm, telling him that Stromberg had wired them from Biarritz to cable Hammett asking about the story. Why Stromberg couldn't have cabled Hammett directly is not all together clear.

By December of 1937 it looks like Stromberg and Hammett were still battling it out. By this time the Hacketts had fleshed out Hammett's idea into a screenplay, but Stromberg was not satisfied. "I'm in the middle of the usual so-this-script-is-done battles with my own dear producer," wrote Hammett to Hellman, "who insists that it's all right, but it's not exactly like the two previous scripts. The Hacketts sit on the sidelines and tremble while Hunt and I pace the floor and yell at one another. My latest line of attack is to point out that since he doesn't seem to know what was good and what bad in the previous two pictures they were so far as he is concerned just lucky flukes."

It seems they finally had worked things out and an acceptable screenplay was ready by early 1938. But then another problem which had not been foreseen interrupted the start of the third *Thin Man* film — William Powell's fight with rectal cancer. Though the public wasn't made aware of the severity of Powell's condition, the studio had to temporarily shelf plans to make the third film. Powell had an operation in March 1938 and then again in January of 1939; in the meanwhile, he was quite weak and definitely not up to the back-breaking schedule of making a motion picture. There was some talk of recasting the part with either Reginald Gardiner or Melvyn Douglas, but, that too, was quickly discarded. To the public there could be only one "Thin Man" and that was Bill Powell, and if they had to delay the picture until he was able to — they would.

Finally, in mid-July of 1939, seven months after his last surgery, Bill returned to MGM and *Another Thin Man* was finally ready to go before the cameras. While Bill was given a clean bill of health from his doctors, Myrna Loy thought, "He still seemed a bit frail when we started *Another Thin Man*, but he wasn't giving up a thing." Stromberg and Van Dyke made sure that he would be on a schedule which wouldn't over-tax him. Powell only had to work six hours per day (10-4), and all the principles were assigned stand-ins so that the stars (particularly Powell) wouldn't have to be present on the set during camera set ups and lighting. According to author Charles Francisco in his biography of Powell, *Gentleman: The William Powell Story*, Bill was given a standing ovation by the cast and crew on his first day back on the set. "Powell, looking remarkably fit and tanned, seemed embarrassed by the attention. He held up his hands and the familiar grin began to play at the corners of his mouth as he tried to think of something funny to say. The applause stopped, and Bill found that he couldn't speak. Myrna Loy rushed over to him and gave him a kiss and a big hug. Woody Van Dyke supplied the proper ending to the emotionally charged scene, 'All right,' he bellowed, 'what are we wasting time for? Let's get to work.'"

Screen tough-guy (and later innovative producer) Sheldon Leonard made his film debut in *Another Thin Man* and in his autobiography, *And the Show Goes On*, recalled the experience: "The year was 1939. Actually, I had committed to the picture almost a year earlier, but it had been postponed when Powell was stricken with cancer of the colon. The dramatic surgery that was necessary to cope with that type of cancer was relatively new and crude. Powell had come through it well and was ready to go to work, but the suave, urbane, glamorous star had to cope with the indignity of a colostomy bag. I had to do a fight scene with him. 'Be gentle with him,' I was warned. Someone should have told him to be gentle with me. When we shot the scene, the recuperating invalid tossed me around like a beach ball. He was a remarkable man. Some years ago I visited with him in Palm Springs. He was well into his eighties, looking tan and fit, and still playing an excellent game of tennis."

Leonard also recalled working with Woody Van Dyke. "In the course of time, I learned that Van Dyke's approach to a shooting schedule was unique. He made no secret of it. In his words, 'I finish the picture nice and fast. No fooling around. Print take one. I finish three or four days ahead of schedule and they give me a bonus. Then I go back (with retakes and editing) and really make my picture."

Leonard also recalls in the book that Van Dyke "taught me a lot." He explained, "Early in the shooting schedule there was a scene in which I was to be shot while trying to scale a parapet. When the bullet hit me, I was to stagger, then fall onto the narrow top of the parapet, balance there briefly, and then tumble off onto a pile of mattresses off camera. It was tricky. The damned parapet was narrow and the surface was covered with gravel. Every time I hit it I left skin behind, not to mention the cuts and bruises that I carried away with me. Take after take, either I flinched, thus lousing up the shot, or Van Dyke wasn't pleased with it for some other reason. When he finally Okayed a print, I was a mess of scrapes and bruises. He called me over. He said, 'Look, kid. I just gave you a first class screwing. I took advantage of your inexperience. Don't ever let any other director make you do stuff like that. Don't even sit down in a hard chair without calling for a stunt man. That's how they make their living. When you do hazardous stuff, you're keeping a qualified stunt man from making a paycheck. They're a tight group and they don't like things like that. One day you'll be doing a fight scene somewhere without a stuntman and a fist will come flying out of nowhere and you'll be picking your teeth up off the floor."

This film introduced Nick Charles, Jr. According to contemporary newspaper articles of the time, the studio found eight-month-old William Anthony Poulson, "after rejecting several hundred babies." Poulson was signed on for seven weeks' worth of work at a slightly higher salary than normal which his parents put away for his future college education because they didn't expect their son to continue working in the movies. Indeed, according to IMDb, young Mr. Poulson never did appear in another motion picture.

When MGM was making the trailer to *Another Thin Man*, they played up the fact that Bill was back. "Happy Days are here again!"

begins the trailer, which ends with "Welcome Back, Bill Powell!" Who could blame them? *Another Thin Man* became one of MGM's top hits of the year. Bill and Myrna both attended the preview of the picture at the Academy Theater in Inglewood, California, and when Bill made his first appearance on screen the audience "nearly took the roof off" with applause and cheers.

According to a contemporary newspaper article: "After a year and a half, William Powell is back before the camera and he and Myrna Loy are kissing each other for a scene in *Another Thin Man*. Director W.S. Van Dyke, who doesn't believe in fooling around with any scene, makes a couple of takes and announces that he is satisfied. As the camera crane, inevitable on Van Dyke sets, is pulled back, the still photographer for the company makes a quick setup and asks Myrna and Bill to go into a clinch again. They hold the kiss and he snaps the picture. 'Now, just one more,' says the still man, 'and Miss Loy can we have your eyes open this time.' Van Dyke snorts impatiently, 'You make it snappy,' he yells at the still man, 'or we'll just run over you and your Kodak.' There is never a moment's lull on a Van Dyke set. He directs a picture as if he were leading a charge of the marines." (*Union Town* (PA) *Morning Herald*, 7/28/39, Harrison Carroll, *Behind the Scenes in Hollywood*.)

SUPPORTING CAST
VIRGINIA GREY (March 22, 1917-July 31, 2004)

Virginia Grey was one of the busiest ladies on the screen from the late '30s and into the '40s, her glamorous good looks used to good effect in several films. She was born on March 22, 1917, in Edendale, California. Her father, Ray Grey, was an actor who worked as one of the Keystone Kops and director (for Mack Sennett), and her mother was a film cutter, so young Virginia was a studio brat; growing up around soundstages and stars. One prominent story has it that one of Virginia's babysitters was none other than Gloria Swanson. Virginia's first film role came at the age of nine when she was discovered walking on the lot one day and cast as little Eva in the 1927 adaptation of Harriet Beecher Stowe's *Uncle Tom's Cabin*.

She worked in other films over the next few years usually in bits or walk-ons and by the time she graduated high school she made plans on studying nursing and put acting behind her. But that changed in 1936 when MGM decided to sign her to a contract. She did bit parts in such films as *The Great Ziegfeld*, starring William Powell, and *Our Relations* with Laurel and Hardy.

Her first notable part was as Bruce Cabot's love interest in an interesting little "B" called *Bad Guy*. She then worked opposite Richard Arlen in *Secret Valley* (1937). She first came to the attention of Woody Van Dyke that same year when he cast Virginia as Ray Bolger's girlfriend in *Rosalie*. In 1938 she was cast as eye candy in the Clark Gable-Myrna Loy-Spencer Tracy action film *Test Pilot*. It was the first time she would work with Gable, who found the 21-year-old irresistible; an affair soon began which would last on-and-off for several years. She would work again with Gable as one of his bevy of chorus girls in *Idiot's Delight* two years later. MGM executive Howard Strickling told Gable biographer Lyn Tornabene, "Clark and Virginia had a great relationship. If he was lonesome, you know — I mean Virginia was always there. I mean, if he was in a mood, Virginia was there, you know." It is said by some that the never-married Grey stayed unattached for the rest of her life because of the man who got away — Gable.

She continued to plug along in small roles in popular films such as *The Hardys Ride High*, The Women and then larger roles in "B" films such as *Thunder Afloat*. Her part in *Another Thin Man* turned out to be a prominent role in an "A" picture and did a great deal to advance her career at MGM, at least temporarily. She was loaned out to Warner Brothers for *Three Cheers for the Irish*; cast as Charles Coburn and Beulah Bondi's daughter in *The Captain Is a Lady*; played the ingénue (opposite Tony Martin) in the Marx Brothers' *The Big Store*; worked with Red Skelton in *Whistling in the Dark* and was put in *Tarzan's New York Adventure*. The final film of her MGM contract was Tish in 1942, sixth-billed below lead Marjorie Main. During the war years, when she wasn't busy working at the studios, she was a constant presence at the Hollywood Canteen and on war bond tours.

From MGM she went to Republic, where she worked with their big cowboy stars like Gene Autry in *Bells of Capistrano*, Roy Rogers in *Idaho* and John Wayne in *Flame of the Barbary Coast*. One of her most interesting Republic films was *Strangers in the Night* about a girl who invents an imaginary daughter to replace the one she could never have. She was later reunited with her *Tarzan* co-star Johnny Weissmuller in *Swamp Fire* and *Jungle Jim*. She was rescued from "B" budgets with a decorative role in Cecil B. DeMille's *Unconquered* and in 1948 she played straight woman for Abbott and Costello in *Mexican Hayride*. After this, she may have had her all-time best role, in RKO's *The Threat*, where she played a café singer held hostage by escaped convict Charles McGraw. She had another good part in the cult classic *The Bullfighter and the Lady* (1951) directed by Budd Boetticher (and produced by John Wayne). She appeared increasingly on television (*Playhouse 90, Goodyear Theatre, The Millionaire, The Red Skelton Show, The Jack Benny Program*), but by the mid-'50s her fortune turned around for a time with good supporting roles in such successful films as *The Rose Tattoo, All that Heaven Allows* and *Jeanne Eagels*.

Grey kept busy during the '60s with television work and in such films as *Back Street, Bachelor in Paradise, Portrait in Black,* and *Madam X*. In the mid-'60s she appeared in strong parts in two cult films: as a bordello madam in Samuel Fuller's *The Naked Kiss* and as a middle-aged woman seeking love while on vacation in Acapulco in *Love Has Many Faces*. Grey continued to work up to the middle-'70s, when her last part was in a small role in a television mini-series, *The Money Changers*, based on an Arthur Hailey novel. She died of heart failure on July 31, 2004, at the age of 87.

RUTH HUSSEY (October 30, 1911-April 19, 2005)

Ruth Hussey excelled at playing smart and sophisticated, if somewhat world-weary, women who could lighten the mood with a witty or self-depreciatory observation about her surroundings or herself. She was talented and pretty enough to be a star, but the studios never really gave her the chance, but she graced many fine films with her presence.

She was born Ruth Carol Hussey, on October 30, 1911, in Providence, Rhode Island. One of her ancestors was a purchaser of Nantucket Island off of Massachusetts. Her father died when she was only seven years old, a casualty of the 1918-1919 flu which had also claimed the life of Myrna Loy's father. She attended Brown University (or rather Pembroke College, which was then Brown's girl school), where she graduated (with a degree in Philosophy) in 1933. She later said that despite trying out for many school productions she never got offered a role while at Pembroke. She did study drama as a post-graduate at the University of Michigan and worked in summer stock for two seasons.

When she returned to Providence in 1935 she got a job as a fashion commentator on a local radio station as well as occasional jobs as a model. She also traveled to New York City where she signed with a talent agent who booked her for a role at the Providence Playhouse. Her New York connections landed her modeling work with the John Robert Powers Modeling Agency. While living in New York, Hussey lodged in the legendary Rehearsal Club Hotel for women that inspired the play and later movie *Stage Door*. In 1937 Hussey joined the national touring group for the play *Dead End* and when they played their final engagement at a theater in Los Angeles, she was "discovered" by MGM talent scout Billy Grady and signed to a standard MGM contract which initially paid her $150 per week with options every six months.

Hussey was often cast in large roles in "B" films and small roles in "A" pictures. One of her earliest films was *Madam X* opposite Gladys George. She made appearances in the MGM series pictures: *Judge Hardy's Children, Maisie* and *After the Thin Man*. She worked well with Robert Young, a second-level MGM leading man at the time, as his leading lady in films like *Rich Man, Poor Girl* and *Honolulu*. She played Edward G. Robinson's wife in *Blackmail*. Hussey was cast in the small role as a secretary by George Cukor in *The Women* (1939), and this proved to be fortunate for the intelligent young actress. Cukor took a liking to her talent and cast her again the next year in two big films: the kindly "other woman" opposite Joan Crawford in *Susan and God* and, most memorably, as the knowing photographer opposite James Stewart's reporter in *The Philadelphia Story*.

Hussey never had a better role before (and, sadly, was never given an equal opportunity again) and she certainly made the most of it. It was one of the most sophisticated films of its time and still holds up. Hussey later said that director Cukor became a mentor to her. "He gave me one piece of advice that I always use, 'Keep your emotions near the surface so that you can call on them when you need to.'" Hussey was a huge success in the film and was nominated for an Academy Award for Best Supporting Actress; losing to Jane Darwell in *The Grapes of Wrath*.

This was her best period of activity with good roles in quality films like *Northwest Passage* (with Robert Young again); as Robert Young's social-climbing wife in the excellent *H.M. Pulham, Esq.*; and playing First Lady to Van Heflin's President Andrew Johnson in *Tennessee Johnson* in 1942, the final film of her MGM contract. She then went to RKO to star opposite Ginger Rogers in the Edward Dmytryk-directed, Dalton Trumbo-written *Tender Comrades*. For Paramount she made her other memorable film (after *The Philadelphia Story*), playing Ray Milland's sister in the psychological haunted house drama *The Uninvited*. After this, her film offerings declined, but she was used to good effect in *The Great Gatsby* with Alan Ladd, *Mr. Music* with Bing Crosby, as Jerry Lewis' mother in *That's My Boy* and Mrs. John Philip Sousa opposite Clifton Webb in *Stars and Stripes Forever*.

By the 1950s, with good film roles drying up, she turned increasingly to television with strong parts on many anthology series such as *Studio One* and *General Electric Theater*. She played the Virgin Mary three times on *Family Theater* and was nominated for an Emmy in 1955 for a television version of *Craig's Wife*. In between she also appeared more frequently on the New York stage, appearing in productions of *State of the Union* (with Ralph Bellamy), *Goodbye, My Fancy* and *The Royal Family*.

Hussey's last feature film was in 1960 when she was cast as Bob Hope's wife in the adult comedy *The Facts of Life*. After that she continued to appear on television, including working with her good friend Robert Young in an episode of *Marcus Welby M.D.* and the television movie *My Darling Daughter's Anniversary* in 1973. Soon after, she retired from active show business work.

Hussey had married talent scout C. Robert Longenecker in 1942. Longenecker told friends that after he saw Hussey in the film *Fight Command* that he was determined to marry her and they did after a seven-week courtship. They would have a son and daughter. In her spare time Hussey was an accomplished artist of watercolors. She also designed the family's vacation home in Lake Arrowhead, California. Her son later said, "My mom enjoyed sketching floor plans for years and we were all thrilled when she was able to make her architectural talent a reality."

Of her career Hussey would later say, "It [Hollywood] treated me well. I learned a lot about acting and I even got a mink coat." But by her own admission she wasn't a driven actress, "I just faded out of sight, I guess. I didn't seek work, but producers also didn't seek me." This suited Hussey fine, since it allowed her the time she wanted to spend with her family and her other interests. She died on April 19, 2005 at the age of 93 following complications from a recent hospital stay for appendicitis. (Sources include *Washington Post*, 4/21/05, "Always a Lady," *Classic Images*, August 2007, Colin Briggs and Gordon Leslie Hunter.)

OTTO KRUGER (September 6, 1885-September 6, 1974)

Otto Kruger became known to many moviegoers for his villainous roles; playing crooks, Nazis, and various other shady men, usually suave and debonair, but no less menacing. He later summed up his career: "For a while I played sad husbands, then I got nothing but lawyers. Then I was a doctor, and during the war I specialized in Nazis. Lately I've been playing sugar daddies." But along the way he was also given the opportunity to play some nice guys in some interesting films.

Kruger was born in Toledo, Ohio, on September 6, 1885. He was the grand nephew of South African president Paul Kruger. His early career was spent on the stage and he made his Broadway debut in *Natural Law* in 1915 when he was 30 years old. He also made his first film that year. However, he would only make a few more films before returning to the New York stage, where he would appear in a succession of plays between 1915 and 1932, including prominent roles in *The Royal Family, Counselor-at-Law* and *Private Lives*.

He returned to Hollywood in 1933 where he would stay for most of the rest of his career. His first film was *Turn Back the Clock* for MGM. That same year he appeared in Woody Van Dyke's *The Prizefighter and the Lady*, played Barbara Stanwyck's German husband-turned-spy in *Ever in My Heart*; and had a more sympathetic role as an adoptive father in Ann Harding's *Gallant Lady*. He even began appearing in a few leads (*The Crime Doctor, The Women in His Life, Springtime for Henry*), and made a proper Dr. Livesey in *Treasure Island* and played a psychiatrist who comes under the spell of *Dracula's Daughter.*

During the '40s he played more than his share of extreme villains, including Nazis in such films as *The Man I Married,* Alfred Hitchcock's *Saboteur, Hitler's Children* and *Tarzan's Desert Mystery.* During this time he also had prominent roles in such films as *Dr. Ehrlich's Magic Bullet, Corregidor, Murder, My Sweet,* and the District Attorney (not unlike his DA of *Another Thin Man*) in *Wonder Man.* During the war years, Kruger, who was an ardent gardener, worked as a food coordinator for the Los Angeles County Agricultural Department. In the late '40s Kruger went back to the Broadway stage, where he had hits with *Laura* and *A Time for Elizabeth.*

He returned to the screen sporadically after that. One of his best-known roles from the 1950s was that of the judge who skips town rather than help Gary Cooper face the man he sentenced in *High Noon.* He was also memorable in the hugely popular *Magnificent Obsession.* Kruger retired after playing a small role in the 1964 *Sex and the Single Girl,* starring Natalie Wood and Tony Curtis. He was in fragile health ever since suffering a stroke while appearing in the pre-Broadway tryouts for *Advise and Consent* in 1960. Kruger died at the Motion Picture and Television Hospital on his 89th birthday on September 6, 1974, following a series of small strokes. He was survived by his widow, Sue, and a daughter and three granddaughters. (Sources include *Hayward* (CA) *Daily Review,* 9/1/74, *Pasadena Star News,* 9/7/74.)

SHELDON LEONARD (February 22, 1907-January 10, 1997)

Sheldon Leonard had one of the most recognized faces in the movies — and voices. He was tall, dark, stocky, and had a menacing face with a voice out of Damon Runyon. Inevitably, Leonard would usually be cast as tough guys and often gangsters. But there was more to Sheldon Leonard than met the eye. His friends knew him as a well-educated and well-spoken man. He later became one of the most celebrated and successful television producers.

Leonard was born Sheldon Leonard Bershad in New York City, on February 22, 1907. He attended Syracuse University on a football scholarship, and was involved in water polo and the campus theater, becoming the president of the campus dramatic society. After graduating he secured an executive job on Wall Street. However, the stock market crash of 1929 meant the loss of this job, and to make ends meet he decided to become an actor. When he auditioned for roles he didn't look or sound like a romantic lead or the Wall Street executive he was, but as a hood, and he played several gangster roles on Broadway in such plays as *Hotel Alimony, Fly Away Home* and *Having Wonderful Time.* At the same time his distinctive voice made him a natural for radio and one of his best remembered roles was as a racetrack tout on *The Jack Benny Program,* where he would motion over to Benny and say in that distinctive voice, "Hey, bud . . . come here a minute" and then try to talk Benny into making a bad bet.

His role in *Another Thin Man* was only his fourth film and it was typical of the parts he played. The only variety is that at times the parts were comic and more clearly Runyanesque rather than menacing. The films include *Tall Dark and Handsome, Taxi, Mister, Weekend in Havana, Lucky Jordan* and *Hit the Ice.* In the mid-to late-'40s he appeared in three memorable films — *To Have and Have Not, It's a Wonderful Life* and *Decoy.* He continued to work into the 1950s as a movie actor with roles in *Money from Home* and *Guys and Dolls,* but he was appearing more often in television with a regular recurring role on *The Danny Thomas Show* as well as *The Jack Benny Program.*

It was as a partner with Danny Thomas that Leonard began to create and produce several well-regarded and long-running television series. According to the Museum of Broadcast Communication (MBC), "For nearly two decades, from the early 1950s through the late '60s, Sheldon Leonard was one of Hollywood's most successful hyphenates, producing — and often directing and writing — a distinctive array of situation comedies, of which three can be considered classics (*The Danny Thomas Show, The Andy Griffith Show The Dick Van Dyke Show*)." Of his decision to get into the creative end of the business Leonard once said, "Somebody said, 'if you don't like the way we're doing it — why don't you do it yourself' and the next thing I knew I was a director and then I became a producer from being chronically dissatisfied with directors."

As a television producer Sheldon Leonard was well known for his commitment to the quality of his scripts and he made it a rule to hire the best writers in television such as Danny Arnold, Garry Marshall and the team of Bill Persky and Sam Denoff.

Among the other television series that Leonard produced were *Gomer Pyle, U.S.M.C.* (spun off from *The Andy Griffith Show*), *I Spy, Good Morning World, My World and Welcome to It, Shirley's World* and *The Don Rickles Show*. *I Spy* was especially important due to Leonard's decision to cast an African American, comedian Bill Cosby, opposite Robert Culp, as one of the leads of the series. Cosby became the first black man to star in a dramatic television series and *Variety* dubbed him "Television's Jackie Robinson." Leonard himself later said of his casting of Cosby, "After that I felt I had left my mark on television." Cosby, in 1988, paid tribute to Leonard: "I could feel the support and that was very important. People who've worked for Sheldon will tell you that his good qualities rubbed off on them."

At this point Leonard still made occasional appearances in front of the cameras, usually sending up his own gangster persona, such as his appearance as "Big Max" Cardova on a 1964 episode of *The Dick Van Dyke Show*. He also made appearances on *Sanford and Son, The Cosby Show, Matlock, Murder, She Wrote* and *Cheers*. Leonard became, during the course of his producing career, one of the most honored men in the television industry winning three Emmys, a Golden Globe and an array of other honors from the television industry as well as recognition from such groups as the B'nai B'rith and NAACP for his work in forging brotherhood among all people. Leonard retired in the early '90s and devoted himself to his wife, two children and four grandchildren. He died in 1997, at the age of 89, shortly after being feted by the Director's Guild of America (DGA) for his accomplishments in the industry. (Sources include: *Variety*, January 1997.)

MARJORIE MAIN (February 24, 1890-April 10, 1975)

Marjorie Main made a career out of playing direct, no-nonsense types whose bark was worst than her bite. She eventually became a star in her own right playing "Ma Kettle" in a series of films which helped save Universal from financial straits. Damon Runyon once wrote of Main, "It is difficult for me to reconcile the name Marjorie with Miss Main's appearance, and her manner. She has a dead pan, square shoulders, a stocky build, a voice like a file, and an unhurried aspect. She has a stride like a section boss. She has bright, squinty eyes. She generally starts off looking as if she never smiled in her life, then suddenly she smiles from her eyes out."

Main was born, appropriately enough, in a cornfield near Acton, Indiana. Her birth name was Mary Tomlinson, the daughter of a fire-and-brimstone minister. Main was impressed by her father's dramatic voice; whether delivering a sermon or reading Dickens to his family while seated under a shade tree, the Rev. Tomlinson knew how to deliver his lines. The family's black maid took the young Marjorie to a Negro jubilee where the fascinated youngster enjoyed the skits which were performed and the spirituals which were sung. This awakened in her an interest in the theater. When she was determined to become an actress, her father balked because to his fundamentalist beliefs and upbringing show business and show people equaled sinfulness and wickedness. But Marjorie proved persuasive and talked her father into paying for her to attend Hamilton College, where she studied dramatics but told her father it was to teach rather than act.

After graduating she talked her father into allowing her to go on the Chautauqua circuit — one of those traveling tent shows — where she promised him that she would only perform Shakespeare. She earned $8 per week playing Katherine in *The Taming of the Shrew*. It was on the Chautauqua circuit that she met the man she would eventually marry, Dr. Stanley Krebbs, himself a former minister, who lectured on psychology. It was with Krebs that Mary Tomlinson chose Marjorie Main as her stage name. "There's a main street, main entrance, main event, main everything," the actress later explained. Dr. Krebs chose Marjorie for the first name. Giving herself a stage name was in part to appease her father who still opposed his daughter working as an actress. From the Chautauqua circuit Marjorie began performing with touring companies throughout the United States and eventually made her way to Broadway where she appeared in such prestigious Broadway hits as *Burlesque* (opposite a young Barbara Stanwyck), *Dead End* and *The Women*.

Main made her film debut in 1931 with a small role in *A House Divided*. She made relatively few films and devoted most of her time to the stage up until 1937. By now Main was a widow (Dr. Krebs died in 1935) when she repeated her role as the slum mother in the film version of *Dead End* memorably slapping Humphrey Bogart hard across the mouth and calling him a "dirty yellow dog." Indeed, for a woman who would eventually be known for her comedy roles, many of her memorable early roles were in dramatic parts. The same year she appeared as Barbara Stanwyck's mother in *Stella Dallas*. But the big break came when she signed with MGM in 1939, where, again repeating a stage role, she appeared in *The Women*. It was another MGM film that put her on the map at the studio, when, billed ninth, she appeared in the Wallace Beery film *Wyoming*. Her comic scenes with Beery reminded the studio of the chemistry he had in the early '30s with Marie Dressler. The studio upped Main to co-starring status with Beery in a series of films, including *Barnacle Bill*, *The Bugle Sounds*, *Jackass Mail* and *Bad Bascomb*. They had chemistry on screen, but off screen Main detested Beery for his bad manners and what she considered his unprofessionalism in changing his lines mid-scene.

In addition to working with Beery, MGM kept Main busy in many other pictures during her fourteen years with the studio: *Honky Tonk, Meet Me in St. Louis, The Harvey Girls, Summer Stock, The Belle of New York* and *The Long, Long Trailer*. During the '40s Main appeared in more than thirty films and became a recognizable face (and voice!) but remained unpretentious. She traveled to and from the studio by bus and ate many of her meals in studio cafeterias. She seldom socialized in the "Hollywood" way by going to parties.

It was on loan out to Universal that she landed the role of a lifetime — the boisterous Ma to Percy Kilbride's slow-moving, slow-speaking Pa Kettle in *The Egg and I* in 1947. Main and Kilbride stole the movie lock, stock and barrel from stars Claudette Colbert and Fred MacMurray. The film was a huge box office hit and Main was nominated for an Academy Award as Best Supporting Actress. In 1949 the studio decided it wanted to do a sequel, sans Colbert and MacMurray, starring Ma and Pa Kettle. The film was made for $400,000 and went on to gross $2 million. To cash in the studio began a series of films featuring Ma and Pa Kettle which by December of 1951 had produced three highly profitable films and led to *Colliers* to write, "The hottest box-office couple in Hollywood today are no enraptured celluloid lovebirds, but a thin, tattered little man who looks like a fugitive from a corn patch, and a broad-beamed, stringy-haired woman with the voice of an Iowa hog caller. Percy Kilbride and Marjorie Main have never evoked bobby-soxers' squeals or spinster's sighs, and in any compilation of famous screen lovers it is doubtful that they would receive even honorable mention. Still, as Ma and Pa Kettle, the harum-scarum hero and heroine of a continuing series of low-budget comedies, they have brought into the theaters an audience that Hollywood thought it had lost long ago." The noted producer Jerry Wald (*Mildred Pierce, Johnny Belinda*) weighted in his opinion on why the Kettle films were so popular by stating the movies were, "warm, human and humorous, like the early Will Rogers pictures." The series continued profitably until Kilbride decided to retire shortly after completing *Ma and Pa Kettle at Waikiki* in 1955. Main continued on with two more Kettle pictures without Kilbride, but the magic was gone. Main retired after completing *The Kettles on Old MacDonald's Farm* in 1957.

Even though she was retired, she was still recognizable thanks to television showings of her old pictures, especially the still-popular *Kettle* films. She would look back fondly on the old days, "I kinda liked the fuss. But I did enough acting to last me . . . 'Course I miss it, now and then. But I just wait a while and the mood passes." At the time of her death, at age 85, in 1975, Main was a very wealthy woman with homes in Beverly Hills, Palm Springs and at a mountain resort in Idyllwild, but she kept up each home herself; never hiring a housekeeper. (Sources include *Colliers*, 12/8/51.)

TOM NEAL (January 28, 1914-August 7, 1972)

Tom Neal made a career out of playing tough guys. Maybe the reason he was so effective at such roles was because in real life he was a tough guy who often went to the same extremes that some of his screen characters did. His greatest role was actually one of his most sympathetic: as a piano player who hitches a ride to California to be with his girlfriend and ends up accidentally killing two people in the *film noir Detour*. Little did Neal know at the time of its making that this film would be somewhat prophetic of what was to come in his real life.

Neal was born on January 28, 1914, the product of a wealthy family. He went to top schools, including Northwestern and Harvard University. His family wanted Neal to become an attorney, but Neal had an eye on an acting career. He did have talent and the brawny, dark good looks to be noticed and began performing in stock at West Falmouth, Massachusetts. In 1935 he made his Broadway debut in an anti-war drama, *If This be Treason*. Neal had a touch with scandal even then when he became engaged to a former Follies girl who had once been the girlfriend of a gangster. His father made sure that Neal knew that if he went any further with this relationship he would have his son disinherited from the million-dollar-plus family fortune. After a couple more Broadway productions he was signed, in 1937, by MGM.

Neal made his screen debut in the Andy Hardy picture *Out West with the Hardys* in 1938. Neal had small parts in many films over the next few years. In two of his early film appearances he worked with outstanding directors like Jacques Tourneur in *They All Came Out* and Fred Zimmermann in a short called *Help Wanted*. His role in *Another Thin Man*, playing the personal secretary (with a secret) of C. Aubrey Smith, was one of his first prominent roles in an A picture. But it really didn't lead to more "A"-level films and Neal continued to be a useful utility leading man or supporting player in programmers like *The Courageous Dr. Christian* and *Sky Murder*.

After not having his option picked up by MGM Neal went the freelancing route and appeared in films at most of the studios in town — major and minor: *The Flying Tigers, China Girl, Bowery at Midnight*, the serial *Jungle Girl* and *She Has What it Takes*. Neal then had a prominent role, which garnered its share of good reviews at the time, playing an U.S.-educated Japanese man in *Behind the Rising Sun* directed by Edward Dmytryk for RKO in 1943.

In 1945 Neal took the starring role in Edgar M. Ulmer's *noir* classic *Detour*, today considered one of the all-time best in the *noir* category. That same year Neal also appeared in Ulmer's *Club Havana*.

In 1946 Neal was used effectively at Universal in the mystery-suspenser *Blonde Alibi* playing a man suspected of murder. But more usual were his appearances in minor films like *The Brute Man*, *The Hat Box Mystery* and *The Case of the Baby Sitter*; and minor Westerns like *Apache Chief*, *Red Desert* and *The Daltons' Women*.

More and more it was Neal's personal life that was getting attention, not the films he made. In 1951 he was involved in a very public brawl with actor Franchot Tone over actress Barbara Payton (who was involved with Neal, but would later, briefly, become Tone's wife). One-time boxer Neal made mincemeat out of poor Tone, who suffered a fractured cheekbone, broken nose and a brain concussion. Problems like this, caused by Neal's explosive temper, made him unemployable. His Hollywood career was virtually over by the mid-'50s.

Neal was briefly married to actress Vicky Lane from 1948-1950. His second marriage, from 1956 to 1958, to Patricia Fenton, produced a son, Tom Neal, Jr., but he became a widower when Patricia died of cancer. Because he had become virtually unemployable in Hollywood, Neal moved to Palm Springs where he became the night manager of a nightclub/restaurant. He also operated a landscaping business. In 1961 Neal married for the third time, to Gail Bennett, a receptionist at the Palm Springs Tennis Club. This was a troubled marriage — and by 1965 the couple had separated. On April 1, 1965, Neal came to a restaurant owned by a friend of his and gave him the shocking news that he had just killed Gail — adding to the disbelieving friend, "It's not an April Fool's joke; it's true." Police arrived the next day (called by Neal's attorney) where they discovered Gail lying on a couch, partially covered by a bed spread. She had been shot behind the right ear with a .45 automatic. Neal surrendered to police.

When it was discovered that a public defender was going to represent Neal, Neal's friends decided he deserved better legal representation than that and several people in Palm Springs and Hollywood contributed to it (including Mickey Rooney, Blake Edwards, Dorothy Manners and, of all people, Franchot Tone). With this money Neal was able to get a prominent Palm Springs attorney to defend him. On the stand Neal said that he and his estranged wife were discussing a possible reconciliation when Neal said he wasn't sure that it was a good idea because she was allegedly "fooling around with all these guys." Apparently, according to Neal, this upset Gail, who was reclining on the couch with Neal on his knee next to her, and Neal was soon facing the barrel of a .45. According to Neal, he began struggling with her over the gun and she accidentally shot herself. The pathologist who performed the autopsy told the jury that Neal's account of the shooting was "unlikely." The jury deliberated for ten hours and then returned with the verdict of "involuntary manslaughter." Neal was sentenced to 15 years in prison. He was paroled on December 6, 1971 and told reporters that all his problems in his life had been caused by women. He moved back to Hollywood, where he died of a heart attack on August 7, 1972 — he was only 58. In *Detour* Neal uttered this immortal line, "Fate, or some mysterious force, can put the finger on you or me for no good reason at all." In Neal's case, fate had more than a little help from Tom Neal. (Sources include ***Bucks County Courier Times***, 8/8/72 & ***Palm Springs Life*** 5/07.)

C. AUBREY SMITH (July 21, 1863-December 20, 1948)

C. Aubrey Smith, more than any other actor, represented the stiff upper lip personification of the British Empire in motion pictures and, according to film historian Barry Monush, "could so marvelously evoke the spirit of England with the simple puff of his pipe." Long faced, with bushy eyebrows and a handlebar mustache, Smith looked every bit the Britain abroad.

He was born Charles Aubrey Smith, on July 21, 1863, the son of a London physician and was educated at Charterhouse School and Cambridge University. In school Smith didn't aspire to be an actor; he was an acclaimed British athlete. He played soccer for the Corinthians and cricket while at Cambridge. He became known as "round the corner Smith" due to his distinctive playing style and was involved in numerous champion matches around the empire. Upon graduation, he made plans of following the footsteps of his father into medicine, but ultimately he became a stockbroker. He later settled in South Africa during 1888-1889, where he tried his luck as a gold prospector. At age 29 Smith finally tried his hand at acting and launched a stage career with a London repertory company. One of Smith's first big successes on the London stage was playing Black Michael in *The Prisoner of Zenda*. In 1896 he married Isobel May Wood, and they would be devoted to one another for fifty years, and would produce one child. His greatest success on the London stage was succeeding the brilliant actor/stage manager Sir Herbert Beerbohm Tree as Professor Henry Higgins in *Pygmalion*. He managed to make the role his own. He appeared in several silent films, mostly made in London, but his major career during the '20s was alternating between the London and New York stage. Among the plays he performed in on Broadway were *Hamlet, The Constant Wife* and the lead role in *The Bachelor Father*.]

His real film career began in 1931, when he was already 68 years old, when MGM asked him to recreate his stage role of a rich but lonely old man who seeks out his three illegitimate children in *The Bachelor Father*. He had an uncredited role in Woody Van Dyke's *Trader Horn*. He then played an assortment of screen fathers: Leslie Howard's in *Never the Twain Shall Meet*; Robert Montgomery's in *The Man in Possession*; Franchot Tone's in *Bombshell*. Reunited with director Van Dyke, he was Jane's father who goes to Africa in search of an elephant's graveyard and loses his daughter to *Tarzan the Ape Man.* When he wasn't somebody's father, he often was cast as a pastor, such as his roles in *Guilty Hands* (again for director Woody Van Dyke) and *Polly of the Circus*. He played a variety of roles in several different types of films: he was the corrupt chairman of a cosmetics firm in the stylish comedy *Trouble in Paradise*; Greta Garbo's servant in *Queen Christina*; excellent as Freddie Bartholomew's grandfather in *Little Lord Fauntleroy*; an old actor who takes a liking to Katharine Hepburn in *Morning Glory*; a Roman General in *Cleopatra*; Ray Milland's father in *The Gilded Lily*; the Duke of Wellington in *The House of Rothschild*; the Prime Minister in *Clive of India*; Lord Capulet in *Romeo and Juliet*; Old Col. Williams befriended by Shirley Temple in *Wee Willie Winkie*; the Duke of Argyle in an adaptation of Robert Louis Stevenson's *Kidnapped*; and the crusty old industrialist who fears for his life in *Another Thin Man.* Hollywood certainly kept Smith busy during the '30s, appearing in 65 films between 1931 and 1939.

When he wasn't in front of the camera, Smith was the unofficial head of the so-called "British colony" in Hollywood, a sort of empire in exile which included Basil Rathbone, Nigel Bruce, Boris Karloff, Leslie Howard, Ronald Colman, David Niven, Laurence Olivier and Vivien Leigh. This group would get together for Sunday teas at Smith's Beverly Hills home. He was also the captain of the Hollywood Cricket Club which had its field on the north end of Griffith Park in the Hollywood Hills.

He slowed down a bit during the '40s, but he still managed to make twenty-six films between 1940 and 1948, including his Col. Julyan in Alfred Hitchcock's *Rebecca*; Robert Taylor's father in *Waterloo Bridge*; the Bishop in the Spencer Tracy version of *Dr. Jekyll and Mr. Hyde*; Col. Forsyth in *The White Cliffs of Dover*; one of the murder victims in *And Then There Were None*; the ghost in *Beyond Tomorrow*; a Scotland Yard detective in *Secrets of Scotland Yard*; the Chief Justice in *Unconquered*; and his final film, released after his death, playing Mr. Lawrence in *Little Women.*

Despite spending the war years in California, Smith was knighted in 1944, and was now Sir. C Aubrey Smith. In his final years Smith kept working despite loss of hearing and a recurring heart ailment. Shortly after filming *Little Women* Smith developed pneumonia and died peacefully at his Beverly Hills home. He was 85. (Sources include: *Berkshire Evening Eagle* 12/21/48, *Modesto Bee*, 12/29/48.)

REVIEWS:

"Powell, absent from films for more than eighteen months, comes back just where he left off, looking exceedingly fit after his long and successful battle with ill health and revealing, in the pleasure experienced in watching his portrayal, how sorely he has been missed."

The Hollywood Reporter, November 10, 1939

"In the gay tradition of its predecessors, howbeit a trifle more forced in its gayety, is *Another Thin Man*, latest of the Dashiell Hammett series to reach the Capitol's screen. With William Powell back in domestic harness as Nick Charles, with Myrna Loy as the almost too-perfect helpmate, and with — of all people — a Nick Jr. to guarantee the continuance of the series, this third of the trademarked *Thin Men* takes its murders as jauntily as ever, confirms our impression that matrimony need not be too serious a business and provides as light an entertainment as any holiday-amusement seeker is likely to find."

New York Times, November 24, 1939

"*Another Thin Man* is a double homecoming as the theater looks at it — the return of the popular 'Thin Man' stories to the screen, and ditto, William Powell. Powell's illness kept him out of pictures for nearly two years. He looks a little thinner, whiter, and more fragile, but he's still the smoothie theater patrons liked to see then, and still do."

Lincoln (NE) *Sunday Journal and Star*, December 10, 1939

"Made as a quickie in 14-days by Producer Hunt Stromberg and Director W.S. Van Dyke II, the first *Thin Man* revealed some surprising facts:

• Suave William Powell made a better raffish detective-husband than a romantic lover.

• Exotic Myrna Loy made a better wife than a siren.

• A wire-haired terrier named Asta (formerly Skippy) was the best canine actor since Rin Tin Tin.

• To the incredulous delight of U.S. cinemillions, two people could be in love though married.

• The *Thin Man* formula (exciting murder mystery plus fast, racy dialogue plus an equable, wise-cracking, Scotch-bibbing married couple plus real people in a weird jumbling together of underworld and overworld) was good for several more workings.

Another Thin Man is the third working. Shot in 36 days with extreme care by the same producer and director, again using a script by Frances Goodrich and Albert Hackett, it brought back William Powell as smart Detective Nick Charles, Myrna Loy as Nora, his imperturbable wife, Asta (cranky and snappy after a nervous breakdown) as their dog. It had the *Thin Man's* pace, bounce and snappy dialogue, exciting murder and air of amiable dipsomania. Nick and Nora take the pandemonium that passes for their domestic life with the same unquenchable good humor, poise, charm and thirst. But the spontaneity seems a little forced, the pace, jokes and charm a little grimly predetermined."

Time, December 11, 1939

"*** Murder strikes at a Long Island estate and the screen's favorite lush-detective couple . . . move in to solve it, although motherhood has slowed down Nora's drinking a bit. Enjoyable third entry in the series."

Leonard Maltin

Another Thin Man Photo Gallery

Nick and Nora are now parents of Little Nicky, as Asta looks on.

From Left to Right: Patric Knowles, Virginia Grey, Tom Neal, Myrna and Bill in *Another Thin Man*, 1939. COURTESY OF LAURA WAGNER.

Nick and Nora being held at bay by Sheldon Leonard in *Another Thin Man*.

The writers of the first three *Thin Man* films, Frances Goodrich and Albert Hackett.

CHAPTER SIX

SHADOW OF THE THIN MAN

CAST: William Powell (Nick Charles), Myrna Loy (Nora Charles), Barry Nelson (Paul Clarke), Donna Reed (Molly Ford), Sam Levene (Lt. Abrams), Alan Baxter ("Whitey"), Harry O'Neill (Major Jason I. Sculley), Dickie Hall (Nick, Jr.), Stella Adler (Claire Porter), Loring Smith (Link Stephens), Joseph Anthony (Joe Macy), Louise Beavers (Stella), Asta.

COMPANY CREDITS: Major W.S. Van Dyke II (Director), Hunt Stromberg (Producer), Irving Brecher and Harry Kurnitz (Screenwriters), Robert J. Kern (Editor), David Snell (Original Music), Cedric Gibbons (Art Direction), Edwin Willis (Set Direction), William H. Daniels (Cinematographer).

PRODUCTION DATES: August 3-late August of 1941. Released: November 21, 1941 (New York). Black and White. 99 minutes.

SYNOPSIS:

The film opens with a happy and content Nick Charles walking with his young son, no longer the infant he was in the prior adventure, now about four or five years old, and, if the uniform is any indication, he is in military school. Nick is walking while holding a newspaper which is inside a children's storybook. He has Nick, Jr. on a leash, who, in turn, is holding Asta on a leash. Our first look at Asta has him emerging from behind some bushes obviously doing what a dog has to do. It's apparently Nick's turn to take Nicky to the park and as they sit down on a bench, Nicky asks Nick to read him a story. Of course Nick makes up a story

Poster for the third sequel, *Shadow of the Thin Man*.

("Once upon a time") based on the racing form he is reading in the morning paper! Nicky is wise to him and finally tells Nick to just read him the racing form. Meanwhile, Nora and the Charleses' maid Stella (Louise Beavers) are watching father and son from Nick and Nora's penthouse window. Nora keeps wondering when Nick will be returning, but is happy that they are having father/son time together. Stella, looking at the scene in binoculars, can't believe that Nick Charles is sitting happily reading Nicky a story on the park bench. Suddenly, Nick says to Nicky, "Nicky, something tells me that something important is happening somewhere and I think we should be there." Cut to Nora, who is shaking up a cocktail! Stella is certain that Nick has returned to their apartment because he somehow, by intuition, heard the cocktails being mixed. Nick is again retired and happily enjoying his family and managing Nora's money. But, naturally, behind the happy domestic existence, lurks murder on the horizon.

This time they are back in San Francisco. So far, the first four films have been divided between the two coasts. In *The Thin Man* and *Another Thin Man*, the Charleses are in New York while in *After the Thin Man* and *Shadow of the Thin Man* they are in San Francisco.

On a lark, Nick and Nora decide to have some adult playtime away from little Nicky and go to the races. On their way Nick is pulled over by a police officer for driving too fast:

NICK (to Nora): Thank Goodness, neither one of us was driving.

The officer asks Nick for ID and, as Nick hesitates to open his wallet, the officer says, "Wider, wider."

NORA: You see, dear, if you went to the dentist when you should he wouldn't have to follow you around on a motorcycle.

Naturally, the officer recognizes the famous Nick Charles, detective, and as he is writing Nick a ticket the officer asks Nick what case he's working on. "Right now, trying to get out of a ticket," says Nick. Nick explains to the officer that he and Nora are off to the races, and after giving the ticket to Nick (no, the officer didn't fix Nick's ticket), he offers to escort Nick and Nora to the racetrack. While en route, there is a terrific commotion, several motorcycled police officers and an ambulance with Nick and Nora in the middle, but it turns out they are all on their way to the same place: the race track.

At the track, Nick and Nora learn that a jockey who lost a race the previous day, Gomez, has been murdered, possibly for throwing the race. Nora gives a reply which would make Marie Wilson proud: "My, they're strict at this track." Nick joins his old sparring partner, Lt. Abrams (Sam Levene, in a repeat appearance from *After the Thin Man*), in the jockey dressing room as Abrams begins his investigation. Naturally, the reporters present all assume that Nick Charles is out of retirement and on the case. Nick tries to assure them that he's not on the case, as he tried to do in the first two films. While insisting that his detective days are over, Nick can't help but be intrigued when one of Gomez's jockey pals tells the police that he believes that Gomez had been murdered because he refused to throw a race.

That night, Nick is visited by Major Sculley (Henry O'Neill) and a Paul Clarke (Barry Nelson), an investigative reporter looking into the murder and allegations that the jockey had been murdered. Major Sculley beseeches Nick to help investigate the death. But Nick is adamant that his days as a detective are over. The Major tells Nick that he's the only man who can solve the case, to which Nora, who is just walking into the room, replies, "Nick can do anything." Nick tells her, "My, what big ears you have." But Nick still insists that he is retired as a detective, and, besides, he is going to take Nora to a wrestling match that night. This is Nora's first wrestling match and she gets so involved in the proceedings that she suddenly grabs Nick around the neck and attempts to hold him in a half-nelson.

While at the wrestling match another reporter, "Whitey" (Alan Baxter), a rival of Paul Clarke's, blackmails racketeer "Link" Stephens (Loring Smith) girlfriend, Claire Porter (Stella Adler), into giving him an expensive diamond bracelet. Naturally, at the fights, Nick is surrounded by many of his less-than-reputable old "friends" — and Nora is in her element. One such friend is "Rainbow" Benny Loomis

(Lou Lubin), who goes to Stephens' upstairs office, but hides when he hears Whitey come in and demands that Stephens pay him hush money to keep his name out of the papers. It turns out that Whitey owes Benny $8,000, which is one of the reasons why he was shaking down both Stephens and his girlfriend.

Meanwhile, in a nearby restaurant, we are introduced to Paul's girlfriend, Molly Ford (Donna Reed), who is helping him in his investigation while working undercover as Stephens' secretary. Though it is against her better judgment, she winds up giving Paul her key to the office door. Later, Paul uses the key to search Stephens' office, where he discovers a notebook which may have some incriminating evidence. It is at this point that Paul is confronted by Whitey who demands the notebook. The two reporters get into a fight and when Paul knocks his head against the desk, Whitey grabs the notebook. As Whitey is about to make his escape, he is shot dead; meanwhile, a night watchman observes Benny running down the stairs.

After the wrestling match Nick and Nora again run into Lt. Abrams, who informs them of Whitey's murder. They join Abrams interrogating a still dazed Paul in Stephens' office. Nora, as usual, is on the side of the underdog, and she is sure that Paul is innocent of any wrongdoing and urges Nick to take on the case after Paul is arrested by Lt. Abrams. Nick reluctantly agrees to look into things.

Once again, as in every *Thin Man* film, Nick takes Asta with him to investigate. This time they go to the racetrack where Nick searches the jockey room; it is there that Nick discovers evidence that Gomez wasn't murdered, but had accidentally killed himself. But he still believes that there is some kind of tie-in between Gomez killing himself and the murder of Whitey. So he tricks Abrams into making a statement that the police are convinced that Gomez and Whitey were both killed by the same person and that Paul is being released from police custody. Meanwhile, Nick pays a visit to Claire who says that she hardly knew Whitey, but her mounting anger makes Nick doubt what she is saying. Then Nick and Asta pay a visit to Whitey's apartment, where the diamond bracelet that Whitey had forced Claire to give him is found. Suddenly, Claire arrives at Whitey's apartment and Nick and Asta hide so that he can observe her movements. She is searching for something — no doubt the bracelet — which Nick then confronts her with. She admits to Nick that it is her bracelet and that Whitey had blackmailed her for it, but doubts that Stephens knew that she had once been Whitey's girlfriend. She also makes Nick aware of the money that Whitey owed to Benny — the $8,000.

That night Nick and Nora meet Paul and Molly for dinner and Nick runs into Benny and tells him that the night watchman had observed him leaving the premises the night of Whitey's murder. Nick also discovers that a very nervous Benny is wearing a bullet-proof vest. Paul then calls Col. Sculley telling him that Nick needs information, and Sculley agrees to meet them at Benny's apartment building. When Nick, Nora, Abrams and Paul meet Sculley at Benny's apartment building he takes them directly to Benny's room where they discover Benny's hanging body. Nick observes marks around the neck which are inconsistent with suicide and believes that Benny was murdered. Abram's disagrees and points out the lacerations:

NICK: Yes, but not raw lacerations like that. I think he was strangled first with a rough, heavy cord, a rope. And then the stage was set for this overturned chair, the chandelier, the sash. And another thing: When Benny skipped out of Mario's [the restaurant] tonight, he was wearing a bulletproof vest.

ABRAMS: What?

NICK: It's not on him anymore.

ABRAMS: Maybe he took it off.

NICK: Or it was *taken* off.

ABRAMS: By who?

NICK: By whoever hung him there. Our murderer didn't want us to know Benny was living in fear of his life.

They also find remnants of the notebook that Whitey had taken from Paul when they had scuffled just prior to Whitey being murdered.

Nick begins to put two-plus-two together and calls for all the suspects to assemble the next day in Abram's office. As usual, all the suspects have some kind of motive for the killing, but a vital clue is disclosed by Nick: Benny had only lived in the apartment building for *three hours* prior to his murder. When the murderer is revealed by Nick, he makes an attempt to shoot Nick, but brave-hearted Nora jumps him.

BEST LINE:
NORA (to Stella): He's [Nick, Jr.] getting more like his father every day.

STELLA: He sure is. This morning he was playing with a corkscrew.

THE WRITERS:
HARRY KURNITZ (January 5, 1908-March 18, 1968)
Harry Kurnitz was a noted playwright and screenwriter who was once considered the "court jester" to a Hollywood group which included such luminaries as Cole Porter, Billy Wilder, John Huston, Moss Hart and George S. Kaufman. He was noted for his self-depreciating sense of humor. "What I remember mainly about Harry's courtship," his one-time fiancée, actress Patricia Englund, once said, "is that I couldn't stop laughing."

Kurnitz was born on March 18, 1908 and spent his early career as both a reporter and pulp mystery writer, writing mysteries under the pen name Maroo Page. He was invited to Hollywood in 1938 to adapt one of his mysteries, *Fast Company* (which was directed by *Song of the Thin Man's* Edward Buzzell), for the screen. The film starred Melvyn Douglas as an antique book collector who solves mysteries with Florence Rice as his interfering wife. The film was more than a little inspired by the successful husband-wife *Thin Man* novel and inspired two sequels, the best being the second, *Fast and Loose* (also written by Kurnitz), which starred Robert Montgomery and Rosalind Russell.

Kurnitz stayed in Hollywood and at MGM for the next few years writing two back-to-back screenplays for William Powell and Myrna Loy (*I Love You, Again* and, in collaboration with Irving Brecher, *Shadow of the Thin Man*). His other screenplays include the very popular Robert Walker-Donna Reed wartime comedy *See Here, Private Hargrove* (for which Kurnitz was nominated for his only Academy Award for his screenplay) and its sequel *What Next, Corporal Hargrove?* He contributed to the William Powell-Hedy Lamarr film *The Heavenly Body*, and contributed the story to *The Thin Man Goes Home* (the script was by Robert Riskin). After the war Kurnitz went to Warner Brothers, where he wrote *Adventures of Don Juan* for Errol Flynn, My Dream is Yours for Doris Day and *The Inspector General* for Danny Kaye.

In the 1950s he began writing for the Broadway stage, writing the shows *Reclining Figure* and *Once More with Feeling. Once More with Feeling* proved to be a moderate success and was made into a film in 1960 starring Yul Brynner. Other films he wrote during the '50s include *Tonight We Sing, The Love Lottery, Land of the Pharaohs*, and in 1957 collaborated with Billy Wilder on the film version of Agatha Christie's *Witness for the Prosecution* (for which he received an "Edgar" award (so named for Edgar Allen Poe) from the Mystery Writers of America). According to Wilder biographer Ed Sikov, "Billy specifically picked Harry Kurnitz to write this murder mystery because Kurnitz was not only an Anglophile but also an experienced writer of mysteries."

In the '60s Kurnitz wrote the story for what became the Howard Hawks film Hatari!, as well as screenplays for *Goodbye Charlie* and *How to Steal a Million* (released in 1966, it was his last film). His greatest success of the decade was writing the play *A Shot in the Dark* and later helping to adapt it to the screen for the Blake Edwards film starring Peter Sellers as Inspector Clouseau. This took great effort since the Clouseau character was not in the original play. He was nominated for a Tony Award for writing the musical *The Girl Who Came to Dinner* in 1963.

Kurnitz died of complications from a heart attack on March 18, 1968; he was only sixty. At the time of his sudden death, Kurnitz was preparing to work again with Billy Wilder; this time on the film which ultimately became Wilder's The Private Life of Sherlock Holmes. (Sources include *Long Beach Independent Press-Telegram*, 3/29/68.)

IRVING BRECHER (January 14, 1914)

Several men connected in some way with the Marx Brothers were associated with some of the *Thin Man* films (Nat Perrin and Edward Buzzell, for example), another is Irving Brecher, who contributed to screenplays for two of the Marxes' films, *At the Circus* and *Go West*. In addition to his work as a motion picture writer he was an innovative radio and television writer-producer, creating the popular radio/television series *The Life of Riley*. He was known among his friends for his abundance of wisecracks and as one of the best "gag" men in the business. Mervyn LeRoy called Brecher, "The undisputed king of gag men, living or dead." S.J. Perelman called Brecher, "one of the three quickest wits in America," the others being George S. Kaufman and Oscar Levant.

Brecher was born on January 14, 1914, in New York City. By the time he was 19 Brecher was working as an usher at the Little Carnegie Playhouse and occasionally writing gags for stage performers like Milton Berle. Berle was known in the industry (and often lampooned by himself) for stealing gags by other comics. Brecher thought that he could get Berle's attention by placing an ad in *Daily Variety* which said that his (Brecher's) gags were "Berle proof." This did get Milton's attention and Berle called Brecher up and said, "This is Milton Berle!" Brecher thought it was a friend playing a practical joke and hung up, but Berle called back and convinced Brecher he was who he was and told him, "If you're so damn smart be over at the Capital Theater tonight . . . and bring some jokes." That was the start of his professional career. It was with Berle that Brecher got his start in radio as the writer of Berle's *Gillette Community Sing*.

At age twenty-four Brecher was brought to Hollywood by producer-director Mervyn LeRoy and put under personal contract at $650 per week. He wrote the screenplay *New Faces of 1937* (which starred Berle) and then wrote uncredited dialogue for the film *Fools for Scandal* (LeRoy told Brecher, "The screenplay's just not funny enough. I need you to punch it up") and *The Wizard of Oz*, which was produced by LeRoy. He always downplayed his contribution to *The Wizard of Oz.* "I wrote some amusing stuff for the Cowardly Lion, and the exaggerations, the silliness of the wizard." Then came his two Marx Brothers films. It was a dream come true for Brecher who had grown up idolizing the Marx Brothers and saw many of their stage shows. He had worshipped Groucho since the time he was a kid. "When I was a teenager, the night editor of the *Yonkers Herald Statesman*, where I worked, gave me a movie pass — worth twenty-five cents, to see *Animal Crackers* and I was on the floor. I stayed in the theater and watched it a second time. I couldn't get it out of my head. I started to do my own version of Groucho Marx." One of his brightest memories of *At the Circus* is the scene where Eve Arden stuffs some cash that Groucho wants down the front of her leotard. Groucho wanted a wisecrack to get out of the scene and director Edward Buzzell and producer LeRoy immediately summoned Brecher to the set. "And then I said, 'How about this? There's got to be some way of getting the money back without getting in trouble with the Hays' Office." Groucho loved the line, but Buzzell didn't think that audiences would get it and refused to film it. LeRoy asked director S. Sylvan Simon to shoot the line and, according to Brecher, the result at the preview was two minutes of solid laughter.

After working with the Marxes, Brecher's next project was *Shadow of the Thin Man* in collaboration with Harry Kurnitz. This was the first *Thin Man* film not written by Hackett and Goodrich, which made Brecher a bit nervous. "The first three were of a consistently high level, but each was lesser than the other, so we hoped that we could put some new life in an aging series — and I think we succeeded." He then worked on the screenplays for a series of delightful MGM musicals: *Ship Ahoy, Best Foot Forward, DuBarry was a Lady, Yolanda and the Thief, Ziegfeld Follies* and *Summer Holiday.* But the best, and probably the best of his career, was 1944's *Meet Me in St. Louis.*

During the '40s Brecher created a radio show, a sitcom about a good intentioned but not terribly bright family man named Chester A. Riley. In its initial conception the role was tailored for Groucho Marx, but it didn't sell — later the character was changed to adapt to the talents of character actor William Bendix and the radio show sold and became a huge hit running for seven years. It later was adapted into a movie (also directed by Brecher) and television show which initially starred Bendix and later, in his first big television role, Jackie Gleason. It was Brecher who came up with Riley's trademark saying, "What a revoltin' development this is." Brecher's final film as a screenwriter was the 1963 musical *Bye, Bye Birdie*, based on the popular Broadway show.

During the '50s, apparently without his knowledge, Brecher had been blacklisted. He was shown a list of affiliations he belonged to which he was told were suspect (Hollywood Democratic Committee and Bundles for Russia, for example). He had wondered why his phone hadn't been ringing with offers of work. He had been living off the licensing fees of his television shows. Brecher was told that to get off the blacklist he needed to appeal to two of the biggest anti-communist reactionaries in the industry, character actor Ward Bond and Carpenters Union chief Roy Brewer. "Ward Bond, that prick," Brecher later said, "and Roy Brewer . . . you had to write them a letter explaining your past associations. They would either clear you or condemn you to death. And I wrote the letter — the worst job I ever did."

Now 93 years young, Brecher still stays active giving interviews about his long career and appearing at nostalgia shows. He is also in demand to give eulogies at funerals. "I like to do eulogies, but only if I can make people laugh at the services. There was this one where I was looking down, and I can't read my own notes. I said, 'This morning my eyesight was so bad I couldn't find my hearing aid.'" (Sources include *Forward*, 8/3/01.)

THE BACK STORY:

William Powell and Myrna Loy share a soundstage for a major MGM film for the third time in fourteen months with *Shadow of the Thin Man*. In April of 1940 they shot *I Love You, Again*. They then reunited in February of 1941 for Love Crazy and then on August 3, 1941 began three weeks of principal photography on *Shadow of the Thin Man*, the Charleses' fourth adventure in seven years.

This film is important as the last featuring director W.S. Van Dyke and producer Hunt Stromberg. By this time the Van Dyke-Stromberg relationship had cooled. As early as 1938, after a period of eleven years of working closely as a producer-director team, Stromberg appeared to be getting frustrated by Van Dyke's work. He wrote a memo to Van Dyke about what he thought were some of the problems he was observing in the rushes of their latest picture together, *Sweethearts*: "Important lines lost in unnatural speed . . . Discrepancies like this are occurring in practically every scene . . . Proving that there is no reading of the script (by you) nor understanding of the story. All coming under the head of gross carelessness and arrogance since these scenes are not being interpreted in any degree of consistency with the main story idea, nor even the characterization idea . . . If we continue like this there will be unreasonable amount of retakes." Stromberg went so far as to say, "So far as I am concerned this can be the last picture, as it seems that our past wonderful relationship cannot be continued on this basis." Was Van Dyke's reputation as a speed fiend finally catching up with him and he was now getting careless? Despite this memo, Stromberg and Van Dyke did work together again on three pictures, including *Another Thin Man* and *Shadow of the Thin Man.*

This was also the first *Thin Man* film not written for the screen by Frances Goodrich and Albert Hackett. Stromberg assigned Irving Brecher and Harry Kurnitz to adapt a story by Elliot Paul to screenplay. Brecher was assigned to the picture on the recommendation of Melvyn LeRoy to Hunt Stromberg. Brecher later said that he found Hunt Stromberg, "the most able producer of my experience." That is saying a lot since Brecher worked with some very strong and talented producers in his time, including LeRoy and Arthur Freed, who were responsible for so many of the classic MGM musicals of the '40s and '50s. Here is what Brecher had to say about the writing of *Shadow of the Thin Man*: "I was assigned to do the script of *Shadow of the Thin Man* with a friend of mine, Harry Kurnitz. The story was by Elliot Paul, but there wasn't a helluva lot of story and it had a lot of problems. Kurnitz and I worked together for a little while and then Kurnitz left to do something else and I worked alone. Stromberg was an education. Here was a man who made you write better than you thought you could. He was indefatigable in terms of taste. He was never in a hurry, always encouraging. If he disapproved of something, he didn't just say, 'It's no good,' he told you why. He was a sick man, in great pain all the time, but a wonderful man. I wrote that for him, and I think that one made me feel more of a writer than just, you know, a comedy man."

The cinematographer on *Shadow of the Thin Man* was William H. Daniels. Daniels was born in Cleveland, Ohio, on December 1, 1901. Educated at USC, he later became known around MGM as Greta Garbo's favorite cameraman. She requested him for nearly every picture after their first, *Flesh and the Devil*, and he served as director of photography on some of her greatest films, including *Love, Anna Christie, Grand Hotel, Anna Karenina, Camille,* and *Ninotchka*. He had worked with Powell and Loy, too, in *Double Wedding* and the previous *Thin Man* film, *Another Thin Man*. In the mid-'40s Daniels had a contract dispute with the studio which led to his leaving, but it didn't stop his career. In 1948 he was the director of photography of the very realistic *The Naked City*, which was shot on location in New York City. He also did such gritty films as *Brute Force* and *Winchester '73*. In the late '50s thru the middle-'60s Daniels graduated from being Garbo's favorite cameraman to being Frank Sinatra's in such films as *Some Came Running, Never So Few, Can-Can, Von Ryan's Express* and *Marriage on the Rocks*. Daniels served as President of the American Society of Cinematographers from 1961-1963 and died on June 14, 1970 shortly after filming *Move* with Elliot Gould.

Of *Shadow of the Thin Man*, Myrna Loy would say, "I don't recall much [about the film] except that Bill's prediction about Nick Charles, Jr., came true. He was already off to military school." It turns out that when the Hacketts got Nora pregnant and introduced Nick, Jr., in *Another Thin Man*, Bill confided in Myrna, "Why do we want this kid? First thing you know he'll be in kindergarten, then prep school, then college. How old will that make us?" Myrna recalls that Bill, then in his mid-forties, was "very conscious of aging." One of the things he did to hide the aging process was dye his hair. "When I saw him in the hospital after his operation, it amazed me to find him with gray, almost white hair. I never knew he'd been dyeing it all those years. He really didn't like being seen that way, even by his screen wife. 'There's a factory down here that gives off silver dust,' he explained. 'It blows through the window into my hair.'"

This would be the final Nick and Nora adventure for nearly four years, and even then it took some doing in getting Myrna Loy to return to play Nora Charles.

SUPPORTING ACTORS:
STELLA ADLER (February 10, 1901-December 21, 1992)

Stella Adler acted in only three films in her career but she can be thanked for helping revolutionize the American cinema through her work as an acting teacher and coach and influencing such actors as Marlon Brando, Robert De Niro, Warren Beatty and Candice Bergen.

Adler was born on February 1, 1901 in New York City. She was the youngest daughter of Yiddish theater actors Jacob P. Adler and Sarah Adler. In addition to her parents, all of her siblings eventually became actors and performed on the New York stage. It was eventually estimated that by 1939 fifteen members of the Adler family were contributing to the Yiddish theater and Group Theater in New York. The Adler family owned a theater, and it was in this theater, at the age of four, in 1905 that Adler made her debut as an actress in the play *Broken Hearts*. At the age of eighteen she went to London, where she worked for a year in the play *Elisa Ben Avia*. She would then spend the next ten years performing on stages throughout the United States and Europe. It is estimated that during those years she appeared in over one-hundred plays as an actress.

In the late '20s Adler began appearing on the Broadway stage and over a ten-year period she appeared in thirteen Broadway shows, none of which was really a huge hit. It was as part of the Yiddish theater that she made her biggest impact, adapting classical plays into Yiddish — Shakespeare, Ibsen, Tolstoy, among others. She also played female as well as male parts in some of these productions.

In 1931 Adler joined the prestigious New York Group Theater. This theater was formed by such theater luminaries as Harold Clurman, Lee Strasberg and Cheryl Crawford. The Group Theater was a cooperative ensemble which believed in presenting contemporary material which emphasized realism, not only with its material but by the way the actors presented the material. The principles of acting taught by the Group Theater were heavily influenced by

Konstantin Stanislavsky's "Method" where the actors attempted to find theatrical truths by replicating real-life emotions and creating characterizations which came from within the actors themselves based on their own experiences, emotions and memories. It was with the Group Theater that Adler performed in such plays as *Success Story, Awake and Sing* and *Paradise Lost* (the latter two by one of the Group Theatre's great playwrights, Clifford Odets). In 1934 Adler took leave from the Group Theater and traveled to Russia where she studied for five weeks in the Moscow Art Theater, and had private lessons with Stanislavsky himself.

Despite her success as a stage actress she wanted what many actors dreamed: to become a successful film actress and, in 1937, she went to Hollywood to pursue this goal. But her unconventional looks didn't work in her favor and she wound up appearing in only a few films, of which her role in *Shadow of the Thin Man* is probably her most prominent. She also served as an associate producer at MGM during those years. Giving up on her film dreams, Adler returned to the New York stage where she alternated between performing and directing. As a performer she appeared in *Sons and Soldiers* in 1943 and later that same year directed *Manhattan Nocturne.*

She didn't return to the Group Theater, however, as she began to feel uncomfortable with their ideas and politics. For instance, Lee Strasberg interpreted the "Method" through memory exercises which Adler thought was "sick" as well as misguided. Instead, she began teaching with the New School in the mid-'40s. It was here that she was tutor and mentor to the young Marlon Brando. (Brando would later write, "Little did she know that through her teachings she would impact theater culture worldwide. Almost all filmmakers everywhere in the world have felt the effects of American films, which have been in turn influenced by Stella Adler's teachings. She is loved by many and we owe her much.") Adler maintained that "the theater exists 99% in the imagination" and believed that the actor must come to terms with the emotional origins of the script and to "read between the lines" of what the playwright is trying to put across rather than primarily drawing on their own experiences as Strasberg had taught. Her motto was, "You act with your soul. That's why you all want to be actors, because your souls are not used up by life." In 1949, with her second husband, Harold Clurman, Adler established her own acting school, The Stella Adler Conservatory of Acting.

She was now devoting more time to teaching and less to acting. She made her final appearance as an actress in the play *He Who Gets Slapped* in 1946 and staged her final Broadway play, *Sunday Breakfast*, in 1952. She also became an adjunct professor of acting at the School of Drama at Yale University where she taught script analysis. At her own school she began teaching courses for advanced students and professional actors and attracted lecturers such as Sir John Gielgud and Arthur Laurents. In 1960 Adler and Clurman divorced and she later married Mitchell Wilson, a union which lasted until his death in 1973. She never remarried. In the '80s she wrote an influential book on her principles of acting, *Stella Adler on Acting*. She stayed active almost to the end. She died on December 21, 1992 of heart failure in her sleep at the age of 91. Robert De Niro would recall her as "the first teacher who actually inspired me on stage. Stella would say 'your talent lies in your choice.' Her sense of what character should be enabled her to teach acting in its purest form." (Sources include *West Virginia Chronicle-Telegram*, 12/22/92, *Oakland Tribune*, 7/3/04.)

LOUISE BEAVERS (March 8, 1902-October 26, 1962)

Louise Beavers was an African-American character actress who became one of the first actors of her race to play a role which was equal to that of the white lead when cast opposite Claudette Colbert in the original version of *Imitation of Life*. Despite her superb performance in this film, Beavers never got another opportunity to so dominate a movie. She was often in competition with Hattie McDaniel (Mammy in *Gone With the Wind*) for roles and believed that she was often on the losing end of the competition once saying, "I get the parts Hattie McDaniel turns down."

Beavers was born on March 8, 1902, in Cincinnati, Ohio. At the age of eleven her family settled in Pasadena, California and she attended public schools. At an early age she aspired to be a doctor, but in that day and age it was difficult for an African-American woman to follow such dreams and she drifted into work as a domestic. She began her show business career as a minstrel singer. (On occasion in films, such as *Holiday Inn* (1942), Beavers had an opportunity to display her singing voice.) She performed for some years as part of an act called "Lady Minstrels." When she went to Hollywood, it wasn't as an actress but as the maid to silent film star Leatrice Joy (as well as actress Lilyan Tashman). But she soon got an opportunity to appear as an extra in several films before making her first impact on the screen playing the cook in the 1927 silent film, *Uncle Tom's Cabin*.

In mainstream Hollywood films African-American actors were played mainly as (1) slow-witted comic relief (especially male actors) or (2) as (sometimes) sassy maids, the dominant role that Beavers played throughout much of her career. But she always made the most out of the part, no matter how small, and often gave her characters more personality just by her presence. She played maids in such films as *Back Pay, Our Blushing Brides, Girls About Town, Bombshell, The Dark Horse,* and *What Price Hollywood?* Hollywood had the idea that black actresses had to be jovially fat, yet, in "real life," Beavers wasn't naturally overweight, but the studios wanted her plump and insisted that she eat extra servings of food so that she would have the "right look" for the "Mammy" types of roles that were often the only parts available to black actresses in that era. Beavers said she wanted to do more serious roles — perhaps on the stage — but with the Depression raging on she took what she could get. "Money was scarce so Hollywood won."

In 1933 Beavers had perhaps her most famous "maid" role, playing Pearl, Mae West's maid, in *She Done Him Wrong*.

PEARL: Oh, Miss Lou, you's so rich.

LOU: I wasn't always rich . . . I was once so poor I didn't know where my next husband was comin' from.

Pearl is not only a servant but a confidant to the Mae West character. In fact, Beavers played this confidant to the white heroine in several of her films. "Beavers was a perfect foil and background flavor for such Depression heroines as Jean Harlow, Mae West, and Claudette Colbert," writes author Donald Bogle, "women forced by the times to be on their own, yet needing someone in their corner to cheer them up when things looked too rough, to advise them when personal problems overwhelmed them."

Then in 1934 came *Imitation of Life*, where two women, one white (Claudette Colbert) and one black (Beavers), with children, decide to pool their money together and go into business. For the time this was a very progressive concept. Of course, it had its limits since it was Colbert's business know-how, along with Beaver's "Aunt Jemimah" image and recipes which makes their business successful. But the film also was groundbreaking in attempting to address social issues such as light-skinned Negroes vs. dark-skinned Negroes. (In the film Beaver's daughter is light skinned and can easily pass as white.) Beavers convincingly played her role as a cook (in real life Beavers detested cooking) and captured the pathos of having a child who doesn't want to publicly acknowledge her as her mother. The making of the film couldn't have been a pleasurable one for Beavers. In an early scene a child playing the young daughter of the Beavers character screamed that she didn't want Beavers to play her mother because "she's black!" Then the front office decided to punish Beavers for successfully having the word "nigger" removed from the *Imitation of Life* script (with the help of the NAACP) by having her say the word "Negro" repeatedly in front of lily-white executives. But despite this she gives a superb performance which should have been nominated for an Oscar, but wasn't. Hollywood columnist Jimmy Fiddler objected at the time, "I also lament the fact that the motion picture industry has not set aside racial prejudice in naming actresses. I don't see how it is possible to overlook the magnificent portrayal of the Negro actress, Louise Beavers, who played the mother in *Imitation of Life*. If the industry chooses to ignore Miss Beaver's performance, please let this reporter, born and bred in the South, tender a special award of praise to Louise Beavers for the finest performance of 1934."

After that Beavers would have one more fairly substantial role, and one which let her truly stretch her talents, in *Rainbow on the River*, in which she played an ex-slave who raises a white boy after the Civil War. Other than that it was the usual assortment of cooks/maids: *Gambling Lady, The Last Gangster, Made for Each Other* (offering Carole Lombard such tidbits as "Enduring hardships is like eating watermelon. You just have to learn to spit out the seeds and enjoy the melon"), *No Time for Comedy, Shadow of the Thin Man, Holiday Inn* (perhaps with the exception of *Imitation of Life*, her best-known role), *Tennessee Johnson, Mr. Blandings Builds His Dream House* (saving the day at the end when her character comes up with a slogan which saves ad-man Cary Grant's job: "Not ham! Wham! If you ain't eating Wham, you ain't eating ham!"), and *Good Sam*. One of her last substantial roles was playing Jackie Robinson's mother in *The Jackie Robinson Story*.

In the 1950s she began to appear on television, taking over for Hattie McDaniel as *Beulah* (as a maid, but the lead character) and as a regular on *The Danny Thomas Show*. She also appeared on stage with Mae West in the mid-'50s in places like Las Vegas where she reprised the role of Pearl, Mae's maid from *She Done Him Wrong*. Her final film role was as Lucille Ball's maid in *The Facts of Life* in 1960. (She also played Lucy's maid in the films *The Big Street* and *Lover Come Back*.) Beavers suffered from diabetes for many years and her health caught up with her on October 26, 1962 when she died of a heart attack at age 60. She is buried in the grave of her mother, who died in 1933, at Evergreen Cemetery in East Los Angeles. In 1976 Beavers was inducted into the Black Filmmakers Hall of Fame. (Sources include: "A Look Back on Blacks on the Big Screen," *Michigan Chronicle*, 2/15/94, *Films of the Golden Age*, #44, Spring, 2006.)

BARRY NELSON (April 16, 1917-April 7, 2007)

Barry Nelson was a good-looking and genial secondary leading man who made a greater mark on the Broadway stage than in films, but still managed to grace the movies with his presence in more than two-dozen motion pictures. He is also a regular trivia question as "Who was the first actor to portray Ian Fleming's James Bond?"

Nelson, of Scandinavian heritage, was born on April 16, 1917 in San Francisco, but was raised in nearby Oakland and later attended the University of California at Berkeley. It was at Berkeley that a talent scout from MGM took notice of Nelson in a production of *Macbeth* and signed him to a standard contract. Nelson made his film debut in *Shadow of the Thin Man* as the investigative reporter Paul Clarke. The vast majority of his films were made during the

'40s and include secondary roles in *Johnny Eager, Dr. Kildare's Victory, Rio Rita, The Human Comedy, Bataan,* and *A Guy Named Joe.* He was the co-lead (with Laraine Day) of the 1942 war film *A Yank on the Burma Road* as a truck driver who hauls medical supplies along the Burma Road during World War II. Nelson served in the military, and was stationed stateside. It was while serving in the military that Nelson made his Broadway stage debut as one of the leads in Moss Hart's *Winged Victory*, a part he would recreate in the 1944 film and be billed as "Corporal Barry Nelson."

After the war Nelson made only a few more films, the best being *Beginning of the End*, playing the pilot of the *Enola Gay*, the plane which dropped the first Atomic Bomb. He followed up with *Undercover Maisie, Tenth Avenue Angel*, and then leant his voice (on the loud speaker) in his final film of his MGM contract, *Command Decision*. He then enthusiastically returned to the stage, appearing in such hits as *Light Up the Sky, The Rat Race,* and, especially, *The Moon Is Blue* with Barbara Bel Geddes. In 1956 he returned to Hollywood for a one-shot film as Ginger Rogers' leading man in *The First Traveling Saleslady*. He appeared frequently on television during the '50s, especially in live anthology shows broadcast from New York and on panel shows like *What's My Line?* and *To Tell the Truth*. He also starred in two short-lived television series, *The Hunter* and *My Favorite Husband*. But his most famous (today) television appearance was as the first actor (and only American to date) to play James Bond in a TV version of *Casino Royale*. Nelson played Bond as "Jimmy" Bond, an American. "At that time, no one had ever heard of James Bond," Nelson said many years later. "I was scratching my head wondering how to play it. I hadn't read the book or anything like that because it wasn't well known."

During the 1960s Nelson enjoyed more success on stage, especially in the long-running *Mary, Mary* (later co-starring in the 1963 film with Debbie Reynolds) and as the dentist in love with a young woman while ignoring his devoted nurse (played by Lauren Bacall) in *Cactus Flower*. In the '70s he played supporting roles in two films: the hugely successful *Airport* and the much less successful *Pete 'n' Tillie* opposite Walter Matthau and Carol Burnett. He had one of his biggest personal successes on Broadway in the musical

The Act (opposite Liza Minnelli) in the late '70s and won a Tony Award for his efforts. In 1980 he appeared in his final film, as the hotel manager who interviews Jack Nicholson for the job of keeper in *The Shining*. In the '80s Nelson made some television guest shots and did one more Broadway show, *42nd Street*, before retiring.

In his retirement Nelson and his wife Nanci enjoyed traveling around the country on the lookout for antiques. Nelson was also a devoted Civil War researcher who enjoyed attending Civil War shows and re-enactments of battles. While on an antique trip in Bucks County, Pennsylvania, Nelson quietly died in his hotel room at the age of 89 on April 7, 2007. He had no children. His agent, Francis Delduca, recalled of Nelson, "He was a very naturalistic, believable actor. He was good at both comedy and the serious stuff." (Sources include *Independent* (London), 4/16/07.)

DONNA REED (January 27, 1921-January 14, 1986)

Donna Reed's wholesome and sweet screen persona sometimes hid the fact that she was a marvelous film actress who, on occasion, could even get away with playing against type: such as her Academy Award-winning portrayal of a "hostess" (read prostitute) in the 1953 classic *From Here to Eternity*. But it was her wholesome appeal, highlighted as Jimmy Stewart's devoted and understanding wife in *It's a Wonderful Life* and a long run in her own *Donna Reed Show* (as one of that medium's definitive mother figures), for which she is most fondly recalled today.

Reed was born in Denison, Iowa, on January 27, 1921, as Donna Belle Mullenger. Her parental grandparents were born in England and later immigrated to the United States. She grew up a farm girl, but stood out even at a young age due to her exceptional beauty. She later won a beauty contest in Denison and upon graduating from high school she went to California to attend Los Angeles City College and pursue her dream of acting. At City College she appeared in many school productions and won the title of "campus queen." She was eventually sighted by an MGM talent scout and signed to a contract. Upon signing with MGM, the studio changed her name to "Donna Adams" but within a short period of time the studio changed the "Adams" to "Reed."

Reed had minor roles in *The Get-Away* and, as a secretary, in *Babes on Broadway*, but it was her role as another secretary, in *Shadow of the Thin Man*, for which she received her first substantial notice. She followed up in typical MGM ingénue fashion by appearing in an *Andy Hardy* film and two *Dr. Gillespies*. Her next big part was as Mickey Rooney's sister in one of the best MGM films of the '40s, *The Human Comedy*. She made a fine counterbalance to Robert Walker as his girlfriend in the immensely popular wartime *See Here, Private Hargrove*. She did a fine job as well as the girl Hurd Hatfield loves in *The Picture of Dorian Gray*. John Ford cast Reed as the Army nurse romantically involved with John Wayne in the excellent *They Were Expendable*.

The next year, Frank Capra cast Reed (after major actresses like Ginger Rogers and Jean Arthur turned him down) as Mary Bailey in *It's a Wonderful Life*. This was the first film that Capra and Jimmy Stewart made after having served in the Second World War. Today, the film is considered a classic but at the time of its release it received a mixed critical response and only did so-so at the box office. Reed later recalled, "Working with James Stewart on *It's a Wonderful Life* was the hardest thing I've ever done because he was such a good actor. And Frank Capra was such a fine director, but they were both so intense. They had just returned from the war. It was really my first big role in an important film and everybody was looking for approval but nobody was in a position to give it. I was terrified most of the time."

She followed up with back-to-back films opposite Alan Ladd (*Beyond Glory, Chicago Deadline*); played a reporter who exploits John Derek in *Saturday's Hero*, and then played opposite Derek again as a newspaper editor in *Scandal Sheet*. She made an attractive leading lady for Randolph Scott in *Hangman's Knot* and then was cast as a child welfare worker who falls for John Wayne in the sentimental and underrated *Trouble Along the Way*. Under contract to Columbia she campaigned hard for and finally won the role of the prostitute Alma Burke in *From Here to Eternity*, giving such a strong and believable against-type performance that she won a Best Supporting Actress Academy Award. It should have led to bigger and better film roles but really didn't. She played Dean Martin's girlfriend in *The Caddy* and appeared in a trio of good but minor

Westerns (*Gun Fury, They Rode West, Three Hours to Kill*). She got a chance to play the Indian heroine, Sacajawea, opposite Fred MacMurray, in *The Far Horizons*. Reed had a strong role opposite Glenn Ford as a distressed mother in *Ransom!*

Shortly after this she and her second husband, Tony Owens (with whom she had four children), produced the family comedy *The Donna Reed Show*, which cast Reed as mother and wife extraordinaire Donna Stone. The show ran for eight seasons on ABC and Reed was nominated for an Emmy as Best Actress in a Comedy Series four years in a row (1958-1962), and the show, and the actress, won a battery of other awards from civic and environmental groups.

After the show left the air, Reed took a break from acting and became an activist. It wasn't that she didn't want to work. "I just wouldn't do junk," she later explained. "I didn't like the way films were treating women. Most of the roles were extremely passive — poor stupid souls who couldn't help themselves." Tiring of the carnage from the Vietnam War, she co-founded the organization "Another Mother for Peace." She also became an anti-Nuclear advocate.

In the '80s she returned to acting by appearing in an occasional TV movie or episode of an established series (such as *The Love Boat*), but when Barbara Bel Geddes left *Dallas* in 1984 the producers needed another actress to step into the role of patriarch "Miss Ellie" and approached Reed, who readily accepted. Fans of the show didn't particularly take to Reed's brittle and slightly toned down Miss Ellie and when Bel Geddes was induced to return the following season, Reed was let go — in a humiliating action against a veteran actress. She wasn't even told of her firing until she heard it in the press while on a vacation to Paris. She later filed suit against the production company, Lorimar, and eventually accepted a $1 million settlement.

But her victory was short-lived. In 1986 she was hospitalized for ulcer surgery when doctors discovered that she had inoperable pancreatic cancer. She died with dignity, surrounded by her family in her Beverly Hills home, on January 14, 1986, only two weeks prior to her 65th birthday. In a statement, her *From Here to Eternity* co-star Frank Sinatra said, "I can remember in the beginning, when every guy who saw her on the screen had a crush on Donna, particularly myself. She was a lovely lady, gentle and kind."

REVIEWS:

"Both Stars handle their assignments in a manner that gets the ultimate of laughs."

Variety,
October 22, 1941

"In an off-handed mood, this column might even confess that the whole picture suffers from an excess of the cutes. Although Mr. Powell and Miss Loy play their parts to perfection, the Charles's are beginning to rely — a bit too emphatically on their rare delightful charm. Miss Loy has an out-of-the band-box look which is so helpful amid these lured circumstances."

San Francisco Chronicle,
11/21/41

"After a two-year sabbatical the Nick Charleses are back in town again with *The Shadow of the Thin Man*, which is currently stopping at the Capitol. And the news this morning is that they are still the same merrily married couple, which they are still at home to such motley folks as Rainbow Benny, Spider Webb and Meat Balls Murphy, and that William Powell — Nick, none other — still drinks cocktails with an obvious zest that must be worth millions in advertising to the liquor industry. But delightful people that they are, there is a slight change coming over the Charleses, increasingly noticeable in their visits since *The Thin Man* first appeared in 1934. Nick Jr. is growing to be a big boy now and there isn't quite the same old flashing give and take between mamma and papa. The Charleses, we're afraid, are setting down."

The New York Times,
11/21/41

"Perhaps we are a bit weary of the series for this newest item doesn't seem to come up to the others, or perhaps the humor strains too hard at sophistication and tells too much of the famous detective and his love for downing cocktails and solving complicated crimes instead of letting him get into action."

Commonweal,
11/28/41

". . . Myrna Loy and William Powell can make anything of which they have a part different. It's a substantial piece of film merchandise that will appeal to movie goers as greatly as have its predecessors."

The Piqua (**Ohio**) *Daily Call*,
December 16, 1941

"**** — Another sumptuous serving of sophisticated fun."
Mick Martin and Marsha Porter,
Video and Movie Guide,
2002

Shadow of the Thin Man Photo Gallery

Dickie Hall (as Nick, Jr.) now joins Bill, Myrna and Asta in *Shadow of the Thin Man*, 1941. COURTESY OF SCOTT O'BRIEN.

Nick being pulled over by a cop in *Shadow of the Thin Man*.

Barry Nelson, Bill, Sam Levene, and Harry O'Neill in *Shadow of the Thin Man*.

Nick takes Nora to her first wrestling match in *Shadow of the Thin Man*.

CHAPTER SEVEN

THE THIN MAN GOES HOME

CAST: William Powell (Nick Charles), Myrna Loy (Nora Charles), Lucile Watson (Mrs. Charles), Gloria DeHaven (Laura Ronson), Anne Revere (Crazy Mary), Harry Davenport (Dr. Bertram Charles), Helen Vinson (Helena), Leon Ames (Edgar Draque), Donald Meek (Willie Crump), Edward Brophy (Brogan), Lloyd Corrigan (Dr. Bruce Clayworth).

COMPANY CREDITS: A Metro-Goldwyn-Mayer (MGM) film. Richard Thorpe (Director), Everett Riskin (Producer), Robert Riskin and Dwight Taylor (Screenwriters), Ralph E. Winters (Editor), David Snell (Original Music), Karl Freund (Cinematographer), Cedric Gibbons (Art Director).

PRODUCTION DATES: May 8, 1944-July 14, 1944 with retakes in August and September, 1944. Released: January 25, 1945 (New York). Black and White. 100 minutes.

SYNOPSIS:
Who would have guessed that ultra-sophisticated, debonair Nick Charles, who counts among his friends the very criminals he has sent "up the river," is a product of a small-town respectability? After all, in *Another Thin Man*, Nora tells Nick that her father is as honest as his father and Nick retorts, "Some day you'll find out what a hot recommendation *that* is!" But Nick's dad, Dr. Bertram Charles, as played by Harry Davenport, is the very epitome of small-town respectability and horse sense and his mother, as played by Lucile Watson, is doting and understanding of the fact that father and son

The Fourth sequel *The Thin Man Goes Home* (1944).

haven't always seen eye to eye, especially regarding Nick's chosen profession — being a detective.

This, the fifth *Thin Man* film, opens at a train station with Nick and Nora discussing what they are going to do with Asta; they don't want him to be alone in the baggage car. Nick suggests to Nora that she, "camouflage him under your coat," a suggestion that Nora takes seriously. At that point Asta gets away and within the first two minutes of the film William Powell (or his stunt man) takes two big pratfalls chasing after the playful pup. It is while lying on the ground after the second pratfall that Nick runs into an old police chum who says, "I thought you could handle the stuff, Mr. Charles," speaking, of course, of Nick's legendary fondness for booze. Nick assures him that he has had "nothing but a swig of cider all day" and his flask contains nothing more than apple cider. Nora explains to the disbelieving police officer, "It's true — he's going to visit his parents and they disapprove of drinking." This becomes a recurring bit of business in the film; Nick, believe it or not, staying perfectly sober throughout the film — but hardly anybody believing it. Nick and Nora are on their way to Sycamore

Springs to visit his parents and celebrate Nick's birthday — minus Nick Jr., who, as Nora explains, "just loves kindergarten," and so they decided not to take the little — nuisance — angel along.

On the train, on their way to Sycamore Springs, Nick shares his flask of apple cider with Nora.

NORA: You really like cider?

NICK: Love it — pure juice of the apple — what could be better?

NORA: A dry martini!

NICK: *That* horrible stuff — it almost took the lining off my stomach.

NORA: What did you care? It didn't show.

Poor Nick, doing the best he can to convince himself! At one point on the train a mother asks Nick to please take her baby's bottle, which is full of milk, to the conductor so it can be heated. Nick does so, and when Nora sees Nick with a bottle of milk she exclaims, "Good Grief! Are you on milk now?"

Meanwhile, on the train, Nick runs into another friend, Brogan (Edward Brophy), probably an ex-con but now a greeting card salesman. Brogan tells Nick that he'll probably be looking him up in Sycamore Springs.

Nora tells Nick that she's sure that the people of Sycamore Springs will look at Nick as the "local boy made good" and that Nick's father, Dr. Charles, will happily give Nick a "pat on the back." Nick explains to Nora that his father thinks that he "plays and drinks too hard."

When the train arrives at Sycamore Spring, we are introduced to a local character named Crazy Mary (Anne Revere). Nick goes up to her and asks if she remembers him — she does, "Yes, Nick Charles" or rather "Crazy Nick," as she tells Nora.

Nick and Nora make their way to the home of Dr. and Mrs. Charles. The door is open and they walk in — intending to surprise

Nick's parents. Nick's mother is in the kitchen and is pleasantly surprised; you see, Dr. Charles didn't tell her that Nick and Nora were coming only that she should "set two more places at the table" for dinner that night. Mrs. Charles decides to put Nick right to work fixing an unstable table in the parlor. Nick is on his hands and knees trying to make the flap of the table stay up when it falls down and knocks him on the head putting Nick spread eagle on the floor with his flask falling from his coat. Enter Dr. Charles, who sees Nick flat on the ground with the flask by his hand. Nora doesn't help things by telling him, "I managed to get him here." Nick tells his father, "But it's only cider!" and allows him to taste it. "Why, Nick — it *is* cider!" Dr. Charles exclaims with a voice of unbelieving incredulousness.

After dinner, Dr. Charles asks Nick, "Still a policeman?" in a contemptuous voice. Nora gets her dander up and begins telling Dr. Charles about all the complex cases Nick has solved. "He's more of a genius," than a detective, she tells him, which is why the police always come to Nick for help. Dr. Charles is unmoved:

NORA: Dr. Charles, you are impossible.

DR. CHARLES: Spirited little thing, isn't she.

Nora wishes that Nick could do something while in Sycamore Springs to impress his father and prove what a great detective he is, but Nora is assured that there is no crime in Sycamore Springs. Mrs. Charles tells Nora that the trouble between Nick and his father was due to Nick not following Dr. Charles into medicine. This is followed by another slapstick comedy routine, this time involving Myrna Loy trying to set up a lounge chair while Nick is lingering on a hammock. Despite every effort by Nora she just can't set the darn chair up the correct way; her frustration is total when Nick easily assembles it. But the payoff comes when Nora lies down on it; it collapses under her.

At this point we meet an old school chum of Nick's, Dr. Bruce Clayworth (Lloyd Corrigan), who tells Nora he's just a "small-town doctor." We also meet Laura Ronson (Gloria DeHaven) or as everybody calls her "Laura-belle." Laura wants to be an actress and attends drama school and speaks in a very dramatic-actressy manner. She, like everybody else, assumes that Nick is in town on a case. Laura tells Nick, "I can feel it inside." Nick is sorry to "disappoint your insides," but assures her that he is not on a case. But the town continues to gossip and is convinced that Nick Charles is back in town on some kind of investigation.

Somebody who takes Nick's presence in town very seriously is Edgar Draque (Leon Ames) and his wife Helena (Helen Vinson). It's clear they have something to hide and that Nick might be back in town investigating their activities. It is important that they get a particular painting by a local artist named Peter Berton (Ralph Brookes). It is a photograph of the town's old windmill — why is this painting so important to this couple? Meanwhile, Nora, who is on the look out for the perfect birthday present for Nick, goes to the local art store where she meets the proprietor, Willie Crump (Donald Meek), and she notices the painting of the windmill and believes it would be perfect for Nick because it would bring back childhood memories. Crump tells Nora that he has promised the painting to somebody else, but Nora won't say "No" and offers Crump a great deal of money, more than what the painting is worth. Just after Nora leaves, Helena Draque comes in for the painting. Crump explains that he just sold it to Nora. The Draques determine that they have to somehow get that painting back.

Meanwhile, that night, the artist of the painting, Peter Berton, arrives at Dr. Charles' front door. No sooner does Nick answer the door and Peter begins to tell him that he has something he needs to tell Nick that he collapses into Nick's arms. He has been shot, but no bullet was heard! Nick goes out to investigate and runs into greeting card salesman Brogan in the bushes. Brogan explains that he was just having a smoke. Nora is suspicious of Brogan, but not Nick.

Nick's friend, Dr. Clayworth, performs an autopsy on Berton and comes to the conclusion that he was killed by .45-caliber bullet. Meanwhile, Nick goes on an investigation of his own. He goes to the flat that Berton lived in at Tom's Auto Court. There he learns that Berton had a fight with someone earlier in the week, and that the fight may have been over Laura Ronson. Meanwhile, in Berton's room, Nick finds a clue — a rare cigar wrapper, "Cuban Perfecto," which Nick seems to feel is out of place. Meanwhile, in the background, observing Nick is Crazy Mary who picks up a heavy object and knocks Nick out. Nick stumbles home and everybody assumes that Nick is drunk! Even Nora chastises him for "sneaking out and getting drunk — without me!"

The next day Nick goes to the home of Laura Ronson that she shares with her father, bank president Sam Ronson (Minor Watson). Nick confronts Laura, who only speaks of "poor Peter" and how at times like this she likes to quote the poet "Shelly," to which Nick sarcastically replies, "Me, too." Nick explains to Laura that he had heard that Peter Berton had had a fight with somebody earlier regarding Laura and wants Laura to explain the situation. He also arouses her anger when he tells her that he has found out that her father opposed a relationship between Laura and Berton. Laura has had enough and runs off. Nick then confronts her father and Mr. Ronson says he had no reason not to approve of his daughter seeing Berton. Nick, who noticed that Ronson smokes "Cuban Perfecto" cigars, says to Ronson on the way out, "You might want to explain why you were in Peter Berton's room yesterday." Ronson tells Nick that he had better be careful or else his father, Dr. Charles, may not get the new hospital he has been lobbying for.

Meanwhile, Nick, along with Dr. Clayworth, pays a visit to Crazy Mary at her shack. Dr. Clayworth announces that he is there and walks in, but when Nick follows him in, she demands that they leave. It is obvious that Crazy Mary seems to fear Nick discovering something — but what? Later on, Nick, along with Nora and Dr. Clayworth, pays another visit to Crazy Mary and discover her dead — shot to death. Why did somebody want to do her in? And what did Crazy Mary fear Nick might find out?

In the climax of the film, Nick gathers all the suspects together at Dr. Charles' house. In the drawing room are all the suspects:

Mr. and Mrs. Draque — why is it so important that they get their hands on that painting by Peter Berton?

Laura Ronson — why was Peter Berton fighting another man over her? And is the other man, Tom (Irving Bacon), who has been insanely jealous of another man showing her attention?

Sam Ronson — what was his cigar wrapper doing in Peter Berton's room? And what information does he know regarding Crazy Mary?

Willie Crump — did he know more than he said about the windmill painting?

Brogan — why was he around lurking in the bushes at the time of the murder?

Dr. Clayworth — did he tell all he knows about the autopsy results?

After all is revealed, Dr. Charles gives Nick a big smile and says, "Great work, my boy!" He is truly impressed that Nick has solved this crime using medical science as a backdrop. Finally, Nick has earned his father's respect and admiration. He is so pleased that his chest puffs out and his buttons burst! THE END.

BEST DIALOG:

NICK: A couple of weeks on this cider and I'll be a new man.

NORA: I sort of like the old one.

NICK: Why, darling, that's the nicest thing you've said to me since I got my head caught in that cuspidor at the Waldorf.

THE DIRECTOR:

RICHARD THORPE (February 24, 1896-May 1, 1991)

Richard Thorpe was a highly productive journeyman director who turned out 186 films in a forty-four-year career, and more than thirty of those years were spent at MGM. He was a "Van Dyke-lite" — fast, efficient, and often using the first take, but he didn't process Van Dyke's artistry. Film historian David Thomson put it this way, "We can say that Thorpe's films were seldom interesting, and that Van Dyke's usually were: both were notable for printing the first take, but whereas in Van Dyke's case his films have spontaneity and vigor . . . the reverse is true of Thorpe." Of course, there are exceptions, and over the course of his career Thorpe did make some interesting and worthwhile films.

He was born in Hutchinson, Kansas, on February 24, 1896. He began as an actor in vaudeville, on the stage and in some early silent films, but he soon found his grounding writing and eventually directing films. His first film as a director was in 1923 and over the next six years he churned out 66 mostly routine programmers; he was especially adept at turning out low-budget Westerns of the sort that were probably filmed over two or three days.

In 1934 Thorpe was hired by MGM. "Metro plucked Richard Thorpe from poverty row . . . and brought him along as an unpretentious all-rounder, a young Woody Van Dyke. It didn't work out . . . Thorpe was hardly anything but a by-the-numbers director, albeit a busy one: sixty-six films for MGM in thirty years." Of course, it's true that he did do films mostly for a poverty-row company named Chesterfield Pictures, but he also, prior to joining MGM, did some films for more established and profitable studios like RKO and Universal, yet without exception in the "B" category. But it is true that it was his speed and efficiency which caught the eye of MGM and that was the key reason why they signed him. Despite directing many fine films, it's doubtful he ever directed any so-called "classic" films, but he brought his pictures in on time and usually under budget; something Louis B. Mayer could certainly appreciate.

His first really important picture at MGM is *Tarzan Escapes* (1936), the third in the series of *Tarzan* films which starred Johnny Weissmuller and Maureen O'Sullivan. In fact, Thorpe ended up directing four of the *Tarzan* films (*Tarzan Finds a Son!*, *Tarzan's Secret Treasure* and *Tarzan's New York Adventure*, being the others).

In 1937 Thorpe got his chance in a really prestigious picture and he made the most of it, and it's probably the best film of his career: *Night Must Fall*, featuring Robert Montgomery as a psychotic murderer. It's atmospheric, moody, and very well done. It is a minor classic of the cinema of the '30s and while it wasn't a huge financial success, it did win critical plaudits, and under Thorpe's direction Montgomery was nominated for an Academy Award (as was Dame May Whitty, in the Supporting Actress category).

MGM entrusted some of its biggest stars to Thorpe. He first directed William Powell and Myrna Loy in the 1937 screwball comedy *Double Wedding*; Robert Taylor in the boxing drama *The Crowd Roars*; and Mickey Rooney in the excellent *The Adventures of Huckleberry Finn*. This film was made in 1939, the same year that *The Wizard of Oz* was released. Thorpe was originally assigned to direct *Oz*, but was released after about a week. In the press it was announced that George Cukor was taking over because Thorpe was ill. (Cukor was also reassigned and eventually the primary director of *The Wizard of Oz* would be Victor Fleming. All of Thorpe's footage was scrapped.)

In the '40s Thorpe directed a series of moderately-budgeted but entertaining Wallace Beery Westerns (*20 Mule Team, Wyoming, The Bad Man, Barnacle Bill*), which were perfect matches for Thorpe. The films made money and the crotchety Beery seemed to accept and work well with Thorpe. (Thorpe would also direct Beery in his final film, *Big Jack*, in 1949.) In addition, he had a big success for producer Dore Schary's "B" unit with the well-done *Joe Smith, American*, which starred Robert Young. Another good wartime film was *Cry 'Havoc,'* a patriotic story of army nurses, which starred Margaret Sullavan. MGM also handed him the reins to Joan Crawford's last film of her 18-year MGM contract, *Above Suspicion*. In 1944, Myrna Loy finally — reluctantly — decided to make *The Thin Man Goes Home*. It was the first Thin Man film not directed by Van Dyke, but the studio thought that they could come close to the original and gave Thorpe the opportunity — and indeed, he does direct a funny and entertaining entry in the series. Thorpe also proved to be a competent director of musicals, perhaps not the great musicals that MGM is remembered for (such as those made under producer Arthur Freed) but on a more minor scale (for producer Joe Pasternak); entertaining films like *A Date with Judy* and *Three Little Words*. He also helmed three of Esther Williams' early films, *The Thrill of Romance, Fiesta* and *This Time for Keeps*.

During the early '50s Thorpe had a string of box office hits, including *The Great Caruso* (with Mario Lanza), and then three big costume pictures, *Ivanhoe, The Prisoner of Zenda* and *All the Brothers Were Valiant*. These films were often produced in tandem with producer Pandro Berman, who later explained his reasoning for choosing Thorpe to handle such important and big-budgeted films. "I picked Mr. Thorpe before I had any cast," Berman told the AFI in the early '70s after a screening of Ivanhoe. "I picked him for a very specific reason. At that time he was the most efficient, fast-moving, competent, physical director that we had at Metro. I knew that this was going to be a tough picture to make physically."

However, Joan Fontaine cast as Rowena in *Ivanhoe*, would recall that Thorpe, "cared more about the performances of the horses than the actors." In 1958 Thorpe was handed the directorial reins to what many consider to be Elvis Presley's all-time best film, *Jailhouse Rock*. Thorpe would then direct Presley again four years later in one of Elvis' colorful travelogues full of songs and pretty girls, *Fun in Acapulco*. In fact, during the late '50s and early '60s, the sixty-plus-year-old Thorpe specialized in "youth" films at MGM, including *The Honeymoon Machine, The Horizontal Lieutenant, Follow the Boys* and *The Truth About Spring*. In 1967 Thorpe, the last remaining contract director at MGM, directed the final film of his career, a Glenn Ford Western, *The Last Challenge*, and then quietly retired.

Of Thorpe, James Mason would say, "His reputation for requiring only one take is why we don't remember his films." Of course people who love movies fondly recall many of his films, but as John Ford said in his classic Western *The Man Who Shot Liberty Valance*, "When the legend becomes fact, print the legend." The legend is that Richard Thorpe is primarily a second-rate director. Yet the gems among the 186 films he directed prove that he could, when given interesting material, rise to the occasion. Myrna Loy in her autobiography lamented the fact that *The Thin Man Goes Home* would be the first *Thin Man* film without Van Dyke, but had this to say about Thorpe: "Richard Thorpe was a good director and it turned out to be a funny movie. Some of the sequences are hilarious." Thorpe died on May 1, 1991, in Palm Springs, California, at the ripe age of 95.

THE WRITER:
ROBERT RISKIN (March 30, 1897-September 20, 1955)

Robert Riskin is best remembered for the films he wrote for director Frank Capra, including *Lady for a Day, Mr. Deeds Goes to Town*, and he won an Academy Award for his screenplay for the 1934 Claudette Colbert-Clark Gable classic *It Happened One Night*. Riskin became so identified with the sentimentality of the so-called "Capra-corn" that he seems an odd choice to scribe *The Thin Man Goes Home*, and, indeed, Riskin himself had many doubts about the job, but in the end he took the it, and in no small measure because his brother Everett was the producer of the film. While Riskin found the job tedious, he did produce a first-rate, very funny script with the comedy elements overweighing the drama.

Riskin was born on March 30, 1897, in New York City. He attended public schools in both New York City and Baltimore. He left school at the age of 13 to help support his family by working in a textile mill. Riskin entered the world of films in 1914 when he was only 17, acting as a studio manager on two short films which were made in Florida. By the 1920s he was a freelance writer based in New York writing various scenarios for stage and films. He eventually began developing these scenarios into plays for the New York stage. With his brother, Everett, Riskin began producing some of these works. Two of them, *Illicit* and *Bless You Sister*, were moderately successful, but the Riskin brothers didn't make much money out of it.

In 1931, like many young writers looking for some easy money, Riskin went to Hollywood and was signed by Columbia Pictures. He adapted his play, *Bless You Sister*, into a film script, which was retitled *The Miracle Woman*, which a young Columbia contract director, Frank Capra, planned to make into a film starring one of his favorite actresses, Barbara Stanwyck. There is a story that when Capra began to explore adapting *Bless You Sister* into a film he was at a meeting of Columbia executives and was speaking very excitedly about the project, and apparently Capra didn't realize that the writer of the play was also present and sitting in the back of the room. After Capra finished his exuberant presentation, Riskin approached him. "I wrote that play. My brother and I were stupid enough to produce it on Broadway. It cost us almost every cent we had. If you intend to make a picture of it, it only proves one thing: You're even more stupid than we were." Thus began one of the most famous writer-director relationships in motion picture history. Bob Thomas, in the book *King Cohn* (about ruthless Columbia Pictures chairman Harry Cohn), wrote that Riskin was "a man whose gentle humanity was reflected in the Capra scripts." Riskin often did his writing in longhand while sitting on a porch outside the writers building at Columbia. According to Thomas, Riskin, "wrote each script as if he were telling a story, completing a final version in two weeks. He never reread the first draft and he never rewrote."

That same year, 1931, Capra asked Riskin to punch up the dialogue to his film *Platinum Blonde*, which introduced to wide audience acceptance Jean Harlow. He then went on to write *Shopworn* for Barbara Stanwyck and *Three Wise Girls* for Harlow. Riskin was especially adept at capturing the flavor and dialog of the modern working woman. He and Capra next teamed in *American Madness*, about the relationship between a banker (Walter Huston) and an ex-con (Pat O'Brien) who will do anything — even go to jail — to protect the banker from finding out some indiscreet information regarding the banker's wife. Their next film is one of their best: *Lady for a Day* (1933), with May Robson making a brilliant "Apple Annie." This film found wide audience and critical success, and Riskin received his first Academy Award nomination for his screenwriting. When he wasn't working for Capra, Riskin was busy working for other directors, such as two interesting films directed by Edward Buzzell, *Virtue* and *Ann Carver's Profession*, which starred Fay Wray. This film was Riskin's introduction to Wray, best known as King Kong's best girl, and within a decade the two would marry.

After the success of *Lady for a Day*, Capra and Riskin teamed for their greatest film, *It Happened One Night*, which not only was a huge success with audiences but was *the* film of the year sweeping the Oscars with Best Actor going to Clark Gable, Best Actress to Claudette Colbert, Best Director to Capra and Best Screenplay honors to Riskin. The film was also the year's Best Picture. This was the period when Capra could do no wrong. He was acclaimed as the greatest director of his age and his films had high expectations and Riskin, as his primary writer, came along for the ride. In the next four years Riskin wrote such Capra classics as *Broadway Bill* (a film which also featured Myrna Loy), *Mr. Deeds Goes to Town*, *Lost Horizon* and *You Can't Take it With You*. Riskin was again nominated for Oscars for his work on *Deeds* and *You Can't Take it With You*. Riskin was rarely working on other films which didn't include Capra, but one exception was *The Whole Town's Talking*, a rare excursion into screen comedy by director John Ford, and featuring Jean Arthur in one of her first noteworthy roles.

By the end of the '30s Riskin was tiring of working with Capra. He felt that Capra was taking too much credit for their film collaborations and implying that it was he, Capra, who was really responsible for the scripts. Capra often said that it was up to him to tone down "Riskin's Manhattan-bred cynicism." While Capra obviously shaped the films to his own unique vision of the little man winning out over tremendous odds and overwhelming obstacles, it was Riskin who added a dash of wit, satire and sophistication to the Capra films. They would only collaborate on one more picture, *Meet John Doe*, and then go their separate ways. There is one story that suggests the bitterness Riskin felt toward Capra: Riskin brandished an empty piece of white paper in front of Capra's face and said, "Put the famous Capra touch on *that!*"

In 1942 Riskin married Fay Wray and they would have two children (he also adopted Wray's daughter from an earlier marriage). With the United States at war, Riskin, like Myrna Loy, wanted to devote the war years to wartime activities and he became an advisor to the British government on how to use film as propaganda. He also worked for the Office of War Information and created the Overseas Motion Picture Bureau, and served as its chief from 1942-1945. Riskin's only wartime film was *The Thin Man Goes Home*, which he finally consented to write as a favor to his brother, but as mentioned earlier, it was not a job he enjoyed — despite overall positive results.

After the war he only wrote only four more films. He produced and wrote *Magic Town*, which was a Capra-*esque* story about a pollster and a school teacher in an idealized small American town. But, as directed by William Wellman, it didn't quite mesh and wasn't particularly successful at the box office. Ironically, Riskin's final film as a screenwriter was *Here Comes the Groom*, a Bing Crosby vehicle for Paramount, which was assigned to Frank Capra to direct. Capra's post-war reputation had also declined and he no longer was the driving force behind the films he made, but rather, simply, a hired hand. Needless to say, Riskin was nominated for his fifth and final Oscar nomination for his screenplay.

By this time Riskin's health had declined, having suffered a debilitating stroke in 1950. His wife, Fay Wray, put her career on hold and acted as caregiver to him. He showed little improvement over the next five years, however, and he would never write again (though he had several scripts he was developing at the time of his stroke). He was honored for his artistry by his fellow writers with the Laurel Award in June of 1955 (and also in appreciation for the fact that Riskin was one of the organizers of what became the Screen Writers Guild). On September 20, 1955, Riskin died at the age of 58.

THE CINEMATOGRAPHER:
KARL FREUND (January 16, 1890-May 3, 1969)

Karl Freund may be best known today for his innovation in pioneering the three-camera method of filming for television with a live audience, case in point, I Love Lucy, but he is also one of the cinema's great directors of photography with his heyday being his work at Universal during the '30s in their bread-and-butter genre, the horror film.

Freund was born on January 16, 1890 in what is now the Czech Republic. He got his early cinema experiences at the age of 15 as a movie projectionist, and by the age of 17 he had advanced to being a camera operator shooting newsreels. By the 1920s Freund was working at Germany's UFA Studios where he worked closely with such pioneering directors as Fritz Lang and F.W. Murnau. In Murnau's *Letzte Mann, Der (The Last Laugh)*, Freud filmed a drunk scene with the camera secured to his chest with a battery pack on his back to help him maintain his balance. The result enabled him to stumble about producing shots which suggested intoxication. One of Freund's great silent films was Lang's *Metropolis*. By 1930 Freund, whose reputation as a cinematographer was now established worldwide, emigrated to the United States and found work at Universal where he filmed one of that studio's biggest hits up to that time, the anti-war *All Quiet on the Western Front*. Who will ever forget that last shot where Lew Ayres' hand reaches out for the beauty of the butterfly, only to go limp when the brutality of war is revealed and a sniper shoots him dead? We never see his face — there is no long shot — only a shot of the outstretched arm and hand which tells the story. (It was, in fact, the director Lewis Milestone's hand that was used for this final scene, subbing for Ayres.) The film was selected as the Best Picture of 1930 by the Academy.

The Universal horror films which Freund photographed were very much influenced in terms of lighting and atmosphere by his Germanic background. Freund shot *Dracula* and *Murders in the Rue Morgue*, and then the studio entrusted him to direct *The Mummy* in 1932. He directed six other films for Universal over the next two years, but none matched his work on *The Mummy*. In 1935, when he moved over to MGM, Freund was given the director's reins to *Mad Love*, and together with that other great director of photography, Gregg Toland, and starring Peter Lorre, they created a film which captured the best of European avant-garde in a Hollywood film. Unfortunately, this would be Freud's final film as a film director. He returned to working the camera and was assigned some of Metro's best films of the era, including the intricate musical numbers set on a rooftop in *The Great Ziegfeld*, co-shot *Camille* with William H. Daniels and was solo cameraman for Garbo's *Conquest*. His work photographing *The Good Earth*, which included that amazing scene involving millions of advancing grasshoppers, won him an Academy Award. Other films he worked on during the '30s included *Parnell, Conquest*, and, on loan out to Columbia, *Golden Boy* in 1939.

MGM kept him busy for much of the next decade with assignments as cinematographer on *The Earl of Chicago, Pride and Prejudice, Blossoms in the Dust, Tortilla Flat, A Yank at Eton, The Seventh Cross, A Guy Named Joe, The Thin Man Goes Home*, and *Undercurrent*. He also photographed two films which featured an actress with whom he would end his career on a high note with, Lucille Ball, in *DuBarry Was a Lady* and *Without Love*. After leaving MGM in 1946, Freund went to Warner Brothers, where his only real film of distinction was John Huston's studio-bound *Key Largo*. Other than that he filmed minor Westerns starring Joel McCrea (*South of St. Louis*), Errol Flynn (*Montana*) and Gary Cooper (*Bright Leaf*), which would be Freud's last motion picture as a cinematographer.

He was rescued by Lucille Ball and Desi Arnaz and signed by their studio, Desilu, becoming cameraman for such shows as *Our Miss Brooks, December Bride*, and especially *I Love Lucy*. At this time in television most shows were filmed live and on kinescope which distorted the picture because the images were actually filmed off of a television screen. Desi Arnaz, the producer of the series, and a television innovator in his own right, wanted *I Love Lucy* to look lush in glorious black and white and shot like a motion picture would be — on film. Another advantage for filming on film was that the shooting, like a motion picture, could be halted, if need be, if mistakes occurred, allowing the actors to do another "take." Yet *Lucy* was to be shot before a live studio audience, like a live show, because it was found that Ball worked best when she had an audience to work off of. With a studio audience it was near impossible to work with one camera (which was how it was done in films) and required the actors to perform a scene several times for long shots, medium shots and close ups. Freud's solution was another of his innovations, shooting the series with three cameras which would allow one camera each to shoot simultaneously the close ups, medium shots and long shots. Later these shots would be edited together. This was an innovation at the time, and now it's the accepted way of shooting live situation comedies. Of his experience in filming (and lighting) *I Love Lucy*, Freud would later say, "Despite the 43 years I've devoted to cinematography, I must admit that I was scarcely prepared for the many problems which were to confront me upon my initial excursion into the realm of television." He was up to the task.

After completing his work on the *Lucy* show in 1957, Freud retired from work in films and television and devoted his time to work on behalf of Photo Research Corporation, a laboratory for the development of new cinematographic techniques that he had founded in the mid-'40s. Freud, who never married and had no children, died of natural causes on May 3, 1969 at age 79.

THE BACK STORY:

The back story of the fifth *Thin Man* film is one of the most interesting of the entire series. For the first time the producer would not be Hunt Stromberg, who left the studio in 1941 and formed his own independent film production company which released its pictures through United Artists. Also, for the first time, the director wouldn't be W.S. Van Dyke, who died in early 1943. The producer selected was Everett Riskin, who produced some interesting and successful films, including *Holiday, Here Comes Mr. Jordan, A Guy*

Named Joe and *Kismet*. Riskin asked his brother, Robert, to write the screenplay for the newest *Thin Man* picture, a job that Riskin, who wrote many of the outstanding films of the thirties directed by Frank Capra, didn't look forward to with enthusiasm, but did more so out of loyalty to his brother.

According to his biographer, Riskin, "could not achieve any affinity with the characters; he felt that there was little room to develop personalities that had already been so well established in the earlier films. . . . Working with director Richard Thorpe . . . and with the help of fellow writer Dwight Taylor, Riskin looked to create more melodrama and less tough detective narrative in his first screen treatment of the story." In the Spring of 1942, while Riskin was in Hollywood laboring away on the screenplay, his wife Fay Wray was appearing in a play in Cambridge, Massachusetts. He wrote Wray, calling the film work, "dreadfully dull" and that he wasn't even sure "what the scenes are about." Like many of his films for Capra, Riskin set the story in a small town, rather than in New York City or San Francisco, as previous *Thin Man* films had been set. He felt that the small-town atmosphere would be a nice change of pace for Nick and Nora and allow them to interact with different types than the mugs and slickers they usually dealt with. Nick is neutered in this film; he doesn't drink a drop of hard alcohol. In the script it's because his parents do not believe in liquor, but in actuality it's because the studio itself wanted to tone down (during the war years) alcohol consumption as a fun-loving gag. In the end it would take Riskin more than two years to come up with an acceptable script (co-authored by Dwight Taylor and based on a story by Riskin and Harry Kurnitz). If it was Riskin's objective to make the film "more melodramatic" than earlier films, it certainly doesn't show through in the final picture, which is among the lightest of *Thin Man* releases.

Certainly the studio wanted the film put in production two years sooner than it actually was. The problem wasn't so much because of the screenplay, but was due to problems securing the services of Myrna Loy. Myrna wanted very much to devote her time to the war effort, specifically the Red Cross, and to her new husband, John Heinz. But MGM wanted her services for a series of films. According to Executive Committee Meeting notes, of April 21, 1942, Myrna's upcoming projects were discussed and topping the list was *The Thin Man's Rival* (the working title of the film which would ultimately become *The Thin Man Goes Home*). She was also slated to work in the coming months in *Above Suspicion* with Walter Pidgeon and *Strange Adventure* with Spencer Tracy. (The MGM Executive Committee comprised, among others, Louis B. Mayer, Eddie Mannix, Harry Rapf, Sam Katz and Dore Schary, and their purpose was to review upcoming projects for MGM contract players and make decisions on what films to cast them in, among other details.)

The start of the *Thin Man* film was proposed as "on or about June 15th." Myrna made it clear, however, that she had no intention of working on a new *Thin Man* film or any of the other projects that the Executive Committee had wanted her for. Eventually, she was put on suspension by the studio, but they kept trying to entice her to do *The Thin Man* and she kept telling them "No."

By December of 1942, the Executive Committee was seriously discussing replacing Myrna as Nora Charles. Here are the notes of December 15: "There was a lengthy discussion about 'The Thin Man' with regard to the replacement of Myrna Loy. Everett Riskin and Al Litchman [another Executive Committee member] felt that a test of Frances Gifford showed that she wasn't ready for this type of role. Among others mentioned were Jean Arthur, Loretta Young, Ann Sothern, Merle Oberon and Marsha Hunt. Benny Thau is to contact Bill Powell about his making a test with Marsha Hunt. She seemed to be the one most favored." So it is clear that MGM *was* seriously considering replacing Myrna if they were already making tests of other actresses, and that it wasn't, as some believed, simply publicity by the studio in hopes that it would cause Myrna to return to the fold if she actually believed it possible that another actress would be cast as Nora. (This author had the opportunity to ask Miss Hunt about the rumors that she was considered to replace Myrna Loy, and she said that she was never asked to do a test with William Powell. "I never had to test for anything at Metro." She also said that when she heard "the rumors," years later, that she had been strongly considered to play Nora, "I had never been so flattered in my life, but I don't think they ever realistically considered replacing Myrna." (Interview with Marsha Hunt, 6/14/07.) (Marsha would later appear opposite William Powell in 1949's *Take a False Step*.)

Even more intriguing are the comments made in the January 19, 1943 Executive Committee Meeting notes: "There was a discussion about Lucille Ball for 'The Thin Man' and there is to be a meeting with Mr. Mayer, Mr. Mannix, Mr. Katz, Mr. Lichtman, Mr. Thau and Bill Powell in relation to Bill Powell's two pictures 'Stars Can Wait' [which ultimately became *The Heavenly Body*] and 'The Thin Man'; as well as discussion of the two parts for leading lady in each of these pictures." Is it possible that MGM was seriously considering Lucille Ball as a replacement for Myrna Loy as Nora Charles?

Eventually, MGM did leak a name to the press as a possible replacement for Loy — Irene Dunne. "*The Thin Man* pictures had always been big money-makers," recalled Bill Powell, "and naturally the MGM boys were eager to keep them going. They announced new Noras, like Irene Dunne, from time to time, merely as a ploy, I suspect, to lure Myrna back — but every time such sacrilege appeared in the columns, there was uproar. The studio was deluged with fan letters. The fans wanted Myrna, and they didn't want anybody else. I wanted Myrna, too." The bottom line is that the studio finally did catch on, that replacing Myrna Loy in her signature role would cause an uproar among the movie-going public, and waved the white flag. But their appeals to Myrna, along with the public outcry for a new *Thin Man* film, finally wore Loy out and in May of 1944 she finally relented and went before the cameras for what would be her only film of the war years, *The Thin Man Goes Home*.

Myrna's return from New York to Hollywood was a day of glee for Bill Powell as he recalled in Myrna's autobiography, "When Myrna wired Mr. Mayer that she was ready to start business again at the old stand, I learned that she was arriving on the Chief, so I borrowed Asta for the day and rushed out to Pasadena to meet her. As she got off the train, I quickly told her that Asta and I had just arrived from Palm Springs and that I thought it was a hell of a nice gesture on her part to come three thousand miles to meet me. Myrna looked weary and a bit thin, I thought. 'When the studio sees you,' I said, 'they'll change the title of our picture from The *Thin Man Goes Home* to *The Thin Woman Comes Home* . . . the first day of the picture, everybody wanted to hug and kiss Myrna. I've never seen a girl so popular with so many people. Everybody from wardrobe was over on the set, everybody from makeup, everybody from property; everybody from a mile around, it looked like. There were big signs across the stage flamboyantly announcing, WELCOME HOME, MYRNA or DON'T LEAVE US AGAIN, MYRNA . . . The second day, we got down to the business of bringing Nick and Nora to life again."

During the making of this film Myrna Loy performed a vigorous jitterbug with Arthur Walsh, the national "jitterbug king." According to a contemporary article (published on 6/10/44), Myrna was coached by her black maid Teresa, who was the jitterbug champ of Harlem. The article says that Teresa went so far as to bring "jive records" from her home "because the studio music wasn't in the groove." When the sequence was filmed Myrna said that Arthur "is doing all the work. I just follow him around and do a lot of faking."

This same article makes note that in the film there is no sign of Nick, Jr. and that he is only mentioned once, very quickly in passing. This was no accident "The real reason the baby isn't in the picture is that the studio found he just got in the way of things." (This was exactly the reason why the Hacketts made Nora pregnant at the end of the second picture, as a way of discontinuing the series.)

As for Asta, he was aging. The original Asta was still alive, but he was slowing down. What MGM did now was to use two doubles to do the trademark Asta leaping and jumping and only used the original Asta for close-ups. But, according to one article, Asta still got around. He ran off and ended up visiting a nearby set where Fred Astaire and Gene Kelly were rehearsing (for their joint dance number in *The Ziegfeld Follies*). The assistant director thought that he was a stray who had accidentally got on the lot and hustled him away. "The gent has taken a ribbing ever since. People remind him that Asta earns more than he does." (Hollywood by Erskine Johnson, NEA, *Frederick* (MD) *Post*, 6/10/44.)

SUPPORTING CAST:

LEON AMES (January 20, 1902-October 12, 1993)

Leon Ames played more than his share of fathers in a film career that spanned better than fifty years. But a closer look at his credits shows a large variety of roles and, in both of the *Thin Man* films in which he appeared, *The Thin Man Goes Home* and *Song of the Thin Man*, Ames played nobody's dear old dad, but a prominent murder suspect in each.

Ames was born Leon Waycoff on January 20, 1902, in Portland, Indiana, the son of Russian Immigrants. In the early '20s Ames (or Waycoff) joined the Charles K. Champlin theatrical company, out of Pennsylvania, as a business manager but eventually, thanks to his velvet voice and good looks, began to act in productions, often in the romantic juvenile roles. In 1933, as Leon Waycoff, Ames made his Broadway stage debut in the comedy *It Pays to Sin*. In fact, Ames kept his given name well into his career and his early film roles between 1931-1936 he is listed in the credits as Leon Waycoff. One of Ames' most prominent roles was as the romantic lead in Universal's 1932 version of *Murder in the Rue Morgue*. But most of his roles in his earlier films were not in substantial parts, but he did appear in many prestige productions such as *State's Attorney* (with John Barrymore); *Thirteen Women* (starring Irene Dunne and Myrna Loy as one of her exotic oriental types); *Only Yesterday* (with Margaret Sullavan); *The Count of Monte Cristo* (with Robert Donat) and *Reckless* opposite William Powell and Jean Harlow.

In 1937 Leon Waycoff became Leon Ames and remained so for the rest of his career. His first film using this name was a mystery programmer called *Death in the Air*. He played a variety of non-father roles in such films as *Charlie Chan on Broadway* (as a mobster); *Bluebeard's Eighth Wife* (as a chauffeur); *I Was a Convict* (as an unscrupulous businessman); *Mr. Moto in Danger Island* (as a police commissioner); *Panama Patrol* (as a military man); *Legion of Lost Flyers* (playing an actor). Between 1940 and 1943 Ames appeared in several Broadway shows, including a huge success in *The Male Animal*, with his film career taking a back seat. When he returned to Hollywood in 1944, he signed with MGM and his first major role under this contract would be the first (and greatest) of his "father" roles, playing Judy Garland's dad in the classic *Meet Me in St. Louis* which became one of the studio's all-time great hits. His sturdiness, authoritative voice and overbearing manner hid a heart of mush when it came to his daughters (who also included Lucille Bremer and young Margaret O'Brien). But even after this he didn't get typed into fatherly roles. He followed up in *Thirty Seconds over Tokyo, The Thin Man Goes Home, Son of Lassie* (playing a Norwegian fisherman), and *Weekend at the Waldorf.* Ames had one of his best roles as the determined prosecuting attorney in *The Postman Always Rings Twice.* In fact, his next prominent "father" role wouldn't be until 1948, in the musical *A Date with Judy* as Elizabeth Taylor's dad. The following year he was reunited with his *Meet Me in St. Louis* wife, Mary Astor, to play Mr. March, the father of June Allyson, Margaret O'Brien, Elizabeth Taylor and Janet Leigh, in *Little Women.*

Ames, early in his career, devoted a good deal of his time to helping organize the Screen Actors Guild (SAG). Ames would recall that in 1933 he was approached to come to secret meetings where a strategy was developed to form a union. "The working conditions were unbelievable," Ames recalled. "You'd get a call to the studio to makeup at maybe six o'clock in the morning, or four o'clock . . . you were treated like cattle, you had no place to sit down . . . who ever heard of food — you bring your own lunch, if you could. You began to say 'what the hell is this?' there was no place to sit down, nothing to eat, and the actors began to say 'this is ridiculous.'" He was founding member #15 out of the original 19 members. His early organizing for the SAG is one reason why his roles after 1932 seemed to diminish in size. It was not really until he returned to Hollywood after his years (1940-1943) on Broadway that his parts in films began to become larger. In addition to being one of the founding members of SAG, Ames also served a single term (1957-1958) as SAG president — but his term was a rocky one due to friction between Ames' more conservative views and the more radical wings of the union. Nonetheless, Ames served as an elected officer and Board member from 1945-1979 and was named "President Emeritus" from 1979 until his death in 1993.

During the '50s Ames appeared more regularly in his patented father roles. He was Dean Stockwell's dad in both *The Happy Years* and *Cattle Drive*, and perhaps most memorably, and with a tip of the hat to his dad role in *Meet Me in St. Louis*, as Doris Day's dad in the nostalgic musicals *On Moonlight Bay* and *By the Light of the Silvery Moon*. In 1960 he and Myrna Loy played Paul Newman's parents in From the Terrace. During the 1960s he became a frequent supporting character in Disney films, such as his college dean in *The Absent Minded Professor* and *Son of Flubber* and the Judge of *The Misadventures of Merlin Jones* and *The Monkey's Uncle*. His firm, father-like credibility certainly had a great deal to do with his being cast in these films. His film career slowed down but he continued to appear in movies all the way up to 1986 when he played Kathleen Turner's grandfather in *Peggy Sue Gets Married*.

Professionally, Ames began to appear with more frequency on television. He was a perfect fit playing father roles in *Life with Father* (1952-1954) and *Father of the Bride* (1961). He also appeared as Alan Young's neighbor on *Mr. Ed*. In real-life Ames and his wife, Christina, whom he married in 1938, had two children, a boy and a girl. Ames also had a head for business and in 1946 launched his first automobile dealership, "Leon Ames' Ford" and by the early '60s he had one of the largest automobile dealerships in Southern California. It may be because of his business success that in 1963 his wife was abducted and held for ransom; eventually she was found safe and sound.

Ames died of complications from a stroke on October 12, 1993, at the age of 91. Of his years as a "professional dad" he once said, "I held all the great beauties on my knee. And the hell of it was, they were all thirteen." (Sources include: *Daily Herald*, 10/17/93 & www.sag.com.)

HARRY DAVENPORT (January 19, 1866-August 9, 1949)

Harry Davenport was one of the most familiar faces in American films during the '30s and the '40s. He came to motion pictures at an advanced age and specialized in playing men of sterling character, especially judges, doctors, grandfathers and ministers.

Davenport was born in New York City on January 19, 1866, not even a year after the Civil War ended. He grew up in Philadelphia and came from a family of thespians. His father was a stage actor, E.L. Davenport, and on his mother's side was a famed 18th-century Irish actor. He had a sister who was also an actress. Davenport made his professional stage debut at the age of five in the play *Damon and Pythias*. He made his Broadway stage debut in 1895 in Puddn'head Wilson and over the next forty years would appear in countless plays on the "Great White Way," including *The Belle of New York, Topaze* and, especially successful, *Lightin'*, which ran for three years.

Davenport proved to be more than one of the sterling stage actors of his time; he was also a labor activist. Along with Eddie Foy, Davenport was the co-founder of an organization called "The White Rats." This organization later became known (to this day) as Actors Equity. Davenport and Foy, along with others, refused to appear on stage for several months, virtually closing down all the Broadway houses until they got their demands fulfilled. These demands included initiating a six-day work week and plumbing in dressing rooms. Finally, the producers had no choice but to give in to their demands so that they could reopen their theaters.

Davenport made his debut as a film actor in 1914 and over the next seven years he appeared in several films, especially well known for directing and starring in a series of *Mr. Jarr* comedy shorts. But his real film career didn't begin until 1930, playing a doctor in *Her Unborn Child*. He played a variety of roles, including the philosopher driven to suicide in *The Scoundrel*; a former confederate soldier looking back on the war in *They Won't Forget*; the opera director in *Maytime*; the archduke in *Fit for a King*; the railroad owner in *Paradise Express*; Louis XI in *The Hunchback of Notre Dame*; and the chief of staff in *The Life of Emile Zola*.

His gray-haired integrity made him a natural for judges such as the ones he played in *You Can't Take it With You, The Story of Alexander Graham Bell, Dr. Ehrlich's Magic Bullet, Princess O'Rourke, Courage of Lassie, The Bachelor and the Bobby-Soxer* (as Myrna Loy's crotchety old retired judge uncle), and *That Hagen Girl*, opposite Ronald Reagan and Shirley Temple. By the same token he was perfectly cast as doctors in *Gone with the Wind, The Sisters, Juarez, Music for Millions, Song of the Thin Man, Adventure, Claudia and David* and, in his penultimate film, as *Dr. Barnes in Little Women*. His age made him perfect casting for grandfatherly roles such as in *Should Husbands Work, Money to Burn, Grandpa Goes to Town, Pardon My Past, A Boy, A Girl, and a Dog* and most especially the grandfather of the Smith family of St. Louis in *Meet Me in St. Louis.* Davenport's final film was *Riding High*, directed by Frank Capra and released in 1950, after his death.

Davenport was married twice. With his first wife he had one child, a daughter. With his second wife, actress Phyllis Rankin, they produced two sons and two daughters. His wife preceded him in death. The end for Davenport came on August 9, 1949, when he succumbed to a heart attack at age 83. Davenport was remembered by Bette Davis (with whom he appeared in *The Sisters, Juarez, All This, and Heaven Too, The Bride Came COD*), as "one of the truly great players of all time."

GLORIA DEHAVEN (July 23, 1925)

Gloria DeHaven's first major role at MGM was in the film adaptation of the hit Broadway musical *Best Foot Forward.* It was while making this film that she met June Allyson, who would become one of her closest friends, and, with Nancy Walker, they would steal the film with their rendition of "The Three B's." At the time it was anybody's guess as to which of those two beauties (Allyson or DeHaven) would emerge as the next major MGM female star. Arguably, DeHaven was the sexier of the two and possessed the better singing voice, but it was "girl next door" June Allyson who would knock Van Johnson off his feet in the subsequent *Two Girls and a Sailor* and emerge as a major star. From that point forward DeHaven would often play glamorous, slightly aloof, secondary leads and romantic rivals to the leading ladies.

Gloria Mildred DeHaven was born in Los Angeles on July 23, 1924. Her parents, Carter DeHaven and Flora Parker, were popular vaudeville and film entertainers. Gloria's father also became a director and writer in films, mainly silent films, and Charlie Chaplin chose DeHaven to be his assistant director on the classic film *Modern Times.* Ultimately, Gloria's parents divorced. Of her childhood DeHaven would say, "I'm the product of divorce, show business, very little stability and no roots. We were always traveling."

DeHaven attended the Ken-Mar Professional School in Hollywood and in her spare time made the rounds to studio casting agents. Her father arranged with Chaplin to give Gloria a small part in his film Modern Times in which she played one of Paulette Goddard's little sisters. It is said that as a teenager Louis B. Mayer saw potential in the young DeHaven and was interested in signing her to a contract, but then found out that her agent was somebody he had barred from the MGM lot, and so Mayer (at that time) passed her over. So she began singing with big bands like Bob Crosby and Jan Savitt. DeHaven got another chance when an MGM talent scout saw her performing with the Savitt band in New Orleans and signed her (this time Mayer made no objections) to a seven-year MGM contract (starting at $50/week).

In the next couple of years DeHaven appeared in several films, including *Two Girls and a Sailor* competing with sister June Allyson for sailor Van Johnson — and losing (but doing a terrific job singing "My Mother Told Me"); loaned out to RKO as Frank Sinatra's love interest in *Step Lively*; *Broadway Rhythm*; and then a chance to show her dramatic mettle, first as the spoiled society girl in *The Thin Man Goes Home* and then opposite Van Johnson and Lionel Barrymore in a Dr. Gillespie film, *Between Two Women*, which cast DeHaven as a singer with an eating disorder. While her career hadn't soared to the same heights as her friend, June Allyson, DeHaven was gaining ground. So, it came as a surprise when she decided to retire after marrying actor John Payne in 1944 (they would have two children). It is said that one of the reasons why DeHaven married Payne was to get away from her obsessive, career-driven mother. It is claimed that when informed that she would marry Payne, Gloria's mother yelled, "You can't do this to me!" but Gloria was more than ready to cut that apron string.

In 1946 DeHaven returned to MGM and was cast opposite Mickey Rooney in *Summer Holiday*, a musical remake of *Ah, Wilderness!* The film, which was not released until 1948, was a box office dud. Following this film, DeHaven found out she was pregnant and took another leave of absence. She didn't return to MGM until 1948 and over the next couple of years was cast opposite Van Johnson (again) in crime story, *Scene of the Crime*, in which she plays a singer. She played an unmarried socialite with a child opposite Glenn Ford and Nancy Davis in *The Doctor and the Girl*; Red Skelton's love interest in *The Yellow Cab Man*; and Judy Garland's temperamental sister in *Summer Stock*. In *Three Little Words*, DeHaven got a chance to play her own mother on film and sing "Who's Sorry Now?" MGM also loaned DeHaven to Universal to play opposite Donald O'Connor in *Yes Sir, That's My Baby* and RKO to join Ann Miller and Janet Leigh in *Two Tickets to Broadway*. Shortly after completing this film came the completion of her MGM contract and marriage to Payne. She would only make sporadic film appearances thereafter. In fact, after *Two Tickets to Broadway*, she would appear in only seven more films spread out over 44 years.

Instead, she moved to New York with her children and gave the Broadway stage a try in *Seventh Heaven*. The show only ran a couple of months. But she enjoyed appearing on stage and ended up working in stock productions over the years, including starring roles in *The Unsinkable Molly Brown* and *The Sound of Music*. In the mid-'60s, she appeared in the London stage production of *Golden Boy*, opposite Sammy Davis, Jr. She also began appearing, with some regularity, on television with guest roles both dramatic (*Wagon Train, Burke's Law, The Defenders, Marcus Welby, M.D.*) and in the musical-comedy vein (*The Red Skelton Show, NBC Comedy Hour, Bob Hope*). She took on a recurring role on the soap opera *As the World Turns* from 1966-1968 and she was hostess of the *ABC Prize Movie* for several years, introducing classic films and chatting with the stars between commercials.

After Payne, she married two more times and had two more children. Neither marriage lasted. Her last big screen role was a good one, playing Jack Lemmon's love interest in the comedy *Out to Sea* in 1997. She looked as beautiful as ever, with one reviewer commenting, "Gloria DeHaven has lost none of her charm." Her last television role to date was a 2000 episode of *Touched by an Angel*. After this she retired but is lured out occasionally to appear on the nostalgia circuit.

DONALD MEEK (July 14, 1878-November 18, 1946)

Donald Meek played characters on stage and screen much like his last name — fussy, milquetoast, worrisome, bald-headed little men who are often taken advantage of by others.

Meek was born in Glasgow, Scotland on July 14, 1878, and began his career by appearing as a rabbit in a Christmas pantomime. This led to other appearances in stock productions, including a tour of Australia in *Little Lord Fauntleroy*. At fourteen he came to the United States as part of an acrobatic troupe. He was accepted as an acrobat due to his slender weight (never more than 120 lbs.) and slightness (he was about 5'5"). He gave up acrobatics when he was appearing in a show in Canada and fell off the top of a pyramid and suffered four compound fractures and spent twelve weeks in a hospital. Meek served in the army during the Spanish American War and had lost his hair by the age of 20, after contracting tropical fever. With his slight stature and bald dome, even at an early age (when Meek returned to the stage), he became typed in character parts rather than lead roles. When he was up and moving around again he resumed his acting career and made appearances with stock companies throughout the United States, South Africa, India and Australia, over the next several years.

In 1917, Meek made the first of his many appearances on the Broadway stage in the musical-comedy *Going Up*, which ran for nearly one year. During the 1920s Meek was a constant presence on the New York stage, appearing in fifteen plays during that decade alone. Among the most successful were *Little Old New York, The Potters* (a domestic comedy in which Meek played the lead role as Pa), and Broken Dishes, which ran more than 100 performances between 1929 and 1930 and featured, in a prominent role, Bette Davis. Davis would later recall that just prior to the opening of *Broken Dishes* Meek had lost his fortune in the stock market crash of 1929, yet the day of the crash he came out on stage and gave an effortless performance, "one of the prime examples of the old saw about the show must go on that I was ever to witness," she later said. It turned out to be a mutual admiration society, with Meek telling reporters, "Watch that young lady, within five years her name will be among the top in Hollywood." While the play was not well received, both Meek and Davis were. "The play is slight and even a little worn . . . but Miss Davis and Mr. Meek make it seem fresh and new — and yes, even meaningful," proclaimed the *New York World*.

In 1930, Meek came to Hollywood where he would appear in more than one-hundred films over the next sixteen years. Early in his career he starred in a series of murder mysteries for Warner

Brothers as Dr. Crabtree, such as *The Trans-Atlantic Mystery*, *The Wall Street Mystery*, *The Studio Murder Mystery* and *The Skull Murder Mystery*. He also appeared on Broadway to huge acclaim in the comedy *Oh, Promise Me*, and in 1933 he appeared in the movie version retitled *Oh, Baby!* He followed this by playing George Arliss' scheming son in *The Last Gentleman*. He was Mr. Wiggs in *Mrs. Wiggs of the Cabbage Patch*, the blind man in Peter Ibbetson, the tailor in *The Informer*, Dr. Wacker opposite Errol Flynn's *Captain Blood*, the judge in *The Bride Comes Home*, the Sunday School superintendent in *The Adventures of Tom Sawyer*, and the timid clerk invited to join the family in *You Can't Take it With You*. In 1939 he had colorful roles in two John Ford classics: as the prosecuting attorney up against *Young Mr. Lincoln* and as the timid whiskey salesman befriended by Thomas Mitchell's drunken doctor in *Stagecoach* (perhaps Meek's most memorable role).

During the '40s he played the card shark pretending to be a minister opposite W.C. Fields and Mae West in *My Little Chickadee;* played the pawnbroker in Norma Shearer's last film, *Her Cardboard Lover*; the little old man opposite Bob Hope in *They Got Me Covered*; the German spy opposite Laurel and Hardy in *Air Raid Wardens*; a judge in *State Fair*; and, his final film, as statistician Mr. Twiddle in the Robert Riskin-produced and -written *Magic Town*.

Shortly after completing *Magic Town*, Meek was diagnosed with leukemia. He was admitted to Hollywood Presbyterian Hospital two weeks before he died on November 18, 1946 at the age of 68. He left behind his widow, Belle, whom he married in 1909. (Sources include: *Berkshire Evening Eagle*, 11/19/46.)

ANNE REVERE (June 25, 1903-December 18, 1990)

The austere, steely, iron-jawed Anne Revere was a direct descendant of Paul Revere and many of the characters she played were infused with a New England sense of independence and contrariness — much like the woman who played them. She specialized in playing stern but loving mothers during the greatest period of her Hollywood career.

Revere was born into a comfortable New York family on June 25, 1903. Her father was a stockbroker. Revere graduated from

Wellesley College and then attended the American Laboratory School in New York studying to be an actress. After leaving "the Lab," she spent much of the 1920s traveling with stock companies throughout the country.

Revere made her Broadway debut in 1931 in a play titled *The Great Barrington*, and would appear in several plays over the next three years, until she got her big break in Lillian Hellman's landmark *The Children's Hour* playing Martha Dobie, one of two teachers that a student spreads malicious rumors about, ruining their careers in the process. The play won many awards and is considered one of the highpoints of 1930s Broadway drama. Revere stayed with the play for almost two years.

Revere had made her film debut in 1934 recreating her Broadway role from the play *Double Door*, but no new offers were extended her way, and when the film version of *The Children's Hour* (retitled *These Three*) was filmed in 1936, Revere, despite the rave reviews she received for the Broadway show, wasn't asked to repeat her role for the screen. Instead, the part went to Miriam Hopkins. Revere continued to concentrate on the theater throughout the rest of the 1930s.

In 1940 she was asked to appear in the RKO film *One Crowded Night*, and this time she stayed in Hollywood. Over the next eleven years she appeared, prominently, in motherly roles in more than thirty films. Her big break as a character actress in motion pictures came playing Jennifer Jones' mother in *The Song of Bernadette*, winning her first Academy Award nomination as Best Supporting Actress. She followed that up strongly the following year as Elizabeth Taylor's loving, but practical mother in *National Velvet*, this time taking home the Oscar as Best Supporting Actress. That same year she appeared as town character "Crazy Mary" in *The Thin Man Goes Home*. She played a WAC major opposite Paulette Goddard in *Standing Room Only*, Gene Tierney's mother in *Dragonwyck*, was superb as Gregory Peck's sickly mother in *Gentleman's Agreement* (winning her third and final Academy Award nomination for Best Supporting Actress), and opposed son John Garfield entering the boxing ring in *Body and Soul*. In 1950 she played Montgomery Clift's austere mother in *A Place in the Son*, who ends up telling Clift to make sure his conscience is clear before he meets with execution for the murder of pregnant girlfriend Shelley Winters. This would be Revere's final film for twenty years.

In the early 1950s Revere was blacklisted when she was called before the House UnAmerican Activities Committee and pleaded the fifth when confronted with an unsigned copy of a Communist Party registration card, though she later maintained her innocence and contended that the card was a fake. Others contradicted her, in an effort to save their own careers. People like Larry Parks and Lee J. Cobb told HUAC that Revere had been a party member in the early '40s. She acknowledged that, "I got to know Communists and communism, but I knew it wasn't for me. I'm a free-thinking Yankee rebel and nobody's going to tell me what to do." She pleaded the fifth primarily because she knew that the committee would try and make her testify against others, something she wasn't about to do. She also resigned from the Board of Directors of the Screen Actors Guild.

She went back to New York, and the theater, which was more supportive of actors, directors, writers and others who were blacklisted by Hollywood. During the '50s she appeared in three Broadway shows and also traveled the country appearing in stock productions. In 1960, Revere had one of her greatest stage triumphs, playing Anna Berniers, in another controversial Lillian Hellman play, *Toys in the Attic*. For her performance she was the recipient of a Tony Award. When the film was being cast in 1962, Revere was once again overlooked.

During much of the '60s and '70s Revere and her husband, playwright and director Samuel Rosen, ran an acting school. She was welcomed back to films by the invitation of director Otto Preminger (Preminger had earlier directed Revere in *Fallen Angel* and *Forever Amber* during the '40s) for a small but colorful role in *Tell Me that You Love Me, Junie Moon* in 1970. She also appeared on television, as a regular on the soap operas *The Edge of Night, Search for Tomorrow*, and *Ryan's Hope* in the late '60s and into the 1970s. Her final movie was the horror film *Birch Interval* in 1976 for director Delbert Mann. After some more television work in 1977, Revere retired. Anne Revere died of pneumonia at her Long Island, New York home at age 87, on December 18, 1990. (Sources include: *Syracuse Post-Standard*, 12/20/90.)

LUCILE WATSON (May 27, 1879-June 24, 1962)

Lucile Watson became known for playing opinionated, indomitable, and often patrician mothers in a film career which really didn't start until she was in her middle-50s. Prior to that Watson had wide stage experience appearing in numerous Broadway productions starting in 1902.

Watson was born on May 27, 1879 in Quebec, Canada and later came to New York as a young woman to study at the New York Academy of Dramatic Arts. Her first professional stage appearance came at the age of 23 in *The Wisdom of the Wise*. That same year she would appear in her first major Broadway play, *Hearts Aflame*. She was recognized as a major Broadway star with her performance in *The City* which ran from 1909-1910. She became acclaimed for playing smooth, sophisticated society ladies in drawing room comedies like *The Bridal Path, The Fountain of Youth, Heartbreak House, The Importance of Being Earnest*, and then a long run in *No More Ladies.*

She came to Hollywood in the mid-'30s and her first major role was opposite Helen Hayes in *What Every Woman Knows* in 1934. From then on she began alternating between the big screen and the Broadway stage. By the end of the '30s she was getting typed playing the mothers of such stars as James Stewart, opposing his romance with Carole Lombard, in *Made for Each Other*, Jeanette MacDonald in *Sweethearts*, and most memorably as Norma Shearer's opinionated mother in *The Women*. She had a change-of-pace role as a housekeeper in *Three Smart Girls* opposite Deanna Durbin. While she was playing support to these big stars in the movies, she was still a top star on the Broadway stage, and two of her most memorable stage roles during the '30s were as Mrs. Bennet in *Pride and Prejudice* and then enjoying nearly a year-long run in *Yes, My Darling Daughter.*

In the early '40s she appeared in such films as *Waterloo Bridge* (opposed to her son, Robert Taylor, being involved with Vivien Leigh's prostitute); *Mr. and Mrs. Smith, Rage in Heaven*, and *The Great Lie*, playing not a mother this time but an aunt. In 1941 she returned to Broadway in one of her greatest triumphs, as the mother in *Watch on the Rhine*, which she played for nearly a year. She returned to Hollywood to appear in the film version opposite Bette

Davis and Paul Lukas (who had also appeared in the Broadway production). She was nominated for an Academy Award as Best Supporting Actress but lost out to Katina Paxinou for *For Whom the Bell Tolls.*

She now appeared more regularly in film roles such as *The Thin Man Comes Home* (who would have thought that Nick Charles would have parents as stable and upstanding as Lucile Watson and Harry Davenport?); Barbara Stanwyck's hard-as-nails mother in *My Reputation*; Gene Tierney's status-conscious mother in *The Razor's Edge*; Greer Garson's indomitable mother-in-law in *Julia Misbehaves*; Bobby Driscoll's southern grandmother in *Song of the South*; and memorable as wealthy and proud Aunt March in *Little Women*. After this she only appeared in four more films over the next two years, the last as Ava Gardner's scheming aunt in *My Forbidden Past.*

But she was not yet done with acting. She returned to the Broadway stage in *Ring Round the Moon*; the lead role as a mystery writer who encounters murder in a spooky house in *The Bat*; and her final stage role, in 1953-1954, *Late Love*. She had a television triumph appearing in "The Old Lady Shows Her Medals" as part of *The Hallmark Hall of Fame* in 1952. Her final work as an actress was in the anthology series *Studio One* in 1954. She was now 75 and had a great career behind her and was ready to enjoy her final years in prosperous retirement. She had been married twice, briefly to a fellow actor and later to playwright Louis Evan Shipman, from 1928 to his death in 1933. Ironically, this woman who gained such fame in the cinema for playing mothers had no children of her own. In her last years she was plagued by heart trouble. At one of her final birthday parties, she was asked if she had gone to the doctor for a checkup and Watson replied, "My heart and lungs are fine as long as I blow out those birthday candles in one blow." She did. She died of a heart attack on June 24, 1962 at 83.(Sources include: *Modesto Bee*, 6/25/62, *San Mateo Times*, 6/25/62.)

REVIEWS:

"Thin Man William Powell, an old and expert hand at this sort of thing, has done it four times before. This time he once more has the able help of his original partner, lynx-eyed Myrna Loy, back in films after a four-year absence. There is also, of course, the bottle brushy terrier Asta . . . the fifth time around, the three of them still guarantee a pleasant excuse for putting off household repairs and serious reading."

Time, 11/22/44

"By now the Thin Man series was beginning to show signs of age and the budget of THE THIN MAN GOES HOME was obviously much smaller than those for the previous four films. Still the movie held up well and was popular, and perhaps M-G-M would have been wise to have ended the series with this outing."

Michael R. Pitts, *Famous Movie Detectives*, 1979

"*The Thin Man Goes Home* came late in the series but it's still fairly cheerful. It features William Powell, Myrna Loy, Asta, and Anne Revere, who, carrying a rifle and wearing a felt hat that looks as if it might have been discarded by a janitor, makes a fascinating lunatic."

Pauline Kael, 5001 *Nights at the Movies*, 1982

"**1/2 — Fifth and weakest entry in the series . . . still entertaining but a lesser effort."

Mick Martin and Marsha Porter, *Video and Movie Guide*, 2002

"***Leisurely entry, with even more comedy than usual."

Leonard Maltin, *Movie and Video Guide*, 1992

The Thin Man Goes Home Photo Gallery

Bill and Myrna in a studio portrait (1944).

Nick and Nora with Nick's stable, small-town parents as played by Lucile Watson and Harry Davenport.

The Thin Man Goes Home Bill with Edward Brophy, one of the few actors to appear in more than one of the *Thin Man* films other than Bill and Myrna.

CHAPTER EIGHT

SONG OF THE THIN MAN

CAST: William Powell (Nick Charles), Myrna Loy (Nora Charles), Keenan Wynn ("Clinker"), Dean Stockwell (Nick Charles, Jr.), Patricia Morison (Phyllis Talbin), Leon Ames (Mitch Talbin), Philip Reed (Tommy Drake), Jayne Meadows (Janet Thayer), Gloria Grahame (Fran Page), Ralph Morgan (David Thayer), Don Taylor (Buddy Hollis), Bruce Cowling (Phil Brant).

COMPANY CREDITS: A Metro-Goldwyn Mayer (MGM) film. Edward Buzzell (Director), Nat Perrin (Producer), Steve Fisher and Nat Perrin (Screenwriters) with James O'Hanlon and Harry Crane (additional dialog), Gene Ruggiero (Editing), Cedric Gibbons (Art Direction), David Snell (Musical score).

PRODUCTION DATES: Early January-mid March, 1947. 86 minutes. Black and White.

SYNOPSIS:
This film begins on a gambling boat, the *S.S. Fortune*, where many of New York's most prominent citizens are participating in a fund-raising charity event. Unlike some past *Thin Man* films it doesn't take long before we are introduced to Nick and Nora Charles. Two of Nick's old "friends" are walking about checking out the "dames" on board. One form catches their eyes immediately. Her back is to them as she is standing by a roulette table. One man says to the other, "Check that one out" and the other man goes "Whoo-whoo." At this point Nick Charles, who overheard them, turns and says, "In polite society it's not 'Whoo-whoo' it's pronounced 'Whoo — whom,'"

Three examples of newspaper advertising for *Song of the Thin Man*

and we're off and running. And, indeed, Myrna Loy, at forty-plus, does look beautiful — more mature, obviously, than our first sighting of Nora thirteen years earlier, but still in Nick's words a "dish." As for Nick, William Powell seems a bit thick around the middle, not so much a thin man but a distinguished older-looking man who is developing a paunch. But his charm and humor never deserts him — and much younger women are still giving Nick the eye. Nick wants to take his winnings and go home, which causes Nora to ask, "What's at home?" Nick replies, "You, my pipe, my slippers." Nora shakes her head and says, "You're slipping." Nick counters, "Darling, give me my pipe, my slippers and a beautiful woman, and you can have my pipe and slippers."

On the ship we are introduced to its owner, Phil Brant (Bruce Cowling), who is in love with socialite Janet Thayer (Jayne Meadows) whose antique dealer father David (Ralph Morgan) disapproves of their relationship. He makes it clear to his daughter that she is to break it off; little does he realize that Phil and Janet are planning to elope.

Also on board are sultry blonde singer Fran Page (Gloria Grahame) and band members Buddy Hollis (Don Taylor), a clarinetist, and his friend Clinker (Keenan Wynn). Buddy is playing a solo, despite being drunk. He had been involved with Fran but bandleader Tommy Drake (Philip Reed) took her away for him, though it's clear that Fran still has a soft spot for Buddy. There is an altercation between Buddy and Tommy and this leads to Brant confronting Tommy. Tommy tells Brant that it doesn't matter if he fires him because he is quitting anyway and wants his money. Brant tells him to forget it. If he quits he is out of luck as far as getting any money. The problem is that Tommy badly needs the money since he owes bookie Al Amboy (William Bishop) a great deal of money — $12,000 to be exact. Amboy gets wind that Tommy is planning to quit so he could go on tour for promoter Mitch Talbin (Leon Ames) — and makes it clear to Tommy that he better get the money and be quick about it — or else.

Mitch Talbin and his beautiful and sophisticated wife Phyllis (Patricia Morison) soon arrive, and Tommy tells Mitch that he needs an advance on his wages. Mitch is pulling for his wallet when Tommy spills the beans; he needs $12,000, not just a few hundred bucks. Mitch is unwilling to advance him this kind of money since, as he tells Tommy, anything can happen and Tommy could wind up dead and he, Mitch, would be out of a great deal of money. Incidentally, by the looks that Phyllis Talbin gives Tommy when he appears, it would seem that they have had some kind of past relationship.

Tommy sneaks into Phil Brant's office and is prying open the safe when the door behind him opens and we suddenly see the barrel of an unusual-looking gun. A shot rings out and Tommy falls to the floor, dead. The next morning's papers blare out the news — Bandleader Tommy Drake is dead, and Phil Brant is wanted for the murder.

The next day, Nora and Nick Jr. (Dean Stockwell) are seated at the breakfast table when Nick enters the room looking rather natty. Nora tells him he looks like "a page out of *Vogue*" to which Nick Jr., without missing a beat, says, "Not the page I saw." It's clear that little Nicky has inherited the trademark Charles sly humor — he's a chip off the old block. The scene goes on with Nick Jr. opening up the paper to the comic page and is reading aloud from one which refers to a woman as a "broad." Nora is aghast and reprimands Nick, Jr. for talking that way about women. "But that's what Daddy says," is his defense. Nick says, "I do not! — I say 'doll' or 'dish.'" But never broad.

Suddenly, arriving at the Charleses' front door are Phil and Janet. They explain to Nick and Nora that they have just gotten married. Nick and Nora extend congratulations, without knowing that the morning papers had proclaimed that Tommy was murdered and Phil was wanted for the murder. Phil and Janet tell them. Nick tells Phil the best thing for him to do is turn himself in. What the couple really want Nick to do is investigate the crime. As Nick and Nora are walking them out, a shot rings out. It misses everyone but hits a bottle of champagne that Nick was carrying. Nick goes to investigate. A neighbor comes out and asks if "everybody is okay" and Nick says, "No . . . an old friend went to pieces" (his bottle). As Nick returns, the police arrive and while Nora tries to hide Phil and Janet, Nick leads the cops to them. Phil thanks Nick for double crossing him as he is taken into custody. Nick later explains to Nora that it is safer for Phil to be locked up and in the meanwhile he will continue on with an investigation.

Nick, with Asta, sneaks aboard the **SS Fortune** and finds two clues as he is checking out Phil's office. He is discovered by one of Al Amboy's associates who pulls a knife on Nick. Nick tells his assailant that if he isn't careful he will turn Asta on him, but (as usual) Asta is hiding under a desk. Nick manages to get away and then interviews members of the band who are actually celebrating Tommy's murder. They explain to Nick that he was a hated man and anybody, even the now-missing Buddy Hollis, could have killed him. When Nick notices "Clinker" using a razor blade on his instrument he asks him what he was doing in Phil's office and tells him he found a discarded blade. Clinker explains that anybody could have left it there since it is common for people to use blades on their instruments.

Nick next discovers that the bullet that killed Tommy must have come from an antique gun and so, in the middle of the night, he and Nora pay a visit to Janet and her father, David, the antique dealer. Nick also notices that one of the guns from David's collection is missing. David concedes that he did have the gun with him on the night of the murder, but that he gave Phil the gun; a claim which is disputed by Janet. Suddenly, Janet receives a mysterious phone call. After writing the address down on a pad of paper, Janet excuses herself. Nick and Nora also leave, but not before Nick had taken the next page of paper from the pad and is able to make out the address that Janet wrote down. Janet soon leaves the house and Nick and Nora pursue her in a taxi. Along the way they lose her, but because Nick has the address they soon arrive at the destination. The blaring of a clarinet leads Nick and Nora to an apartment. They open the door and find Fran Page lying on the floor — dead — with a knife in her back. The music is a record that she was playing. Within seconds Janet enters the apartment. Nick and Nora tell her that they were following her and wonder why it is that they got to the destination before she did. Janet explains that the mysterious call that she got was from Fran who had information for her but would only sell it for her for $2500, so she stopped to get the money.

A clue found in the apartment lead Nick and Nora to Poughkeepsie, where they discover Buddy in a sanitarium, and in a daze, recuperating from the trauma. The doctor won't allow Nick to speak with him, telling him he is too ill, but the ever-resourceful Nora sneaks into Buddy's room. She tries to convince him that she was a friend of Fran's but Buddy doesn't buy it and accuses Nora of spying on him. He pulls out a gun — the murder weapon — and declares that he was the one who killed Tommy Drake and takes a shot at Nora, but misses her by a mile. Hearing the shot, Nick rushes to the room. Nick is convinced that Tommy is not the killer; after all, the real killer was able to shoot Tommy through the heart while Buddy easily misses Nora.

When they return to New York, Nick cooks up an idea to trap the real killer. He arranges for Phil to be released from jail and invites all the suspects to gather on the *S.S. Fortune*. He also lets everybody know that Buddy's mental state has improved and that Buddy will make a startling announcement that night regarding the killing of Tommy Drake and Fran. While on board ship, it is Nora who discovers another startling clue. When Al Amboy and his wife Helen (Marie Windsor, in a bit role) arrive, she is wearing an expensive diamond necklace; later in the evening that same necklace is now on the neck of Phyllis Talbin. What is the significance of this? And who done it? You'll have to see the movie to find that information out. After the murderer is found out and dealt with, we return back home with Nick and Nora, and these are William Powell and Myrna Loy's last lines as the carefree Charleses:

NICK: Now Nick Charles is going to retire.

NORA: You're thru with crime?

NICK: No, I'm going to bed.

THE DIRECTOR:
EDWARD BUZZELL (November 13, 1897 (some sources say 1900)-January 11, 1985)

Director Edward Buzzell directed two of the Marx Brothers' MGM films. The connection to the Marx Brothers is quite possibly Buzzell's most lasting claim to fame since the Marx Brothers continue to this day to be admired and appreciated by new generations. Yet the two pictures that Buzzell directed for the Marxes, while quite serviceable, cannot be considered prime Marx.

Buzzell was born in Brooklyn, New York and during the 1920s was a musical-comedy star on Broadway. He went to Hollywood in 1929 to star in the movie version of George M. Cohan's Broadway hit *Little Johnny Jones*, and ended up adapting the play for the screen, as well. The director was Mervyn LeRoy, who would later be a producer and director at MGM at about the same time that Buzzell came to the studio. After this Buzzell appeared in comedy shorts for Vitaphone, but his interests were moving away from the performing end of the spectrum to the production end, and it was in the early '30s that Buzzell began directing shorts for Vitaphone and later feature-length films at Columbia and Universal.

Buzzell's first solid success as a director was *Child of Manhattan* with Nancy Carroll, an adaptation of a Preston Sturges stageplay. Other solid efforts, mostly in the "B" film realm, include *Ann Carver's Profession*, which starred Fay Wray (and written by her future husband and *Thin Man Goes Home* writer Robert Riskin); *The Human Side* (with Adolphe Menjou); *The Girlfriend* (with Ann Sothern); *The Luckiest Girl in the World* (with Jane Wyatt); and *Paradise for Three*, in 1938, starring Robert Young, was Buzzell's first film under a new contract with MGM. Buzzell certainly fit the MGM mode since the films the studio made were, by and large, producer driven rather than having any kind of directorial outlook, and Buzzell delivered in a workman-like and efficient manner and within budget; the thing Metro appreciated the most in any director.

Buzzell's next film, *Fast Company*, is one of his most interesting. It stars Melvyn Douglas as a rare book dealer and amateur sleuth. It contains a nice mixture of comedy and mystery, much in the *Thin Man* tradition. He followed this with a pleasant musical, *Honolulu*, which starred Robert Young, Eleanor Powell and George Burns and Gracie Allen.

It was in 1939 that Buzzell was given the reins to the first Marx Brothers movie for MGM since 1937's *A Day at the Races* (in the interim the brothers had made *Room Service* in 1938 for RKO). This would also be the brothers' first Metro film not produced by their favored Irving Thalberg, who had died in 1937. The producer was Mervyn LeRoy who brought in his old friend Eddie Buzzell to direct. The movie made money, and had some effective gags. The next year MGM made *Go West* with the brothers and, without objections from the Marx Brothers, assigned Buzzell to again direct.

What followed were mostly rather routine films, though a few stood out apart from the others, including *Ship Ahoy* and *Easy to*

Wed. Song of the Thin Man was Buzzell's penultimate film for MGM and a solid, compact job. Of his working relationship with Powell and Loy, Buzzell said at the time, "They are complete professionals and it's a pleasure to come to work every day and watch them at work — so at ease with each other and their characters. It's like a paid vacation."

After leaving MGM (in 1949) Buzzell directed only five more films, the best being *A Woman of Distinction* with Rosalind Russell and Ray Milland, released in 1950 by Columbia. His final film, made in the UK in 1960, was *Mary Had a Little* and he even wrote the title song for that one. During the '50s he also served as a producer of *The Milton Berle Show*. He retired in the early sixties and enjoyed a relatively prosperous retirement in the last quarter century of his life. He died on January 11, 1985.

THE PRODUCER:
NAT PERRIN (March 15, 1905-May 9, 1998)

Perrin produced several films during the late '40s but primarily he was a screenwriter. Like Eddie Buzzell, Perrin worked several times with the Marx Brothers, which usually meant writing gags (if not the complete screenplays) or story ideas for such pictures as *Duck Soup, Monkey Business* and *Go West*, but the fact is he contributed something to virtually every Marx film from 1931 on and, in the process, he became one of Groucho's best friends.

Perrin actually may owe his Hollywood career to Groucho. He was born in New York City in 1905 and planned on a career as an attorney; in fact, he had attended Fordham Law School. But what he really enjoyed doing was writing jokes and submitting them to various comics of the time. Perrin later recalled his first meeting with Groucho: "I'd just finished law school, and I'd been studying very hard. I'd always fooled around writing for the Borscht Circuit, and I was in the law library writing a skit. Somebody looking over my shoulder said, 'that's funny. I know the agent who sold Moss Hart's play *Once in a Lifetime*. I'll get you that agent.' It turned out that his friend was sort of a delivery boy in the woman's office. I didn't want to waste the trip downtown, so I dictated my own letter, signed it, and I took this forgery [a forged letter using Moss Hart's name] and my skit to Brooklyn where the Marx Brothers were appearing at the Albee Theater. I gave the letter I'd done to the doorman, with the sketch. He came out about ten minutes later, and he said, 'Mr. Marx will see you now.' I was shown into Groucho's dressing room. He had the material and liked it. He says, 'We don't use sketches now. We're going to Hollywood to make a picture. We might be able to use a fellow like you. Why don't you come out?' Perrin did and Groucho arranged for the young man to be signed by Paramount.

During the '30s, in addition to writing material for the Marx Brothers, he contributed stories and/or screenplays to several films, including two each for Eddie Cantor (**Roman Scandals, Kid Millions**) and Shirley Temple (**Stowaway, Dimples**), and wrote a comedy-mystery based on SS Van Dine's sleuth Philo Vance, *The Gracie Allen Murder Case*. In the '40s he wrote for Abbott and Costello (**Keep 'em Flying, Pardon my Sarong, Abbott and Costello in Hollywood**) and Red Skelton (**Whistling in Dixie** and **Whistling in Brooklyn**). Perrin liked the then-relaxed atmosphere of writing for MGM. "Metro didn't care if you showed up at the studio or were home or wherever you were . . . You were pretty much on your own. They only cared about the end product."

In 1947 Perrin was allowed to produce the new *Thin Man* film, along with co-writing it. He had considerable success adapting humor with a mystery story in the Skelton pictures, as well as the Philo Vance film, and did an efficient job, but because Powell and Loy were not knockabout comics, like Red Skelton, the material for the *Thin Man* film was more sophisticated and utilized the usual Powell-Loy witticism and comedy byplay and was more focused on the mystery than his other mystery-comedies. In fact, the mystery elements of *Song of the Thin Man* were more upfront than the previous *The Thin Man Goes Home* which seemed to emphasize the comedy more than the mystery. *Song of the Thin Man* has one of the series most solidly constructed plots and mysteries.

Perrin's final two films of the '40s were for Columbia: a good comedy role for Lucille Ball in **Miss Grant Takes Richmond** and Roz Russell in **Tell it to the Judge**. During the '50s Perrin became a television producer and produced a season of the **My Friend Irma** program starring Marie Wilson. He then switched from his usual forte — comedy — and produced the Western anthology program *Death Valley Days*. In the '60s he became the producer of the kooky *Addams Family* television program based on the characters of cartoonist Charles Addams. Series star John Astin (Gomez) would recall Perrin as a "wonderful writer and producer" and was impressed by the fact that the guy who was producing his television show had previously worked with the Marx Brothers. After writing the mediocre Bob Hope comedy *I'll Take Sweden* and Elvis Presley musical *Frankie and Johnny*, Perrin wrote the truly wretched *The Wicked Dreams of Paula Schultz* which starred the cast of TV's *Hogan's Heroes*. It was his final writing credit.

After retiring in the late '60s Perrin lived on another thirty years. In 1977 he was appointed temporary conservator for the estate of his incapacitated friend Groucho Marx where he often had run-ins with Groucho's live-in companion Erin Fleming. He also contributed to several documentaries and books on the lives and careers of the Marxes. Of his Marx Brothers legacy, Perrin would state, "I had more fun on their films than I had on the other films I worked on, very definitely." He died in 1998 at the ripe old age of 93.

THE BACK STORY:

From April to August of 1946 both Bill Powell and Myrna Loy were busy filming two of the most acclaimed films of their careers. Bill was on the Warner Brothers lot shooting *Life with Father* while Myrna was at the Goldwyn Studios shooting *The Best Years of Our Lives*. At the time that the two would reunite at MGM for their final outing as Nick and Nora Charles in *Song of the Thin Man* in January of 1947, *The Best Years of Our Lives* was already breaking box office records and winning acclaim. Myrna Loy had returned to the studio — which had let her go — on the condition that she return for any *Thin Man* films. *Life with Father* would not be released until August of 1947 (nearly a year after principal photography had ended), but with the stage success of the play it was almost assured that Bill, too, would have a huge box office hit, which may be one of the reasons why, ultimately, *Song of the Thin Man* would be released by MGM at about the same time as *Life with Father*.

Writer Nat Perrin would later recall how he came to produce the final *Thin Man* film: "They came to me and said, 'We need a *Thin Man*.' That's when I became a producer, for *Song of the Thin Man*. And I thought, what could we do with the Thin Man this time? And at that time jive talk, the bebop era, had just started. And I had the idea to use that background. And I consulted a man, Harry the Hipster, who played piano in a Vine Street joint. Keenan Wynn and Peter Lawford called . . . 'We want to bring Harry the Hipster over.' And they brought him over and he finished a whole bottle of brandy while playing some crazy songs on the piano. The point is that was the first thing I thought of, the background, and then you develop the line of your story."

Perrin next chose Eddie Buzzell to direct, something he later came to question. "I remember a direction I heard on the sound track of *Song of the Thin Man*. Eddie Buzzell was the director, and I expected him to be better because he had been in the New York Theater as an actor, and I thought he was show wise. Don Taylor was playing a character who played the clarinet, and he has gone wacky from drugs — he's in a sanitarium. It's a very dramatic moment, and I hear the director [Buzzell] say on the sound track, 'Do things with your face!' Now what the heck kind of direction is that?"

The filming of the picture (which extended from early January to mid-March of 1947) was without problems, though Leon Ames, who plays Talbin in the film, later recalled, "Bill Powell was bored with the role." He is also one of the few actors who would later question the widespread belief that Bill and Myrna were as chummy off screen as on. "Here was America's happiest couple," Ames would later say. "For years, the public believed that — and (yet) they never talked. Except when they were in front of the cameras. I'm surprised that they talked even then. Some of the time, they talked to the camera alone and the film was edited together." This is interesting because Ames is one of the few actors to appear in two *Thin Man* films and you would expect that he would have a keen observation of things, but it should also be stressed that he didn't work every day and his roles in each film was relatively small. It is also known that Bill and Myrna each gave themselves space. They had worked together for too long (14 years by this time) and in too many films that they didn't have to spend every moment off camera palling around together. Bill, for instance, often took off for his dressing room between takes and Myrna enjoyed reading or concentrating on her script between scenes and Bill, and others, knew better than to interrupt her.

The wonderful Jayne Meadows had one of her earliest film roles playing Janet Thayer in *Song of the Thin Man*. She would recall Bill and Myrna as "great chums" and enjoyed working with both of them. "I was very fond of both Bill Powell and Myrna Loy and became a good pal of hers," Miss Meadows later said. "Bill gave me the nickname 'Busher' while working on the film, because he said I had the greatest legs this side of Louis B. Mayer's famous filly, 'Busher,' who was not only the number one winning race horse in the world, at the time, but the biggest money-maker as well. Bill was great fun and loved by all — as was Myrna." She would also recall that her stand-in on *Song of the Thin Man* was Gloria Grahame's sister, Joy Mitchum, who was married to Robert Mitchum's brother. "Bill Dana says, 'Ours is an incestuous profession!' We're all somehow related." (By the way, if the actor who plays Jayne's father in *Song of the Thin Man* looks vaguely familiar it's because Ralph Morgan was the brother of MGM character actor Frank Morgan, best known as the wizard in *The Wizard of Oz*.)

Gloria Grahame, who plays sultry nightclub singer Fran Page, wore a stunning gold lame outfit in the film and, according to her biographer, the tight-fitting outfit was "almost pushed to the limit." While a visiting reporter was having an interview with Grahame, Gloria was enjoying a hearty lunch topped off by two bowls of bananas and cream. The reporter, noted that she "had to be a little careful how she sat or gestured, for fear her luscious loveliness might pour out through a seam." Grahame, who would, painstakingly, do her own singing eight years later in *Oklahoma!*, was dubbed here by Carol Arden.

When the film was released in August of 1947, contrary to popular belief, it was a financial success. In the papers of producer Pandro Berman, at the Wisconsin State Historical Society, is the profit/loss sheet of various MGM films and *Song of the Thin Man* ended up with a profit of slightly more than

$500,000 — considering that the film cost just a little more than a million dollars to produce, that is a substantial profit returned to the studio. But by this time MGM was cutting costs and concentrating on "big pictures." They decided to end their series films like *The Thin Man, Maisie,* and *Tarzan.*

Myrna Loy would call *Song of the Thin Man* "a lackluster finish to a great series. I hated it." She would add that "the characters had lost their sparkle for Bill and me, and the people who knew what it was all about were no longer involved. Woody Van Dyke was dead. Dashiell Hammett and Hunt Stromberg had gone elsewhere. The Hacketts were writing other things." Myrna said that "surprisingly" the picture had been well received in England and that Bill had sent her an article he had cut out from *The Hollywood Reporter* which read, "Most of the cricks gave a cordial welcome back to old-timers Bill Powell and Myrna Loy . . ." Bill circled the words "old-timers" and wrote in pencil at the top to Myrna, "Dear old girl! I know you wouldn't want to miss this. Love, Willy (old boy)."

SUPPORTING CAST:
GLORIA GRAHAME (November 28, 1923-October 5, 1981)

Song of the Thin Man was only Gloria Grahame's sixth film, but her *femme fatale* role is the type that would define her career. With her sultry lips and her blonde locks she belonged in the deep crevices of *film noir* — that dark place where knowing women manipulate men who think they are in the driver's seat — but aren't. And, in fact, Grahame was one of the great *noir* stars of her time with such films to her credit as *In a Lonely Place, Macao, The Glass Wall* and especially Fritz Lang's *The Big Heat,* in which she figures in one of the most violent scenes in the history of motion pictures when she gets a pot of scalding coffee thrown into her beautiful face by a sadistic Lee Marvin. *Film noir* historian Marc Dolezal summed up Grahame's effectiveness this way: "The acting of Gloria Grahame, more than any other Hollywood actress, may best embody the essence of what is *film noir.* The characters she portrays in *noir* are tough women with calloused exteriors who are at the same time very fragile and vulnerable, but always attractive."

She was born Gloria Hallward in Los Angeles, California. Her mother had been an actress and, later, an acting coach at the famous

Pasadena Playhouse. Her father was an architect. Louis B. Mayer saw Hallward on stage at the Pasadena Playhouse and, impressed by her beauty, brought her to Hollywood. The studio felt she needed a different name. She kept her real first name and took on her mother's stage last name as her own and Gloria Hallward became Gloria Grahame.

Grahame first came to the attention of moviegoers with her performance as Violet, the bad girl who catches the eye of every man in Bedford Falls, in Frank Capra's perennial classic *It's a Wonderful Life.* Capra was sold on Gloria by MGM casting director Billy Grady who told him, "Two years she's been hanging around here snapping her garters. You can hire her for a cuppa coffee. But you think I can get these jerk directors to listen? She's got real star quality, but nobody will listen." This film was not an MGM film; Grahame was on loan-out to Capra's Liberty Pictures. MGM really didn't know what to do with Grahame, and, in fact, the best of her MGM films and the one which captured her potential best was *Song of the Thin Man.* But MGM didn't specialize in *noir* films, and when they did make one, they had another sultry blonde who was a far bigger name, Lana Turner. MGM sold Grahame's contract to RKO. She excelled in a sympathetic role in *Crossfire,* for which she received her first Oscar nomination for Best Supporting Actress.

Grahame's star shined brightest during the '50s when she appeared in several outstanding films, often cast as the "bad girl" or *femme fatale.* Film critic Rex Reed would later write, "She was sultry, sexy, beautiful and very, very, bad . . . When she was good she was great, but when she was bad she was even better." She was the aspiring actress contending with Humphrey Bogart's temper in Nicholas Ray's *In a Lonely Place.* By this time Ray was Grahame's second husband, having previously been married to actor Stanley Clements (which ended in 1948). Other memorable films of this period include *The Greatest Show on Earth* (as the elephant girl), *The Bad and the Beautiful* (winning an Oscar), *Sudden Fear* (memorably helping Jack Palance menace Joan Crawford), and *Human Desire.* Then came a change of pace playing not the bad, but naughty Ado Annie, the girl who "cain't say no," in *Oklahoma.* Of her performance in *Human Desire* the British critic Judith Williamson would write, ". . . she seems to represent a sort of acted upon femininity, both unfathomable and ungraspable. She slips through the film like a drop of loose mercury. Neither we nor the other characters know whether to believe what she says; elusive as a cat, she is the focus of terrible actions, but unknowable herself."

She was considered difficult by directors and other actors (her bad behavior on the set of *Oklahoma!* is blamed for her career losing its momentum) and soon, despite her undeniable beauty and talent, good roles began to dry up and she returned to the stage. Her private life was equally chaotic. Two years after divorcing Nicholas Ray (in 1952) she married radio and television comedy writer Cy Howard; they had a child, but the union lasted only a few years (of her time with Howard, Grahame would say, "Well, at least he made me laugh"). She then stunned many, in 1960, by marrying the son of her second husband, Nicholas Ray, and, to the surprise of many, this union lasted the longest: sixteen years and produced children. The films she made after 1959 were mostly unmemorable, though she was, as usual, good in them — one of the better ones being the 1980 cult film *Melvin and Howard.* Throughout the sixties and seventies she appeared on the stage. In 1973 she toured with Henry Fonda in the play *The Time of Your Life.* Fonda, a notoriously hard-to-please man, was impressed with Gloria. "The highlight of my recent tour, at least for me, was the ten-minute scene I played with Gloria Grahame. She's a most riveting actress." In her final years she appeared frequently on stage, playing Sadie Thompson in *Rain.* In 1981 Grahame was rehearsing for a play in England when she collapsed. She returned to New York where she was diagnosed with advanced breast cancer. She died on October 5, 1981. She was only 57 years old. (Sources include: *Interview*, 9/1/00.)

JAYNE MEADOWS (September 27, 1920)

Many people recall Jayne Meadows as one of those ultra-sophisticated television panelists on game shows of the '50s and '60s such as *I've Got a Secret*, which was hosted by her husband, Steve Allen. So linked in the public's consciousness is Miss Meadows as Mrs. Steve Allen, that sometimes people forget what a multi-faceted actress and personality she is in her own right.

She was born Jayne Cotter, the daughter of American missionaries in China, on September 27, 1920. She spent her first ten or eleven years in China and spoke the language fluently; in fact, she had to learn English when her family (four children, one of whom was the equally talented actress Audrey Meadows, who would later play the definitive Alice on the legendary television series *The Honeymooners* opposite Jackie Gleason) moved back to the United States. In the late '30s Jayne and Audrey began singing together in clubs and by the early '40s Meadows was appearing with frequency on the Broadway stage, first in the play *Spring Again*. Between 1941 and 1945 Meadows appeared in five Broadway shows, including *Kiss Them for Me*, which featured Richard Widmark and another up-and-coming actress, Judy Holliday.

Meadows was brought to Hollywood by MGM in 1946. The studio had her change her name from Audrey Cotter, because it sounded too much like actress Audrey Totter, to Jayne Meadows. At MGM she was quickly typecast as sophisticated women who had ice water running through their veins. Her first film was *Undercurrent*, which was directed by Vincente Minnelli. Meadows' MGM screen test had been directed by the legendary George Cukor, who was a personal friend of the film's star, Katharine Hepburn. At one point during the filming, Cukor asked Hepburn how she thought Meadows was doing in this, her first film role. Hepburn told the venerable director, "Considering I'm old enough to be her mother and she's playing my rival — I think she's a genius!"

Meadows followed this film up with the *film noir Lady in the Lake*, a Philip Marlowe yarn starring Robert Montgomery, who also directed. Montgomery cast Meadows after accidentally viewing rushes of her work in *Undercurrent* and felt that Jayne would be perfect for the psychopathic murderess of his movie. After this, Meadows went into the final *Dr. Kildare* picture and then the final *Thin Man*. Unfortunately for Jayne, MGM declined to pick up her option after this. But her misfortune became a bit of luck when she was hired by Samuel Goldwyn to appear in *Enchantment*, which became a personal favorite of hers.

In the early '50s Meadows began appearing frequently on television anthology shows, and also occasional film roles. One of the most popular was the 1951 20th Century-Fox film *David and Bathsheba* in which Meadows played Queen Michal, wife to Gregory Peck's King David, whom he divorces to marry Bathsheba (Susan Hayward). In 1954 she married television personality Steve Allen, with whom she would appear frequently with on television, stage and even an occasional motion picture. By this time Meadows was the epitome of New York glamour and sophistication with her frequent appearances on such game shows as *To Tell the Truth, I've Got a Secret* and *What's My Line?*

By the mid-'50s her screen career was virtually over, though she would appear in a few random films in the '80s and '90s like *City Slickers* (playing the mother of Billy Crystal), *Casino* (a cameo with husband Steve Allen), and Rob Reiner's *The Story of Us* (playing Michelle Pfeiffer's mother). She made frequent guest appearances on episodic television, and in the process was nominated for the Emmy Award five times. In 1957 she returned to the Broadway stage in the successful comedy *The Gazebo*. Among the highlights of her television career was a critically acclaimed PBS series she did for several years called *Meeting of Minds*, a talk show (hosted by Steve Allen) where the guests are historical figures who discuss their lives. Meadows appeared several times playing the likes of Cleopatra, Marie Antoinette, Elizabeth Barrett Browning, Catherine the Great, Susan B. Antony and Florence Nightingale. She was also Emmy nominated for an appearance on *St. Elsewhere* in 1987, and appeared on the popular CBS series *Medical Center* for three years.

In 1990 Meadows won acclaim in the off-Broadway production of Neil Simon's *Lost in Yonkers* playing the 85-year-old grandmother of the story and winning the Drama-Lounge Award for Best Actress in the process. Over the years she toured in a one-woman play called *Powerful Women in History* for which she received several awards including the Susan B. Anthony Award, presented by the National Organization of Women (NOW). She and Allen also toured during this decade in *Love Letters*. Allen died suddenly in October 2000, but Meadows is still going strong at 87 and is currently writing her long-awaited memoirs. She has been quoted as saying, "I have this tremendous energy. I just loved and love life. I love it today. I never want to die." (Sources include: www.jaynemeadows.com.)

PATRICIA MORISON (March 19, 1915)

It's interesting that in *Song of the Thin Man* Patricia Morison plays a non-singing role, and yet her most famous roles — on stage — were in musicals — in *Kiss Me Kate* and *The King and I*. The actress who had the singing role in the film, Gloria Grahame, was dubbed. Patricia Morison was often misused in motion pictures, yet, in actuality, it should be said that her role in *Song of the Thin Man*, particularly at its climax, is one of her better opportunities.

Morison was born in New York as Ursula Eileen Patricia Augustus Fraser Morison on March 19, 1914, though some sources claim it to be 1915. Her father was a playwright, and her mother worked for British intelligence during World War I. After graduating from high school, Morison took acting lessons and studied dance with Martha Graham.

In 1933 she made her Broadway debut in a play called *Growing Pains* which folded within a few weeks. She then was understudy to Helen Hayes in *Victoria Regina*, but the indefatigable Hayes never gave her an opportunity to go on. (At one point in the run Hayes did get ill, and couldn't go on, but audiences so anticipated Hayes in the role that they would never accept anybody else, so the play closed until Hayes was able to appear again.) She then appeared with Alfred Drake in the musical *The Two Bouquets*. It was while appearing in this short-lived play that she was discovered by Paramount talent scouts and brought to Hollywood. She was better than competent in such programmers as *Persons in Hiding, I'm From Missouri,* and *Romance on the Rio Grande*. She was then cast in an adaptation of Sinclair Lewis' Mantrap, updated and retitled *Untamed*, opposite Ray Milland. One of the publicity angles that the studio played up was the length of Morison's hair; at 39 inches, it was said that she had the longest hair among Hollywood actresses.

She was Fred MacMurray's leading lady in the Western *Rangers of Fortune* and played the "other woman" opposite MacMurray in *One Night in Lisbon* and Ray Milland in *Are Husbands Necessary?* Morison was disappointed when she was suddenly replaced at the last minute by Veronica Lake in *The Glass Key*. The studio head, Buddy DeSylva, told Morison that she would play heavies not leading lady roles and Morison later said that she got out of her Paramount contract by gaining weight; "I over-ate my way out of the . . . contract."

Morison then went to Monogram for their first attempt at an A-class picture, *Silver Skates*, playing the owner of an Ice Capades-type show. She then had a good part in the Twentieth Century-Fox film *The Song of Bernadette*, playing Empress Eugenie, but it was Jennifer Jones who stole the picture in her first significant film, and winning an Oscar. Morison then played one of the leading roles in the cult film *Hitler's Madman* directed by Douglas Sirk, in a story about Czech resistance fighters trying to free their country from the Nazi grip. One of her most famous films was as a murderess doing battle with Basil Rathbone's Sherlock Holmes in *Dressed to Kill*.

After *Song of the Thin Man* Morison made only a few more films, and many in the industry believed that her time had finally come when she was cast as Victor Mature's suicidal wife in *Kiss of Death*, but when the film was released her part had been drastically cut from the finished product. From that point forward she concentrated her time on the stage and her popular leading roles in *Kiss Me Kate* and *The King and I* (replacing the dying Gertrude Lawrence). She also made television appearances recreating her musical roles on the small screen. In addition to those stage productions, Morison starred in such classic musicals as *Kismet, The Merry Widow* and *Song of Norway*. In the '70s she even took on Vera, the sponsor of *Pal Joey*, on stage opposite Dean Jones.

Now in her 90s Morison is retired from active work as an actress and devotes her time to painting and charitable endeavors. She never married and has no children.

DEAN STOCKWELL (March 5, 1936)

Dean Stockwell was one of the best and most natural of child stars. He was cute with a cherubic face and naturally curly hair, but he never was cloying and went out of his way to avoid the tricks of the child star trade, telling Bob Costa in the late '80s, ". . . frankly I never tried to look cute or sympathetic. If anything, I would try to work against that. Even if it was requested that I be that way. Somehow, I just didn't like that. I just tried to be honest and be myself."

He was born Robert Dean Stockwell, on March 5, 1935, in North Hollywood, California. (His older brother, Guy, born in

1933, was also an actor, mostly on television. Guy died in 2002.) His parents had been stage performers (his father, Harry, voiced the role of the Prince in the Walt Disney animated classic *Snow White and the Seven Dwarfs*) and they allowed him on the stage by the age of seven. In 1943 Dean and Guy made their Broadway debuts playing brothers in the play *Innocent Voyage*. His natural ability shined through and, by the time he was nine, he was under contract to Metro-Goldwyn-Mayer. He would be under contract to MGM for six years and appear in seventeen films.

His first film for the studio was *Anchors Aweigh* playing opposite Gene Kelly and Frank Sinatra. His mother would recall that young Dean met with the producer of the film, Joe Pasternak, and Pasternak asked Dean if he wanted the part of the young boy in the film. Dean replied, "Can I keep the lollypops?" (Pasternak gave him lollypops during the interview), to which Pasternak answered, "Of course." Later, during the making of the film, he made sure that there were a hundred lollypops on the set available for the young actor. That same year he appeared in *The Valley of Decision*. When he wasn't working on a film, he was attending MGM's famed little red school house with Margaret O'Brien and Elizabeth Taylor.

One of Stockwell's biggest early roles was as Nick Charles, Jr. in *Song of the Thin Man*, and Stockwell recalls his screen parents fondly. "I have very positive feelings regarding both of them; they were very sweet people, especially Myrna Loy. And that cute little dog, Asta. I liked that little dog." But his first really significant role came the same year on loan out to another studio, 20th Century-Fox, with Gregory Peck, in *Gentleman's Agreement* (memorably asking the question, "Dad, what is anti-Semitism?"). But in an interview with Craig Edwards in 1995, Stockwell says he didn't enjoy making the film because it was too dark. "I didn't like doing it at all, because it was so serious. In other words, when I would find out I was going to do another movie, my mother would always bring that news to me, and the first question that I would always ask was, 'Is there a crying scene?' And there almost always was, and then I would be totally depressed about that."

It was on loan out again (for RKO) that Stockwell made one of his most famous and popular films of this period and one which called for an actor, and not just a child star — Joseph Losey's *The*

Boy with Green Hair (1948), about a boy who becomes an outcast when his hair turns green. Stockwell's own hair wasn't dyed for the film; he wore a wig which he later told Edwards was a "pain in the ass" to wear.

The next year Stockwell starred opposite his female counterpart as popular MGM child stars, Margaret O'Brien, in the film *The Secret Garden*. He recalled the film itself as "more crying scenes and temper tantrums" but enjoyed working with O'Brien who he recalls as "a very talented little actress." The director of *The Secret Garden*, Fred Wilcox, recalled that Stockwell was "always letter perfect in his lines, so that rigorous rehearsing isn't necessary for him, and might, in fact, dull the sincerity of his performance."

Stockwell's final MGM film was one of his favorites and a very popular one, an adaptation of Rudyard Kipling's *Kim* (1950), which also starred Errol Flynn. He enjoyed making the film and working with Flynn. "*Kim* was great because of Errol Flynn," he told Edwards. "I really liked Errol, he was always very straight with me, not patronizing at all. Very cool. Of all the people I worked with, he was my favorite, along with Dick Widmark and Joel McCrea [S*tars in my Crown, Cattle Drive*]." Of his child actor years Stockwell later recalled to Larry King, "It wasn't easy. No. It wasn't impossible, but it wasn't easy. Look, when it comes down to it, it's a very bizarre form of work. It's work. You go in, and you work eight to ten hours a day. And you have to go to school at the same time, six days a week in those days. So it's a job! That in itself is unusual, for a child to have a job! A paying job!"

The immediate years following his leaving MGM were tough. He was a teenager, and rebellious. He went to regular school and graduated in 1952. He told some interviewers that after this he hitchhiked around the country doing odd jobs. By the late '50s, when he was in his early twenties, he decided to reactivate his film career and got some important roles in some pretty good pictures, including *Gun for a Coward*, a psychological Western which starred Fred MacMurray, and especially *Compulsion* (1958), which he had also done on Broadway (with Roddy McDowall). It was based on the infamous 1920s Leopold and Loeb murders. In the film he was paired with Bradford Dillman and Orson Welles. Stockwell didn't especially care for Welles. "I found him most disagreeable and very badly behaved to other people, bordering on sadistic."

After a lull in the mid-'50s Stockwell was becoming, in the late '50s and early '60s, a top young character lead — not so much a star; they were not always star-making roles but there were juicy parts in films like *Compulsion, Sons and Lovers* and especially *Long Day's Journey Into Night*, which Stockwell recalled as a "great experience" and "one of the highlight films" of his career. Stockwell shared acting honors at the Cannes Film Festival for his performances in *Compulsion* and *Long Day's Journey into Night*. When he wasn't working on a film, he was appearing with great consistency on television, especially in anthology dramas like *General Electric Theater, Playhouse 90* and *Alfred Hitchcock Presents*.

By the mid-'60s Stockwell's movie career had stalled again, and it was frequent appearances on television that kept his name before the public. He met Jack Nicholson for the first time in 1967 when he filmed the counter-generation *Psych-Out* for low-budget AIP. He followed this with a horror film with Sandra Dee, *The Dunwich Horror*, which went nowhere, and a biker movie, *The Loners* (1972), which Stockwell calls a "mess." He had high hopes for *The Werewolf of Washington* (1973), which was a Watergate-themed horror film in which the president of the United States gets bit by a werewolf, but he later conceded that the end result was "disappointing."

Throughout the '70s Stockwell continued to work consistently on television and in films which were on the most part forgettable. It was in the mid-'80s that Stockwell's film career was revived with offbeat roles in celebrated offbeat films like as *Paris, Texas* (*New York Times* film critic Vincent Canby would write, "Mr. Stockwell, the former child star, has aged very well, becoming an exceptionally interesting, mature actor), *Tucker* (playing Howard Hughes), *Blue Velvet*, and *Married to the Mob* (nominated for an Academy Award for his comedy performance as well as receiving the New York Film Critics Award). He called his part in *Married to the Mob* his favorite of his career. "I just felt that that part was just perfect for me and I had a way to approach it that I thought was just right and it turned out that way."

In addition to strong character roles in major films he became a top television star with his performance as Al on *Quantum Leap*.

In the years since he has appeared in such films as *Air Force One, Rites of Passage, The Manchurian Candidate* (2004 remake of classic 1962 film), and *The Deal*. Stockwell became the exception — the child star who managed to evolve into a fully-functioning and successful adult actor. Sixty-two years in motion pictures and still going strong. Stockwell has been married twice, his first wife being the actress Millie Perkins (Anne Frank in George Stevens' 1959 film *The Diary of Anne Frank*). He has two children with his second wife. (Sources include: *American Magazine*, 12/49, *Parents Magazine*, 12/50, *Films in Review*, 1/85.)

KEENAN WYNN (July 27, 1916-October 14, 1986)

A highly talented and respected character actor who could handle any type of role, whether it is slapstick or highly dramatic, Keenan Wynn was one of the top character stars at MGM during the 1940s and for various studios thereafter. He always maintained that he never minded being the second banana. "My billing has always been 'and' or 'including.' That's all right; let the stars take the blame."

He was born in New York City as Francis Xavier Aloysius James Jeremiah Keenan Wynn, on July 27, 1916, the son of popular comedian Ed Wynn, who was Jewish, and his Irish-Catholic wife Hilda. His family had strong ties to show business on both sides. Ed Wynn was at the height of his fame on the American stage at the time of Keenan's birth and his maternal grandfather, Frank Keenan, was a prominent dramatic stage actor. Young Keenan's childhood was an affluent one and he was educated at private schools. When he started in show business many people expected Keenan to follow in his father's footsteps, but Keenan didn't want to be known as a "clown" but as a solid dramatic actor. His earliest acting experience was at the Lakewood Summer Theater in Skowbegan, Maine, where he appeared in several plays in summer stock. He appeared on the Broadway stage in the late '30s and into the early '40s along with making frequent appearances on radio. His big break on stage was appearing in the musical-comedy revue *Two for the Show* (1940), which also featured Eve Arden, Alfred Drake and Betty Hutton. In the late '30s he met the actress Eve Abbott, known as "Evie," who would soon become his wife, acting coach, and advisor, as well as bear him two children.

Wynn was signed by MGM in 1941, but didn't make his first big splash in films until he was cast as Robert Walker's friend in the popular wartime comedy *See Here, Private Hargrove* and its sequel *What Next? Corporal Hargrove.* He played the drunk opposite Walker again and Judy Garland in Vincent Minnelli's charming *The Clock.* He and Lucille Ball practically stole *Without Love* from its stars, Spencer Tracy and Katharine Hepburn. He then worked with Ball again in the 1946 comedy *Easy to Wed*, a remake of 1936's *Libeled Lady*, with Wynn in the Spencer Tracy role and Ball in the Jean Harlow part. The stars were Van Johnson (Wynn's best friend in real life) in the role played by William Powell in the original and Esther Williams in the part played by Myrna Loy. Again, Ball and Wynn stole the film from the nominal stars. The film was directed by Edward Buzzell, who would later cast Wynn in *Song of the Thin Man.* He also excelled in dramatic parts in films like *B.F.'s Daughter* and *The Hucksters*, in which he played a disagreeable star to Clark Gable's advertising man. Shortly after filming *Easy to Wed*, Keenan suffered a near-death motorcycle crash (motorcycles and racing had become his passion) and often at this bedside was his wife Evie and best friend Van Johnson. But the next year Evie and Keenan divorced and Evie married Johnson. This was a bad period for Keenan, who turned increasingly to alcohol. But he had to get on with his work and did so steadily over the next several years in such films as *Neptune's Daughter, Annie Get Your Gun,* and three films with Fred Astaire, *Three Little Words, Royal Wedding* and B*elle of New York.* One of his last films of his MGM contract was *Kiss Me Kate*, where he memorably sang "Bush Up on Your Shakespeare" with James Whitmore. His final film at MGM was *Tennessee's Champ*, a "B" film about boxing in which he had a rare leading role, opposite Shelley Winters.

After leaving MGM, Wynn alternated between parts in films and frequent appearances on television, especially in the dramatic anthology shows which were popular at the time. In 1956, Keenan was teamed for the first time opposite his father in the film *The Great Man.* By this time Ed Wynn had experienced a severe career slide and was reluctant to accept a dramatic role. Keenan and his father had had an awkward relationship with Keenan trying to distance himself from his dad. Keenan once said of their relationship,

"My father was famous, generous, and he loved me — but at a distance. I took up riding a motorcycle as much to worry him and get him to notice me as anything else." It was now up to Keenan to convince his father to do the film and then to work with him on his performance — something that didn't always go easily. This was later dramatized in a *Desilu Playhouse* presentation which starred both Wynns in 1960. Needless to say, Ed did the part, and a new career as a dramatic character actor was launched. He conceded he couldn't have done it without Keenan's help. In 1956, Keenan also appeared in one of live television's great dramatic presentations, *Requiem for a Heavyweight*, as part of *Playhouse 90* (from a Rod Serling script), which also featured his father Ed.

By this time Keenan became a natural at villainous roles in Disney films such as *The Absent Minded Professor* and its sequel *Son of Flubber* playing the money-grubbing businessman who tries to steal Fred MacMurray's formulas. His most famous film is probably *Dr. Strangelove or: How I Learned to Stop Worrying and Love the Bomb* (1964), directed by Stanley Kubrick, playing the hammy Col. Bat Guano. Other film roles during these years included *The Patsy, The Great Race, Point Blank, Finian's Rainbow* (a fourth film with Fred Astaire), *MacKenna's Gold, Viva Max!* and Roger Vadim's *Pretty Maids all in a Row.* In all he would appear in some 200 motion pictures, 250 television programs and over 100 stage productions, making him one of the busiest actors in the business.

Keenan continued on in episodic television and television movies well into the 1980s, never slowing down despite health woes which included heart problems (he had to withdraw from playing the part of Perry White in the first *Superman* film in 1977 due to his heart), and a condition called tinnitus, or ringing in the ears, which affected him during much of the '80s. After a brief second marriage, Keenan would marry again in 1954, a union which would last until his death, and produce three more children. The end came on October 14, 1986 when Wynn finally lost an eight-month battle with cancer. His son-in-law told the press, "His death was peaceful. His family was with him." He was 70. (Sources include: *Syracuse Post Standard*, 10/15/86 & *Chronicle-Telegram*, 10/15/86.)

REVIEWS:

"Powell and Miss Loy, as his always inquisitive wife, fit ideally into the starring roles."

Variety, 7/23/47

"William Powell and Myrna Loy exhibit the same old zest and bantering affection they have always brought to their performances as the Charleses."

New York Times, 8/29/47

"There's a thrill per minute and a laugh per second in the new . . . *Song of the Thin Man* . . . In their latest adventure in hilarious homicide and murderous mirth Nick and Nora tackle the funniest as well as the most spine tingling mystery of their long and successful careers and give off the season's most uproarious action and dialogue while solving it . . . Set down *Song of the Thin Man* on your 'must-see' list . . ."

The **(Annapolis, MD)** *Evening Capital*, 9/3/47

"Mr. and Mrs. Thin Man — William Powell and Myrna Loy, of course, are back! The screens' first lady and gentleman of crime are reunited once more in . . . the most mirth-packed murder mystery yet in the popular series . . ."

The Waterloo **(IA)** *Sunday Courier*, 11/3/47

"The Thin Man's song turns out to be jive, on the beat, reet and ready to fly."

Motion Picture, 1947

"***1/2 — Sixth and final entry in the series, a cut above the previous one because of its involvement in jazz music circles . . . All in all, a worthy effort with which to conclude things."

Mick Martin & Marsha Porter,
Video and Movie Guide, 2002

"**1/2 — In this sixth and final series entry, still amiable and entertaining thanks to the stars chemistry."

Leonard Maltin

Song of the Thin Man Photo Gallery

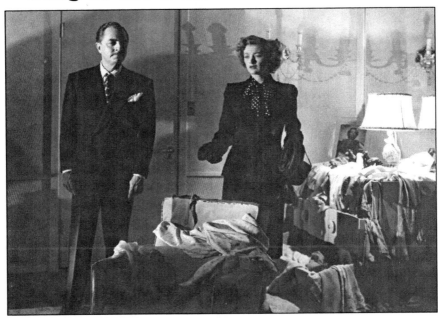

Nick and Nora on the case. PHOTO COURTESY OF LAURA WAGNER

Song of the Thin Man has a jazz background. That's Keenan Wynn to Bill's left.

Nick looking over a photograph of Fran Page (Gloria Grahame).

Dean Stockwell (as Nick Jr.) between Myrna and Bill with Jayne Meadows looking on.

Arguably the best movie series in film history. William Powell, Myrna Loy and Asta. COURTESY OF SCOTT O'BRIEN.

BIBLIOGRAPHY

Adamson, *Joe, Groucho, Harpo, Chico and Sometimes Zeppo*, Simon & Schuster, 1973

Allyson, June (with Frances Spatz Leighton), *June Allyson*, G.P. Putnam's Sons, 1982

Arce, Hector, *The Secret Life of Tyrone Power*, William Morrow & Col, 1979

Bakewell, William, *Hollywood Be Thy Name*, Scarecrow, 1991

Behlmer, Rudy (editor), *W.S. Van Dyke's Journal*, The Scarecrow Press, 1996

Berg, A Scott, *Goldwyn: A Biography*, Alfred A. Knopf, 1989

Bogle, Donald, *Blacks in American Films and Television*, Garland Publishing, Inc., 1988

_____*Toms, Coons, Mulattoes, Mammies & Bucks*, Continuum, 2004

Bosworth, Patricia, *Montgomery Clift*, Harcourt Brace Jovanovich, 1978

Bryant, Roger, *William Powell: The Life and Films*, McFarland & Company, 2006

Cannon, Robert, *Van Dyke and the Mythical City Hollywood*, Murray & Gee, 1948

Capra, Frank, *The Name Above the Title*, MacMillan, 1971

Carey, Gary, *All the Stars in Heaven*, Dutton, 1981

Chandler, Charlotte, *Hello, I Must be Going*, Doubleday, 1978

Chandler, Raymond, *The Simple Art of Murder*, Vintage, 1988

Curio, Vincent, *Suicide Blonde: The Life of Gloria Grahame*, Morrow & Co., 1989

Crowther, Bosley, *Hollywood Rajah: The Life and Times of Louis B. Mayer*, Holt, 1960

Eames, John Douglas, *The MGM Story*, Crown Publishers Inc., 1979

Eliot, Marc, *Jimmy Stewart: A Biography*, Harmony Books, 2006

Eyman, Scott, *Lion of Hollywood: The Life and Legend of Louis B Mayer*, Simon & Schuster, 2005

Fishgall, Gary, *Pieces of Time: The Life of James Stewart*, Scribner, 1997

Fonda, Henry (as told to Howard Teichmann), *Fonda: My Life*, New American Library, 1981.

Fontaine, Joan, *No Bed of Roses*, Berkley, 1980

Fordin, Hugh, *MGM's Greatest Musicals: The Arthur Freed Unit*, Da Capo Press, 1996

Francisco, Charles, *Gentleman: The William Powell Story*, St. Martin's Press, 1985

Fultz, Jay, *In Search of Donna Reed*, University of Iowa Press, 2001

Glitre, Kathrina, *Hollywood Romantic Comedy: States of the Union 1934-1965*, Manchester University Press, 2006

Goodrich, David L, *The Real Nick and Nora*, Southern Illinois University Press, 2001

Hadleigh, Boze, *Hollywood Lesbians*, Barricade Books, 1994

Hammett, Dashiell, *The Thin Man*, Penguin, 2006

Harris, Warren G, *Gable and Lombard*, Simon & Schuster, 1974

Higham, Charles, *Merchant of Dreams: Louis B Mayer, MGM and the Secret Hollywood*, Fine, 1993

Hirsch, Foster, *Acting Hollywood Style*, Henry N. Abrams, Inc., 1991

Johnson, Diane, *Dashiell Hammett: A Life*, Random House, 1983

Kael, Pauline, *Kiss Kiss Bang Bang*, Bantam Books, 1965

_____*5001 Nights at the Movies*, Henry Holt & Co., 1982

Kanin, Garson, *Together Again: The Story of the Great Hollywood Teams*, Doubleday, 1981

Lanchester, Elsa, *Elsa Lanchester Herself*, St. Martin's Press, 1983

LaSalle, Mick, *Complicated Women: Sex and Power in Pre-Code Hollywood*, St. Martin's Press, 2000

Leonard, Sheldon, *And the Show Goes On*, 1st Limelight Edition, 1995

LeRoy, Mervyn (with Dick Kleiner), *Mervyn LeRoy: Take One*, Hawthorn, 1974

Loughery, John, *Alias S.S. Van Dine*, Charles Scribner's Sons, 1992

Louvish, Simon, *Mae West: It Ain't No Sin*, Thomas Dunne Books/St. Martin's Press, 2005

Loy, Myrna (with James Kostsilibas-Davis), *Being and Becoming*, Alfred A. Knopf, 1987

Lyon, Christopher (and Susan Doll), *International Directory of Films & Filmmakers*, Pan MacMillan, 1987

Maltin, Leonard, *Movie and Video Guide, 1992*, Penguin Books, 1991

Martin, Mick (with Marsha Porter), *Video Movie Guide 2002*, Ballantine Book, 2001

Marx, Groucho, *The Groucho Letters*, Simon & Schuster, 1967

McBride, Joseph, *Frank Capra: The Catastrophe of Success*, St. Martin's Griffin, 2000

McClelland, Doug, *Forties Film Talk*, McFarland, 1992

Metress, Christopher (editor), *The Critical Response to Dashiell Hammett*, Greenwood Press, 1994

Monush, Barry, *Encyclopedia of Hollywood Film Actors*, Applause, 2003

Morley, Sheridan, *The Other Side of the Moon: The Life of David Niven*, Weidenfeld and Nicholson, 1985

O'Brien, Scott, *Kay Francis: I Can't Wait to Be Forgotten*, BearManor Media, 2006

Oldham, Gabriella, *First Cuts: Conversations with Film Editors*, University of California Press, 1995

Parish, James Robert (and Don E. Stanke), *The All-Americans*, Arlington House, 1977

Parish, James Robert (and Ronald Bowers), *The MGM Stock Company*, Arlington House, 1973

Peary, Danny, *Guide for the Film Fanatic*, Simon & Schuster, 1986

Pitts, Michael R, *Famous Movie Detectives*, Scarecrow Press, 1979

Quirk, Lawrence J, *The Films of Myrna Loy*, Citadel, 1980

_____*The Complete Films of William Powell*, Citadel, 1986

_____*Fasten Your Seat Belts*, Morrow & Co., 1996

Ragan, David, *Movie Stars of the Forties*, Pentice-Hall, 1985

Reed, Rex, *People are Crazy Here*, Delacorte, Press, 1974

Russell, Rosalind, *Life Is a Banquet*, Random House, 1977

Sarris, Andrew, *American Cinema: Directors & Direction 1929-1968*, Da Capo Press, 1996

Schary, Dore, *Heyday*, Little, Brown, 1979

Schwatz, Thomas, *The Genius of the System: Hollywood Filmmaking in the Studio Era*, Henry Holt & Company, 1988

Scott, Ian, *In Capra's Shadow: The Life of Screenwriter Robert Riskin*, University Press of Kentucky, 2006

Server, Lee, *Screenwriter*, Main Street Press, 1987

Shipman, David, *The Great Movie Stars*, Crown Publishers, 1970

_____ *The Story of Cinema*, St. Martin's Press, 1982

Sikov, Ed, *Screwball: America's Madcap Romantic Comedies*, Crown Publishers, 1989

Steen, Mike, *Hollywood Speaks: An Oral History*, G.P. Putnam's Sons, 1974

Stenn, David, *Bombshell: The Life and Death of Jean Harlow*, Doubleday, 1993

Stevens, George (editor), *Conversations with the Great Moviemakers of Hollywood's Golden Age*, Alfred A. Knopf, 2006

Swindell, Larry, *Screwball: The Life of Carole Lombard*, Morrow, 1975

Thomas, Bob, *King Cohn: The Life and Times of Harry Cohn*, G.P. Putnam's Sons, 1967

Thomson, David, *Showman: The Life of David Selznick*, Alfred A. Knopf, 1996

Tibbetts, John (with James Welsh), *Novels into Films, 2nd Edition*, Facts on File, Inc., 2005

Tornabene, *Lyn, Long Live the King: A Biography of Clark Gable*, G.P. Putnam's Sons, 1976

Watts, Jill, *Hattie McDaniel*, Harper-Collins, 2005

Wayne, Jane Ellen, *The Leading Men of MGM*, Carroll & Graf Publishers, 2004

Widener, Don, *Lemmon*, Macmillan & Company, 1975

Wray, Fay, *On the Other Hand: A Life Story*, Trafalgar Square, 1990

Wright, William, *Lillian Hellman: The Image, The Woman*, Simon & Schuster, 1986

Wynn, Keenan, *Ed Wynn's Son*, Doubleday & Company, 1959

SUPPORTING ACTOR PHOTO GALLERY

The Thin Man

Maureen O'Sullivan.

Nat Pendelton.

Cesar Romero.

After the Thin Man

Paul Fix.

Elissa Landi.

Sam Levene.

Dorothy McNulty.

George Zucco.

Another Thin Man

Virginia Grey.

Ruth Hussey.

Otto Kruger.

C. Aubrey Smith.

Shadow of the Thin Man

Barry Nelson.

Donna Reed.

The Thin Man Goes Home

Leon Ames.

Harry Davenport.

Gloria DeHaven.

Song of the Thin Man

Gloria Grahame.

Dean Stockwell.

Keenan Wynn.

Printed in the United States
131856LV00004B/17/P

9 781593 934002